Wireless Network Securities

By Eugene Weiser

Wireless Network Securities

Copyright © 2013 by Eugene Weiser

Published by Dragonwick Publishing
25429 Brookside Dr
Seaford, DE 19973
www.dragonwickpublishing.com
ISBN # 13 978-1482045093

10 1482045095

Contents

PC

A **personal computer (PC)** is any general-purpose computer whose size, capabilities, and original sales price make it useful for individuals, and which is intended to be operated directly by an end-user with no intervening computer operator. This contrasted with the batch processing or time-sharing models that allowed larger, more expensive minicomputer and mainframe systems to be used by many people, usually at the same time. Large data processing systems require a full-time staff to operate efficiently.

An illustration of a personal desktop computer

Figure 1 The typical desktop computer

Personal computers may be connected to a local area network (LAN), either by a cable or a wireless connection. A personal computer may be a desktop computer or a laptop, tablet, or a handheld PC.

The advances in technology in the 20th century, particularly in the field of communications have produced a revolution in electronics, whose influence is being felt worldwide. A representative part of that revolution has been the advent of the personal computer (PC). Personal computers are computers that are meant to be used by individuals in homes or offices. Their retail prices, size, and capabilities make them practical for use in almost every home and office in the United States and other developed countries. The operation of these computers relies on a small computer chip known as a microprocessor, which governs the functioning of the computer.

All PCs have several basic components that allow them to function and be used. The microprocessor controls everything the computer does, and every process has to go through it first. Computers also have memory, both long-term (read-only memory or ROM) and temporary (random-access memory or RAM), as well as data storage. ROM contains the basic software that allows the computer to boot up and generally does not change; RAM is used to store information that the computer is currently working with, such as open programs.

The microprocessor and memory are contained as part of a large circuit board called the motherboard. The motherboard also acts as an intermediary between the microprocessor and other systems on the computer, such as drives and ports. The hard drive or hard disk is where programs and files are stored. As opposed to the RAM, the hard drive has a large capacity and is meant for long-term storage. This is where the majority of data in personal computers is located.

Another important part that is common to all personal computers is the power supply, which regulates the amount of electricity that the PC is using at a given time. Most computers also have sound cards and graphics cards as well, which are small circuit boards that connect to the motherboard to process audio and video data, respectively. Some modern PCs also include a CD-ROM or DVD-ROM drive, where a disk containing programs or files can be inserted. Programs can be run directly from the CD or DVD, which acts as a form of external data storage for a PC.

Personal computers were first introduced on the market in the late 1970s. Their capabilities and speed left much to be desired in comparison with modern PCs, but because of the advancement they represented, their popularity grew quickly, and PCs began to be developed for everyday household use. Computer games and programs were developed which could be used on household computers, further opening up the market for these devices. By the year 2002, one billion had been sold worldwide since they were first introduced.

History of Personal computers

Personal computers are now a very common item in many houses yet in 1955, there were only 250 computers in use throughout the world. In 1980, more than one million personal computers had been sold and by the mid-1980's, this figure had risen to 30 million. How did this come about?

A computer in 1955 was very large and could not have fitted into a normal room in a normal sized house. They frequently burned out and had a tendency to attract moths into the system that short-circuited them. (Getting a computer 'bug' now refers back to the time when moths were a problem to the early computers).

In the late 1950's, computers got smaller because one of its main components - the valve - was replaced by the much smaller transistor. These made computers far more reliable and therefore businesses took a much greater interest in them. Firms such as IBM could sell a mainframe computer for just under one-half million dollars in today's money.

By the mid-1960's, the microchip was replacing the transistor. A microchip could have several transistors on it. But being smaller, it leads again to a decrease in the size of computers. By 1965, there were 20,000 computers in the world. The most famous was the IBM System/360.

The microchip also leads to computers being made that were small enough to get into the average sized room in a house. By 1970, one microchip could contain 1000 transistors on it. In 1970, a home personal computer would have cost nearly $70,000 in today's money.

In 1971, the microprocessor went on sale. Developed by Ted Hoff of Intel, the Intel 4004 was to revolutionize home computing. The 4004 cost just over £3000 in today's money but by 1972, Intel had produced the 8008 that was far more powerful that the 4004 but cost a tenth of the price of the 4004. Microprocessors had a multitude of uses but they could be used at the heart of true personal computers.

In the early 1970's personal computers were used only by hobbyists. The first 'hobby' personal computer was the Altair 8800 that cost just under $900 in today's money. It had the same power as a computer of the 1950's that cost $1 million.

FIGURE 2 THE MICROSOFT TEAM, 1978.
BILLGATES IN BOTTOM LEFT, PAUL ALLEN
IS BOTTOM RIGHT

In 1975, Bill Gates and Paul Allen developed a program for the Altair that allowed people to write their own programs in BASIC program language. Their newly formed company was called Micro-Soft which was later changed to Microsoft.

In 1975, Apple Computers was founded by Steve Jobs and Steve Wozniac. Apple created the "home/personal computer" that could be used by anybody. The computer - Apple II - was launched in 1977 and was an immediate success. The personal computer was sealed in a neat plastic case, it had a keyboard, video unit and used removable floppy discs. Above all, it only cost $2400 in today's money. The success of Apple II established Apple Computers as the main player in the field of personal computers. By 1980, there were 1 million personal computers in the world.

The personal computer moved into the world of business when Dan Bricklin created a spreadsheet program. His program - called VisiCalc - was designed for the Apple II. It went on sale in 1979 and within 4 years, it had sold 700,000 copies at $250 a time.

IBM launched its own personal computer in 1981. Eventually 85% of all personal computers were to be IBM compatible. Microsoft won the contract to write the operating system for the IBM personal computer. Microsoft called its new operating system MS-DOS. Each copy earned the company $10. During the 1980's, MS-DOS was installed in over 30 million personal computers.

FAX

Fax (short for facsimile), sometimes called telecopying, is the telephonic transmission of scanned printed material (both text and images), normally to a telephone number connected to a printer or other output device. The original document is scanned with a fax machine (or a Telecopier), which processes the contents (text or images) as a single fixed graphic image, converting it into a bitmap, and then transmitting it through the telephone system. The receiving fax machine reconverts the coded image, printing a paper copy. Before digital technology became widespread, for many decades, the scanned data was transmitted as analog.

FIGURE 3 MODERN PRINTER

PRINTER

In computing, a printer is a peripheral that produces a representation of an electronic document on physical media such as paper or transparency film. Many printers are local peripherals connected directly to a nearby personal computer. Individual printers are often designed to support both local and network connected users at the same time. Some printers can print documents stored on memory cards or from digital cameras and scanners. Multifunction printers (MFPs) include a scanner and can copy paper documents or send a fax; these are also called multi-function devices (MFD), or all-in-one (AIO) printers. Most MFPs include printing, scanning, and copying among their many features.

CABLES

Category 5 cable (Cat 5) is a twisted pair cable for carrying signals. This type of cable is used in structured cabling for computer networks such as Ethernet. The cable standard provides performance of up to 100 MHz and is suitable for 10BASE-T, 100BASE-TX (Fast Ethernet), and 1000BASE-T (Gigabit Ethernet). Cat 5 is also used to carry other signals such as telephony and video. In some cases, multiple signals can be carried on a single cable; Cat 5 can carry two conventional telephone lines as well as a single 100BASE-TX channel in a single cable or two 100BASE-TX channels in a single cable.

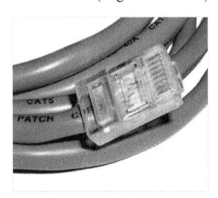

FIGURE 4 CAT 5 CABLES

RJ45 CONNECTORS (8P8C)

The **8P8C (8 position 8 contact, also backronymed as 8 position 8 conductor)** is a modular connector commonly used to terminate twisted pair and multiconductor flat cable. These connectors are commonly used for Ethernet over twisted pair, registered jacks and other telephone applications, RS-232 serial using the EIA/TIA 561 and Yost standards, and other applications involving unshielded twisted pair, shielded twisted pair, and multiconductor flat cable.

An **8P8C modular connector** has two paired components: the male plug and the female jack, each with eight equally spaced conducting channels. On the plug, these conductors are flat contacts positioned parallel with the connector body. Inside the jack, the contacts are suspended diagonally toward the insertion interface. When an 8P8C plug is mated with an 8P8C jack, the contacts meet and create an electrical connection. Spring tension in the jack's contacts ensures a

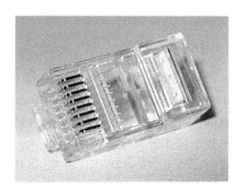

good interface with the plug and allows for slight travel during insertion and removal.

Although **commonly referred to as a "RJ45"** in the context of **Ethernet and category 5 cables**, it is incorrect to refer to a generic 8P8C connector as an RJ45. A telephone-system-standard RJ45 plug has a key which excludes insertion in an un-keyed 8P8C socket. The registered jack (RJ) standard specifies a different mechanical interface and wiring scheme for an RJ45S from TIA/EIA-568-B that is often used for modular connectors used in Ethernet and telephone applications. 8P8C modular plugs and jacks look very similar to the plugs and jacks used for FCC's registered

FIGURE 5 RJ45 CONNECTOR

jack RJ45 variants, although the RJ45S is not compatible with 8P8C modular connectors.

QUIZ

1. Explain briefly what for a Hub works into a network:

- They exist with different number of ports according with the quantity users, the Hubs were named before in legacy networks as concentrators and helped to allow communicate a certain quantity of computers between them.

2. Explain briefly what for a Router works into a network:

- Works as a modem, commonly to communicate one or more networks from to outside the organization, i.e. Sales District of Miami with Sales District in Chicago.

3. Explain briefly what for a switch works into a network:

- It help to segment the network in order to avoid overload the network traffic, the switches were meant to separate two or more networks that in global are part of the same organization.

4. Explain briefly what for a Server works into a network:

- Servers help commonly to share, save, and maintain files that could be read and modified by all the members of one or more departments, it helped also to share printers, or to control user access level security.

5. Explain briefly what for a Printer works into a network:

- Gives the availability to all users involved within a network to send printings to one or more Printers instead of having one per user. It reduces costs.

6. Explain briefly, what for Category Number Five Cables work into a network:

- Are made to connect the Servers, Printers, PC's, FAXES, all together into an organization network

Computer Network Systems

The word "Networking" refers to "connectivity or Links". In computing world, the practice of connecting two or more computing devices together for sharing data could be referred to as Computer Networking. When networks (connectivity between devices) are built with a mix of computer hardware and computer software, it is referred to as Computer Network Systems. The systems must be capable of communicating with each other

A network is a connected collection of devices and end systems, such as computers and servers that can communicate with each other.

k2685847 www.fotosearch.com

Figure 6 A Simple Network Image

In figure 7, we see:

- A cloud represents the Internet or WAN connection.

- A straight line represents an Ethernet link.

(WAN connection and Ethernet link will be discussed in other chapters)

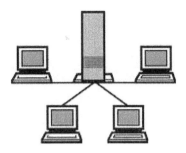

FIGURE 7 INTERNET WAN CONNECTION

The Diagram in figure 8 represents:

- A rectangular box with arrows represents a workgroup switch.

- A tower PC represents a server.

- A desktop or computer and monitor represent an end user PC.

- A straight line represents an Ethernet link.

Computer Network Systems Infrastructure:

A computer network system is made of

1. Distributed application

2. Network infrastructure

Network Distributed application

The Network distrubtion application refers to a network system which provides services to users on other machines, or to other computers. It could also be referred to as a network system that can execute or provide services on two or more computers within a simple connection (network). The objective of a distributed application is to have a network with efficiency of operations through commonly available components used in everyday tasks, sharing files, printing, and storing data. This efficiency results in reduced expenditures and increased productivity.

NETWORK USER APPLICATIONS

The importance of utilizing multiple resources on a data network is having applications that are aware of communication mechanisms. Although many applications are available for users in a network environment, some applications are common to nearly all users.

The most common network user applications include the following:

- **E-mail:** E-mail is a valuable application for most network users. Users can communicate information (messages and files) electronically in a timely manner, to not only other users in the same network but also other users outside the network (suppliers, information resources, and customers, for example). Examples of e-mail programs include Microsoft Outlook and Eudora by Qualcomm.

- **Web browser:** A web browser enables access to the Internet through a common interface. The Internet provides a wealth of information and has become vital to the productivity of both home and business users. Communicating with suppliers and customers, handling orders and fulfillment, and locating information are now routinely done electronically over the Internet, which saves time and increases overall productivity. The most commonly used browsers are Microsoft Internet Explorer, Netscape Navigator, Mozilla, and Firefox.

- **Instant messaging:** Instant messaging started in the personal user-to-user space; however, it soon provided considerable benefit in the corporate world. Now many instant messaging applications, such as those provided by AOL and Yahoo!, provide data encryption and logging, features essential for corporate use.

- **Collaboration:** Working together as individuals or groups is greatly facilitated when the collaborators are on a network. Individuals creating separate parts of an annual report or a business plan, for example, can either transmit their data files to a central resource for compilation or use a workgroup software application to create and modify the entire document, without any exchange of paper. One of the best-known traditional collaboration software programs is Lotus Notes. A more modern web-based collaboration application is a wiki.

- **Database:** This type of application enables users on a network to store information in central locations (such as storage devices) so that others on the network can easily retrieve selected information in the formats that are most useful to them. Some of the most common databases used in enterprises today are Oracle and Microsoft SQL Server.

The Impact of User Applications on the Network

The key to user applications is that they enable users to be connected to one another through the various types of software. As a business begins to rely on these applications as part of the day-to-day business process, the network that the applications operate in becomes a critical part of the business. A special relationship exists between these applications and the network. The applications can affect network performance, and network performance can affect applications. Therefore, you need to understand some common interactions between user applications and the network. Figure 9 characterizes some of the interactions for different types of applications.

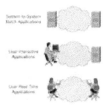

Figure 8 Interactions of different types of applications

NETWORK INFRASTRUCTURE

This type of network systems supports transport of data between computers where distributed applications reside in computers, e.g Ethernet card, Modem, and software or in special network devices like Bridges, Routers, Repeaters, and switches. This means that the network **infrastructure** is the collection of systems that are required for the interconnection of computers running the distributed applications. It is the modern open network interconnectivity currently used in all organizations either open architecture or wireless network.

The simplest form of network infrastructure typically consists of one or more computers, a network or Internet connection, and a *hub* to both link the computers to the network connection and tie the various systems to each other. The hub merely links the computers, but does not limit data flow to or from any one system. To control or limit access between systems and regulate information flow, a switch replaces the hub to create network protocols that define how the systems communicate with each other. To allow the network created by these systems to communicate to others, via the network connection, requires a router, which bridges the networks and provides a common language for data exchange, according to the rules of each network.

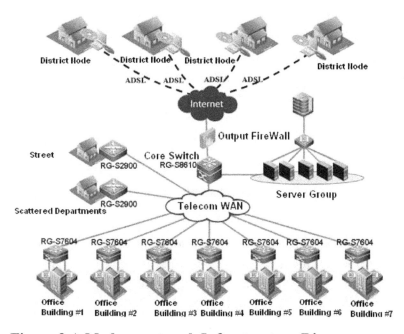

Figure 9 A Modern network Infrastructure Diagram

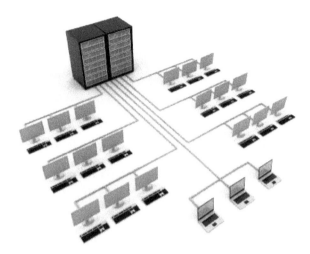

Figure 10 Modern Network Infrastructure Image

When multiple computers in a single household share the same Internet connection, it is considered a basic form of network infrastructure, whether or not the computers also share information with each other. The Internet itself is a more advanced network infrastructure, in which individual systems access a global network that houses information on various systems, and allows access using web standards and protocols, most commonly framed as web addresses, also known as *URL*s.

Office intranets are similar to the global Internet, but operate on a closed network infrastructure accessible only by those within it. This generally consists of a central data store — one or more computers known as *servers* — as well as Ethernet cabling, wireless access points, routers, switches, and the individual computers with access to the central data store. The individual computers connect to the network via either cabling or wireless access. The routers and switches then determine what level of access they are allowed to have, and act as traffic directors to point them to the central data store on the servers. As the individual computers send or receive data, the routers ensure it reaches the appropriate place.

The network infrastructure problem has itself two aspects:

- **Distance**: interconnect remote systems that are too far apart for a direct cable connection

- **meshing**: interconnect systems together; even in the case of systems close to each other, it is not possible in non-trivial cases to put cables from all systems to all systems.

The distance problem is solved by using a network, such as the telephone network with modems (see other chapter). The meshing problem was originally solved easily because the terminals were not able to communicate with each other, but always has to go through a main computer. The mesh in such cases is reduced to a star network. Today this is solved by a complex set of bridges and routers.

THE OSI MODEL

SI 7 Layers Reference Model For Network Communication

Open Systems Interconnection (OSI) model is a reference model developed by ISO (International Organization for Standardization) in 1984, as a conceptual framework of standards for communication in the network across different equipment and applications by different vendors. It is now considered the primary architectural model for inter-computing and internetworking communications. In the late 1970s, the **International Organization for Standardization (ISO)** worked on a seven-layer model for LAN architectures by defining the **Open Systems Interconnection Basic Reference Model (OSI)**. Alongside this The ISO developed a set of protocols that fit within this model. Since then, other models such as the 5 layer TCP/IP model were developed, however the OSI model is still used to map and categorize protocols because of its concise and clear way of representing network functions. Most of the network communication protocols used today have a structure based on the OSI model. The OSI model defines the communications process into 7 layers, which divides the tasks involved with moving information between networked computers into seven smaller, more manageable task groups. A task or group of tasks is then assigned to each of the seven OSI layers. Each layer is reasonably self-contained so that the tasks assigned to each layer can be implemented independently. This enables the solutions offered by one layer to be updated without adversely affecting the other layers. Compatible interconnection of network devices is fundamental to reliable network communications. Developing a set of standards that equipment manufacturers could adhere to went a long way towards providing an open environment for network communications.

The OSI 7 layers model has clear characteristics. Layers 7 through 4 deals with end-to-end communications between data source and destinations. Layers 3 to 1 deal with communications between network devices.

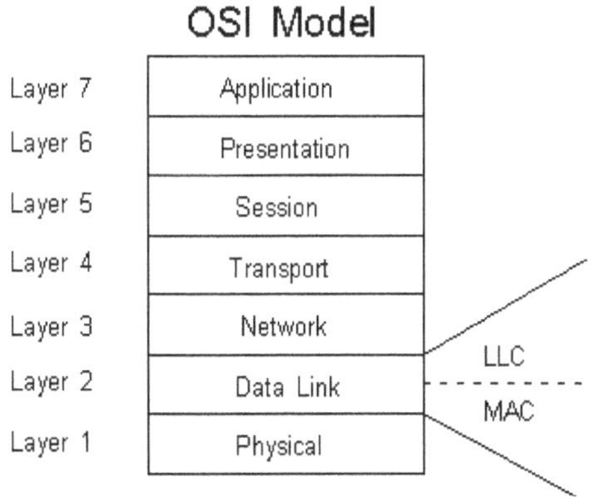

FIGURE 11 EXAMPLE OF AN OSI MODEL

On the other hand, the seven layers of the OSI model can be divided into two groups: upper layers (layers 7, 6 & 5) and lower layers (layers 4, 3, 2, 1). The upper layers of the OSI model deal with application issues and generally are implemented only in software. The highest layer, the application layer, is closest to the end user. The lower layers of the OSI model handle data transport issues. The physical layer and the data link layer are implemented in hardware and software. The lowest layer, the physical layer, is closest to the physical network medium (the wires, for example) and is responsible for placing data on the medium. The IEEE formed the 802 committee in February 1980 with the aim of standardising LAN protocols. This resulted in the IEEE 802 series of committees that sit to develop worldwide standards for communications. Within the OSI model, the Data Link layer was split into two, the Media Access Control (MAC) sub-layer, and the 802.2 Logical Link Control (LLC) sub-layer.

You can make up expressions to remember the order of the 7 layers, for example, 'Angus Prefers Sausages To Nibbling Dried Pork' or 'A Pretty Silly Trick Never Does Please'. I remember it best using the natty expression 'Application, Presentation, Session, Transport, Network, Datalink, Physical'. It just rolls off the tongue!

The OSI protocol set is rarely used today, however the model that was developed serves as a useful guide when referencing other protocol stacks such as ATM, TCP/IP and SPX/IPX.

APPLICATION LAYER 7

It is employed in software packages that implement client-server software. When an application on one computer starts communicating with another computer, then the Application layer is used. Defines interface to user processes for communication and data transfer in network. It provides standardized services such as virtual terminal, file and job transfer and operations. The header contains parameters that are agreed between applications. This header is often only sent at the beginning of an application operation. Examples of services within the application layer include:

- FTP
- DNS
- SNMP
- SMTP gateways
- Web browser
- Network File System (NFS)
- Telnet and Remote Login (rlogin)
- X.400
- FTAM
- Database software
- Print Server Software

PRESENTATION LAYER 6

This provides function call exchange between host operating systems and software layers. Masks the differences of data formats between dissimilar systems. Specifies architecture-independent data transfer format. Encodes and decodes data; Encrypts and decrypts data; Compresses and decompresses data. It defines the format of data being sent and any encryption that may be used, and makes it presentable to the Application layer. Examples of services used are listed below:

- MIDI
- HTML
- GIF
- TIFF
- JPEG
- ASCII
- EBCDIC

SESSION LAYER 5

The Session layer defines how data conversations are started, controlled, and finished. The Session layer manages the transaction sequencing and in some cases authorization. The messages may be bidirectional and there may be many of them, the session layer manages these conversations and creates notifications if some messages fail. Indications show whether a packet is in the middle of a conversation flow or at the end. Manages user sessions and dialogues. This session layer controls establishment and termination of logic links between users. It reports upper layer errors. Only after a completed conversation will the data be passed up to layer 6. Examples of Session layer protocols are listed below:

- RPC
- SQL
- NetBIOS names
- Appletalk ASP
- DECnet SCP

TRANSPORT LAYER 4

This layer is responsible for the ordering and reassembly of packets that may have been broken up to travel across certain media. It manages end-to-end message delivery in network. It also provides reliable and sequential packet delivery through error recovery, flow control mechanisms, and provides connectionless oriented packet delivery. Some protocols in this layer also perform error recovery. After error recovery and reordering, the data part is passed up to layer 5. Examples are:

- TCP

- UDP

- SPX

NETWORK LAYER 3

This layer is responsible for the delivery of packets end to end and implements a logical addressing scheme to help accomplish this. This can be connectionless or connection-oriented and is independent of the topology or path that the data packets travel. Routing packets through a network is also defined at this layer plus a method to fragment large packets into smaller ones depending on MTUs for different media (Packet Switching). Determines how data are transferred between network devices. Routes packets according to unique network device addresses. Provides flow and congestion control to prevent network resource depletion. Once the data from layer 2 has been received, layer 3 examines the destination address and if it is the address of its own end station, it passes the data after the layer 3 headers to layer 4. Examples of Layer 3 protocols include:

- Appletalk DDP

- IP

- IPX

- DECnet

DATA LINK LAYER 2

This layer deals with getting data across a specific medium and individual links by providing one or more data link connections between two network entities. End points are specifically identified, if required by the Network layer Sequencing. Defines procedures for operating the communication links. Frames packets. Detects and corrects packets transmit errors. The frames are maintained in the correct sequence and there are facilities for Flow control and Quality of Service parameters such as Throughput, Service Availability, and Transit Delay.

Examples include:

- IEEE 802.2

- IEEE 802.3

- 802.5 - Token Ring

- HDLC

- Frame Relay

- FDDI

- ATM

- PPP

The Data link layer performs the error check using the Frame Check Sequence (FCS) in the trailer and discards the frame if an error is detected. It then looks at the addresses to see if it needs to process the rest of the frame itself or whether to pass it on to another host. The data between the header and the trailer is passed to layer 3. The MAC layer concerns itself with the access control method and determines how use of the physical transmission is controlled and provides the token ring protocols that define how a token ring operates. The LLC shields the higher level layers from concerns with the specific LAN implementation.

PHYSICAL LAYER 1

This layer deals with the physical aspects of the media being used to transmit the data. The electrical, mechanical, procedural and functional means. This defines things like pinouts, electrical characteristics, modulation, and encoding of data bits on carrier signals. It ensures bit synchronization and places the binary pattern that it receives into a receive buffer. It defines physical means of sending data over network devices and interfaces between network medium and devices. It defines optical, electrical, and mechanical characteristics. Once it decodes the bit stream, the physical layer notifies the data link layer that a frame has been received and passes it up. Examples of specifications include:

- V.24

- V.35

- EIA/TIA-232

- EIA/TIA-449

- FDDI

- 802.3

- 802.5

- Ethernet

- RJ45

- NRZ

- NRZI

You will notice that some protocols span a number of layers (e.g. NFS, 802.3 etc.). A benefit of the seven-layer model is that software can be written in a modular way to deal specifically with one or two layers only, this is often called *Modular Engineering*. Each layer has its own header containing information relevant to its role. This header is passed down to the layer below which in turn adds its own header (encapsulates) until eventually the Physical layer adds the layer 2 information for passage to the next device which understands the layer 2 information and can then strip each of the layers' headers in turn to get at the data in the right location. Each layer within an end station communicates at the same layer within another end station.

TCP/IP NETWORKING PROTOCOLS

The TCP/IP suite of protocols is the set of protocols used to communicate across the internet. It is also widely used on many organizational networks due to its flexibility and wide array of functionality provided. Microsoft who had originally developed their own set of protocols now is more widely using TCP/IP, at first for transport and now to support other services.

TCP/IP PROTOCOL SUITE

Communications between computers on a network is done through protocol suits. The most widely used and most widely available protocol suite is TCP/IP protocol suite. A protocol suit consists of a layered architecture where each layer depicts some functionality which can be carried out by a protocol. Each layer usually has more than one protocol options to carry out the responsibility that the layer adheres to. TCP/IP is normally considered to be a 4 layer system. The four layers are as follows:

1. Application layer

2. Transport layer

3. Network layer

4. Data link layer

1. Application layer

This is the top layer of TCP/IP protocol suite. This layer includes applications or processes that use transport layer protocols to deliver the data to destination computers.

At each layer there are certain protocol options to carry out the task designated to that particular layer. So, application layer also has various protocols that applications use to communicate with the second layer, the transport layer. Some of the popular application layer protocols are :

- HTTP (Hypertext transfer protocol)

- FTP (File transfer protocol)

- SMTP (Simple mail transfer protocol)

- SNMP (Simple network management protocol) etc

2. Transport Layer

This layer provides backbone to data flow between two hosts. This layer receives data from the application layer above it. There are many protocols that work at this layer but the two most commonly used protocols at transport layer are TCP and UDP.

TCP is used where a reliable connection is required while UDP is used in case of unreliable connections.

TCP divides the data (coming from the application layer) into proper sized chunks and then passes these chunks onto the network. It acknowledges received packets, waits for the acknowledgments of the packets it sent and sets timeout to resend the packets if acknowledgements are not received in time. The term 'reliable connection' is used where it is not desired to lose any information that is being transferred over the network through this connection. So, the protocol used for this type of connection must provide the mechanism to achieve this desired characteristic. For example, while downloading a file, it is not desired to lose any information (bytes) as it may lead to corruption of downloaded content.

UDP provides a comparatively simpler but unreliable service by sending packets from one host to another. UDP does not take any extra measures to ensure that the data sent is received by the target host or not. The term 'unreliable connection' is used where loss of some information does not hamper the task being fulfilled through this connection. For example while streaming a video; loss of few bytes of information due to some reason is acceptable as this does not harm the user experience much.

3. Network Layer

This layer is also known as Internet layer. The main purpose of this layer is to organize or handle the movement of data on network. By movement of data, we generally mean routing of data over the network. The main protocol used at this layer is IP. While ICMP (used by popular 'ping' command) and IGMP are also used at this layer.

4. Data Link Layer

This layer is also known as network interface layer. This layer normally consists of device drivers in the OS and the network interface card attached to the system. Both the device drivers and the network interface card take care of the communication details with the media being used to transfer the data over the network. In most of the cases, this media is in the form of cables. Some of the famous protocols that are used at this layer include ARP(Address resolution protocol), PPP(Point to point protocol) etc.

TCP/IP CONCEPT EXAMPLE

One thing, which is worth taking note, is that the interaction between two computers over the network through TCP/IP protocol suite takes place in the form of a client server architecture.

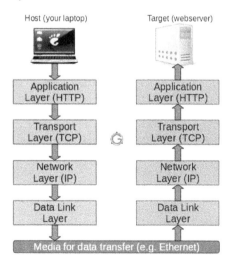

FIGURE 12 DATA FLOW OF A

Client requests for a service while the server processes the request for client.

Now, since we have discussed the underlying layers that help that data flow from host to target over a network. Let us take a very simple example to make the concept clearer.

Consider the data flow when you open a website.

As seen in figure 7, the information flows downward through each layer on the host machine. At the first layer, since http protocol is being used, so an HTTP request is formed and sent to the transport layer.

Here the protocol TCP assigns some more information(like sequence number, source port number, destination port number etc) to the data coming from upper layer so that the communication remains reliable i.e, a track of sent data and received data could be maintained.

At the next lower layer, IP adds its own information over the data coming from transport layer. This information would help in packet travelling over the network. Lastly, the data link layer makes sure that the data transfer to/from the physical media is done properly. Here again the communication done at the data link layer can be reliable or unreliable.

This information travels on the physical media (like Ethernet) and reaches the target machine.

Now, at the target machine (which in our case is the machine at which the website is hosted) the same series of interactions happen, but in reverse order.

The packet is first received at the data link layer. At this layer the information (that was stuffed by the data link layer protocol of the host machine) is read and rest of the data is passed to the upper layer.

Similarly, at the Network layer, the information set by the Network layer protocol of host machine is read and rest of the information is passed on the next upper layer. Same happens at the transport layer and finally the HTTP request sent by the host application(your browser) is received by the target application(Website server).

One would wonder what happens when information particular to each layer is read by the corresponding protocols at target machine or why is it required? Well, lets understand this by an example of TCP protocol present at transport layer. At the host machine this protocol adds information like sequence number to each packet sent by this layer.

At the target machine, when packet reaches at this layer, the TCP at this layer makes note of the sequence number of the packet and sends an acknowledgement (which is received seq number + 1).

Now, if the host TCP does not receive the acknowledgement within some specified time, it re sends the same packet. So this way TCP makes sure that no packet gets lost. So we see that protocol at every layer reads the information set by its counterpart to achieve the functionality of the layer it represents.

OSI comparision with TCP/IP Protocol Stack

OSI #	OSI Layer Name	TCP/IP #	TCP/IP Layer Name	Encapsulation Units	TCP/IP Protocols
7	Application	4	Application	data	FTP, HTTP, POP3, IMAP, telnet, SMTP, DNS, TFTP
6	Presentation			data	
5	Session			data	
4	Transport	3	Transport	segments	TCP, UDP
3	Network	2	Internet	packets	IP
2	Data Link	1	Network Access	frames	
1	Physical			bits	

PORTS, SERVERS AND STANDARDS

On a particular machine, a port number coupled with the IP address of the machine is known as a socket. A combination of IP and port on both client and server is known as four tuple. This four tuple uniquely identifies a connection. In this section, we will discuss how port numbers are chosen.

You already know that some of the very common services like FTP, telnet etc run on well-known port numbers. While FTP server runs on port 21, Telent server runs on port 23. Therefore, we see that some standard services that are provided by any implementation of TCP/IP have some standard ports on which they run. These standard port numbers are generally chosen from 1 to 1023. The well-known ports are managed by Internet Assigned Numbers Authority (IANA).

While most standard servers (that are provided by the implementation of TCP/IP suite) run on standard port numbers, clients do not require any standard port to run on.

Client port numbers are known as ephemeral ports. By ephemeral we mean short lived. This is because a client may connect to server, do its work and then disconnect. So we used the term 'short lived' and hence no standard ports are required for them.

In addition, since clients need to know the port numbers of the servers to connect to them, so most standard servers run on standard port numbers.

The ports reserved for clients generally range from 1024 to 5000. The port number higher than 5000, are reserved for those servers that are not standard or well known.

If we look at the file '/etc/services', you will find most of the standard servers and the port on which they run:

$ cat /etc/services

systat	11/tcp	users
daytime	13/udp	
netstat	15/tcp	
qotd	17/tcp	quote
msp	18/udp	
chargen	19/udp	ttytst source
ftp-data	20/tcp	
ftp	21/tcp	
ssh	22/tcp	
ssh	22/udp	
telnet	23/tcp	

As you see from the /etc/services file, FTP has port number 21, telent has port number 23 etc. You can use 'grep' command on this file to find any server and its associated port.

As far as the standards are concerned, the following four organizations/groups manage the TCP/IP protocol suite. Both the IRTF and the IETF fall under the IAB.

Types of Computer Network Systems models

There are two types of Computer Network Systems Models- Peer to Peer and Client/Server Models.

Peer to Peer Model Systems

The word "peer' represents 'friends' in English language. Peer to peer networking is common on small small networks like the local area networks (LANs will be discussed later), particularly home networks. Both wired and wireless home networks can be configured as peer to peer environments. Computers in a peer-to-peer network run the same networking protocols and software. Peer networks are also often situated physically near to each other, typically in homes, small businesses, or schools. Some peer networks, however, utilize the Internet and are geographically dispersed worldwide.

Home networks that utilize broadband routers are *hybrid* peer to peer and client-server environments. The router provides centralized Internet connection sharing, but file, printer and other resource sharing is managed directly between the local computers involved.

Peer to Peer and P2P Networks

Internet-based peer-to-peer networks emerged in the 1990s due to the development of P2P file sharing networks like Napster. Technically, many P2P networks (including the original Napster) are not pure peer networks but rather hybrid designs as they utilize central servers for some functions such as search.

Advantages of Peer-to-Peer Network Systems Model

You can configure computers in peer-to-peer *workgroups* to allow sharing of files, printers and other resources across all of the devices. Peer networks allow data to be shared easily in both directions, whether for downloads to your computer or uploads from your computer.

On the Internet, peer-to-peer networks handle a very high volume of file sharing traffic by distributing the load across many computers. Because they do not rely exclusively on central servers, P2P networks both scale better and are more resilient than client-server networks in case of failures or traffic bottlenecks.

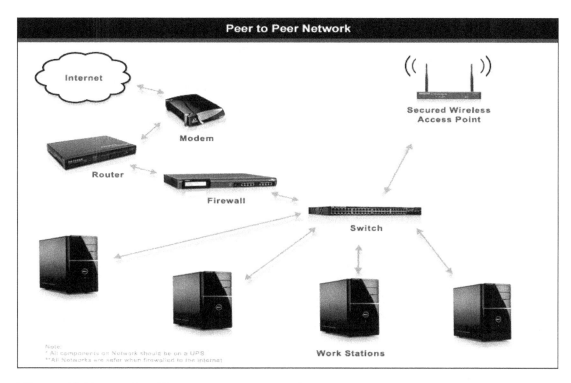

Figure 13 Example of Peer-to-peer network

Peer-to-peer networking enables or enhances the following scenarios: (technet.microsoft.com)

- Real-time communications (RTC)

- Collaboration

- Content distribution

- Distributed processing

- Improved Internet technologies

Real-Time Communications (RTC)

For RTC, peer-to-peer networking enables serverless instant messaging, real-time matchmaking, and game play.

- Serverless instant messaging

RTC exists today. Computer users can chat and have voice or video conversations with their peers today. However, many of the existing programs and their communications protocols rely on servers to function. If you are participating in an ad-hoc wireless network or are a part of an isolated network, you are unable to use these RTC facilities. Peer-to-peer technology allows the extension of RTC technologies to these additional networking environments.

- Real-time matchmaking and game play

Similar to RTC, real-time game play exists today. There are many Web-based game sites that cater to the gaming community via the Internet. They offer the ability to find other gamers with similar interests and play a game together. The problem is that the game sites exist only on the Internet and are geared toward the avid gamer who wants to play against the best gamers in the world. These sites track and provide the statistics to help in the process. However, these sites do not allow a gamer to set up an ad-hoc game among friends in a variety of networking environments. Peer-to-peer networking can provide this capability.

Collaboration

For collaboration, peer-to-peer networking allows the sharing of a workspace, files, and experiences.

An example of a collaboration-based Windows Peer-to-Peer Networking application is Windows Meeting Space, which is included in Windows Vista.

- Project workspaces solving a goal

Shared workspace applications allow for the creation of ad-hoc workgroups and then allow the workgroup owners to populate the shared workspace with the tools and content that will allow the group to solve a problem. This could include message boards, productivity tools, and files.

- Sharing your files with other people

A subset of project workspace sharing is the ability to share files. Although this ability exists today with the current version of Windows, it can be enhanced through peer-to-peer networking to make file content available in an easy and friendly way. Allowing easy access to the incredible wealth of content at the edge of the Internet or in ad-hoc computing environments increases the value of network computing.

- Sharing your experiences

With wireless connectivity becoming more prevalent, peer-to-peer networking allows you to be online in a group of peers and to be able to share your experiences (such as a sunset, a rock concert, or a vacation cruise) while they are occurring.

Content Distribution

Peer-to-peer networking allows the distribution of text, audio, and video and software product updates.

- Text messages

Peer-to-peer networking can allow for the dissemination of text-based information in the form of files or messages to a large group of users. An example is a news list.

- Audio and video

Peer-to-peer networking can also allow for the dissemination of audio or video information to a large group of users, such as a large concert or company meeting. To distribute the content today, you must configure high-capacity servers to collect and distribute the load to hundreds or thousands of users. With peer-to-peer networking, only a handful of peers would actually get their content from the centralized servers. These peers would flood this information out to a few more people who send it to others, and so on. The load of distributing the content is distributed to the peers in the cloud. A peer that wants to receive the content would find the closest distributing peer and get the content from them.

- Distribution of product updates

Peer-to-peer networking can also provide an efficient mechanism to distribute software such as product updates (security updates and service packs). A peer that has a connection to a software distribution server can obtain the product update and propagate it to the other members of its group.

Distributed Processing

Peer-to-peer networking allows computing tasks to be distributed and processor resources to be aggregated.

- Division and distribution of a task

A large computing task can first be divided into separate smaller computing tasks well suited to the computing resources of a peer. A peer could do the dividing of the large computing task. Then, peer-to-peer networking can distribute the individual tasks to the separate peers in the group. Each peer performs its computing task and reports its result back to a centralized accumulation point.

- Aggregation of computer resources

Another way to utilize peer-to-peer networking for distributed processing is to run programs on each peer that run during idle processor times and are part of a larger computing task that is coordinated by a central server. By aggregating the processors of multiple computers, peer-to-peer networking can turn a group of peer computers into a large parallel processor for large computing tasks.

Improved Internet Technologies

Peer-to-peer networking can also provide an improved utilization of the Internet and support new Internet technologies. Historically, the Internet was designed so that network peers can have end-to-end connectivity. The modern-day Internet, however, more closely resembles a client/server environment where communication in many cases is not end-to-end due to the prevalence of Network Address Translators (NATs).

This return to the original purpose of the Internet will enable the creation of a new wave of applications for personal communication and group productivity.

Windows Peer-to-Peer Networking

According to definition posted in Microsoft library explained that Windows Peer-to-Peer networking is a developer platform to create peer-to-peer applications for computers running Windows XP with Service Pack 2, Windows XP Professional x64 Edition, Windows XP with Service Pack 1 and the Advanced Networking Pack for Windows XP, or Windows Vista™. The long-term goal of Windows Peer-to-Peer networking is the following:

To enable people to communicate securely and share information with one another without a dependence on centralized servers, but to work even better when servers are present.

Computers running Windows Vista already have Windows Peer-to-Peer networking installed. For computers running Windows XP with SP2, do the following to install Windows Peer-to-Peer Networking:

1. Click **Start**, click **Control Panel**, and then click **Add or Remove Programs**.

2. Click **Add/Remove Windows Components**.

3. In **Components**, click **Networking Services** (but do not select its check box), and then click **Details**.

4. Select the **Peer-to-Peer** check box, and then click **OK**.

5. Click **next**, and then follow the instructions in the wizard.

For computers running Windows XP with Service Pack 1 (SP1), you can install Windows Peer-to-Peer networking with the Advanced Networking Pack for Windows XP, a free download.

The design of Windows Peer-to-Peer networking incorporates the following principles:

- Secure
- Scalable
- Distributed
- Serverless
- Robust in the face of failure and/or attack
- Self-tuning
- Self-repairing

How these design principles were achieved is described throughout this paper.

Windows Peer-to-Peer Networking and DNS

Another point of contrast between client/server and peer-to-peer networking is the use of the Domain Name System (DNS). Server computers are typically registered in DNS so that client computers can resolve a name to the IP address of the server computer. Client computers are typically not registered in DNS for the following reasons:

- Many client computers have transient connectivity; they connect for unpredictable amounts of time and can be assigned a new IP address for each connection.

- Client computers do not have shared resources and do not respond to requests for resources. Therefore, other computers do not need to resolve the names of client computers. DNS address records for client computers are not necessary.

Peer computers, on the other hand, have resources to share. However, they still have transient connectivity. Peer computers could use DNS dynamic update to register their names, however, very few DNS servers on the Internet support DNS dynamic update. To be successful for peer-to-peer networking, peer computers must not rely on the existing DNS infrastructure. Therefore, there must be a mechanism to resolve peer names to their addresses that does not rely on DNS. For Windows Peer-to-Peer Networking, this mechanism is Peer Name Resolution Protocol (PNRP) and is described in Peer Name Resolution Protocol.

Windows Peer-to-Peer Networking Security

In a peer environment, there are no centralized servers with security databases or that can provide typical security services such as authentication and authorization. For example, in an Active Directory domain, domain controllers provide authentication services using Kerberos. In a serverless peer environment, the peers must provide their own authentication.

For Windows Peer-to-Peer Networking, authentication is provided using self-signed certificates, some of which are formatted as X.509 certificates. Although one usually thinks of X.509 certificates in relation to a public key infrastructure (PKI) that contains a hierarchy of certification authorities (CAs), self-signed certificates are certificates that are created by each peer. Peer networking allows any node to act as a CA and removes the requirement that the root certificate to be deposited in each peer's trusted root store. Each peer generates the public key/private key pair and the certificate that is signed using the private key. The self-signed certificate is used for

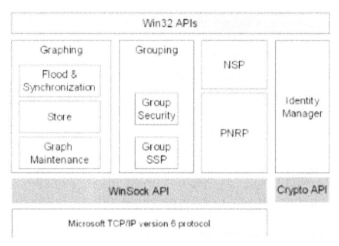

FIGURE 14 WINDOWS PEER-TO-PEER NETWORKING ARCHITECTURE IN WINDOWS XP

authentication and to provide information about the peer entity. Like X.509 authentication, peer networking authentication relies upon a chain of certificates tracing back to a public key that is trusted.

Windows Peer-to-Peer Networking Architecture

The architecture of Windows Peer-to-Peer Networking in Windows XP is shown in Figure 15.

Windows Peer-to-Peer Networking architecture consists of the following components:

- **Graphing** The Graphing component is responsible for maintaining a set of connected nodes known as a graph and providing flooding and replication of data across the graph. The Graphing component uses the Flood & Synchronization, Store, and Graph Maintenance subcomponents.

- **Grouping** The Grouping component is the security layer provided by default on top of a graph. The security layer defines the security model behind group creation, invitation, and connection to the group. In addition, Grouping leverages PNRP as the name resolution protocol - and enables multiple applications to share the same graph. The Grouping component uses the Group Security and Group Security Service Provider (SSP) subcomponents.

- **NSP** The Name Service Provider (NSP) component provides a mechanism to access an arbitrary name service provider. In the case of Windows Peer-to-Peer Networking, peer-to-peer applications use the NSP interface to access PNRP.

- **PNRP** The PNRP component provides peer-to-peer name resolution.

- **Identity Manager** Identity manager enables the creation and management of peer-to-peer identities.

- **Microsoft TCP/IP version 6 protocol** The Microsoft TCP/IP version 6 protocol (IPv6) provides the transport over which Windows Peer-to-Peer Networking operates.

Content and resources can be shared from both the center and the edge of the network. In client/server networking, content, and resources are typically shared from only the center of the network.

A network of peers is easily scaled and more reliable than a single server. A single server is subject to a single point of failure or can be a bottleneck in times of high network utilization.

A network of peers can share its processor, consolidating computing resources for distributed computing tasks, rather than relying on a single computer, such as a supercomputer.

Shared resources of peer computers can be directly accessed. Rather than sharing a file stored on a central server, a peer can share the file directly from its local storage.

Peer-to-peer networking solves the following problems:

1. Allows the processing resources of edge computers to be utilized for distributed computing tasks.

2. Allows local resources to be shared directly, without the need for intermediate servers.

3. Allows efficient multipoint communication without having to rely on IP multicast infrastructure.

CLIENT/SERVER COMPUTER NETWORK MODEL

Client–server computer network system represents a distributed computing model in which client applications request services from server processes. Clients and servers typically run on different computers interconnected by a computer network. Any use of the Internet, such as information retrieval, from the World Wide Web, is an example of client–server computing. However, the term is generally applied to systems in which an organization runs programs with multiple components distributed among computers in a network. The concept is frequently associated with enterprise computing, which makes the computing resources of an organization available to every part of its operation. A client application is a process or program that sends messages to a server via the network. Those messages request the server to perform a specific task, such as looking up a customer record in a database or returning a portion of a file on the server's hard disk. The client manages local resources such as a display, keyboard, local disks, and other peripherals. The server process or program listens for client requests that are transmitted via the network. Servers receive those requests and perform actions such as database queries and reading files. Server processes typically run on powerful PCs, workstations,, or mainframe , computers. An example of a client–server system is a banking application that allows a clerk to access account information on a central database server. All access is done via a PC client that provides a graphical user interface (GUI). An account number can be entered into the GUI along with how much money is to be withdrawn or deposited, respectively. The PC client validates the data provided by the clerk, transmits the data to the database server, and displays the results that are returned by the server. The client–server model is an extension of the object-based (or modular) programming model, where large pieces of software are structured into smaller components that have well defined interfaces. This decentralized approach helps to make complex programs maintainable and extensible.

Components interact by exchanging messages or by Remote Procedure Calling. The calling component becomes the client and the called component the server. A client–server environment may use a variety of operating systems and hardware from multiple vendors; standard network protocols like TCP/IP provide compatibility. Vendor independence and freedom of choice are further advantages of the model. Inexpensive PC equipment can be interconnected with mainframe servers, for example. Client–server systems can be scaled up in size more readily than centralized solutions since server functions can be distributed across more and more server computers as the number of clients' increases. Server processes can thus run in parallel, each process serving its own set of clients. However, when there are multiple servers that update information, there must be some coordination mechanism to avoid inconsistencies. The drawbacks of the client–server model are that security is more difficult to ensure in a distributed environment than it is in a centralized one. The administration of distributed equipment can be much more expensive than the maintenance of a centralized system that data distributed across servers needs to be kept consistent, and that the failure of one server can render a large client–server system unavailable. If a server fails, none of its clients can make further progress, unless the system is designed to be fault-tolerant .The computer network can also become a performance or reliability bottleneck: if the network fails, all servers become unreachable. If one client produces high network traffic then all clients may suffer from long response times.

The client-server model distinguishes between applications as well as devices. Network clients make requests to a server by sending messages, and servers respond to their clients by acting on each request and returning results. One server generally supports numerous clients, and multiple servers can be networked together in a pool to handle the increased processing load as the number of clients grows.

A client computer and a server computer are usually two separate devices, each customized for their designed purpose. For example, a Web client works best with a large screen display, while a Web server does not need any display at all and can be located anywhere in the world. However, in some cases a given device can function as both a client and a server for the same application. Likewise, a device that is a server for one application can simultaneously act as a client to other servers, for different applications.

Some of the most popular applications on the Internet follow the client-server model including email, FTP, and Web services. Each of these clients features a user interface (either graphic- or text-based) and a client application that allows the user to connect to servers. In the case of email

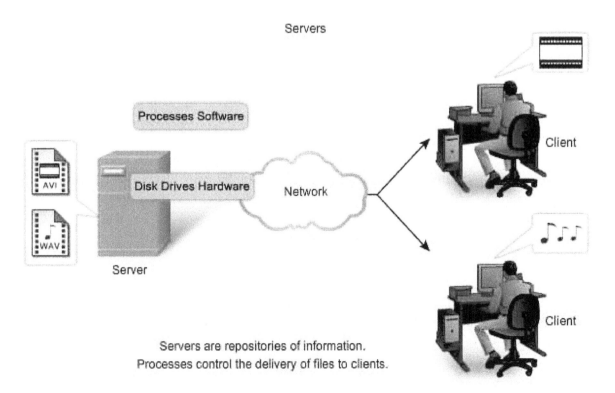

FIGURE 15 PEER TO PEER

and FTP, users enter a computer name (or sometimes an IP address) into the interface to set up connections to the server.

How Client/Server Network model works

The best example of a client server model is web browsers and web servers. To understand how client server networks operate, you need to have a clear idea of what the key terms stand for.

- A client is a machine, typically a personal computer (or mobile, desktop or laptop) that is equipped with network software applications. These applications are designed to request and receive data over the span of the network. In the case of the internet which is kind of like an obscenely big network, the possibilities of sending and receiving data are endless.

- A server is like an enormous warehouse, one that has more memory, bigger disk drives and more super powered central processors, as compared to client machines. A server is a storehouse of files, folders, databases and even more complicated applications. A server is more powerful than a client and can support and process the requests of a large number of clients, at time by networking together many servers the servers can support and enormous amount of clients without being overwhelmed by the load. A server does not necessarily require a display and is usually a separate machine from the client. However this is not a rule.

The process goes like this; the client sends the server a request for data, the server will process the request and produce the closest results to a request and send them back to the client. The machines acting as server and client are usually separate, but this is not a rule. Often a machine, which is acting as a server for another machine, can be a client for other servers. (Some popular client server based applications include email, ftp and web services). Many home networks are unintentionally client server models (the broadband routers used contain DHCP servers that provide IP addresses to the home computers, other network servers include print and backup servers).

The client server approach to networking is beneficial for many reasons, firstly connections do not have to be fixed and can be made per requirement, secondly many users can gain access to database applications, and thirdly creating software is much easier because it supports the modular approach to software building. In addition as opposed to peer-to-peer which is easy to expand, client server networks are more adept with regards to data security.

Advantages of using the client/server computing technology

Cost Effective: From the above it is clear that each component namely the client and server in client/server computing acts as a separate entity that can be connected by network. One of the advantages of having this type of design is it is possible for one to choose system as per the needs of the each component of a client/server computing environment. In other words the system need of system component in client/server computing is different from that of client component. Let us see this in brief. We know that server in client/server computing manages data in database. So for database management the server component system in client/server computing must be a system with more memory and also high processor speed. One has to choose a system for a server in client/server computing satisfying the above need. On the other hand, the system for client component in a client/server computing need not have the above design. That is system representing a client component in client/server computing need not have more memory or high processor speed. But since the client represents user interface or front end application the system must be able to support graphical utilities or applications and also have or support secondary storage as per the needs. So when choosing system for a client component of a client/server application one has to consider this point and make the choice. Thus from the above explanation it is clear that the system chosen for server can be done separately and for client separately as per the needs. This helps the organization to make cost effective system by purchasing systems as per the needs only.

Increased Performance: Performance is also increased without much effort. For instance if a organization decides to go for a system for server side to increase performance this can be done without affecting the user application because client component of client/.server computing need not be disturbed in this case.

Ease of effort and maintenance: Since the client and server component namely the user interface and database management are separated in the design of client/server computing it eases the effort of database administrator and developers. This is because developers can concentrate on user application alone. Also for instance if a user interface change occurs the system can be changed with little effort by making changes only in the client side without making server component changes.

The above are some of the main advantages in client/server computing. Though the advantages are numerous, there are some disadvantage also in client/server computing which made other technology like mainframes to take its shape and popularity. Some of the disadvantages are

We have seen above that the client/server computing is cost effective. It is true, as stated above, because when compared with mainframes the cost of hardware is very less in client/server computing. However, in a client/server computing, it is not that hardware only is present, but other costs included like number of multiple clients' maintenance that includes users, developers, and administrators to maintain database in server side and so on. When we consider all this the cost in client/server, computing is higher.

We know that mainframe is a centralized database managed system. Though the system is costlier in hardware point of view it provides reliable and secured system that is very much needed for big real time applications. This is because in these real times huge applications the main requirement is system must not stop and must run throughout without failure that is achieved by centralized maintained mainframe systems. However, in client/server, computing it is not maintained centrally and the reliability is not much that means if the system was stopped in between then real time huge application would face huge loss in term of productivity and cost.

Thus from the above discussion of advantages and disadvantages it is very clear that one has to make a wise choice of the required technology depending upon the requirement since each technology has its own advantages and disadvantages. For instance in real time huge applications where data handled is much and interconnectivity is for wider area say across the globe and where the system must run without stopping throughout like airline applications, banks it is good to choose mainframe systems. However, if the geographical area covered is small and we need cost effective system is it good to go for client/server computing.

CLASSIFICATION OF COMPUTER NETWORKS

Computer Networks are often classified by their distance and physical or organizational extent or their purpose. Usage, trust level, and access rights differ between these kinds of networks:

A. LAN

    I. VLAN

    II. WLAN

B. MAN

C. WAN

A Local Area Network (LAN) is a network that is confined to a relatively small area. It is generally limited to a geographic area such as a writing lab, school, or building. The interprocessor distance is within 2 miles or (10 meters to 1 kilometer) and the processors are located in a room, a building, or a campus. Computers connected to a network are broadly categorized as servers or workstations. Servers are generally not used by humans directly, but rather run continuously to provide "services" to the other computers (and their human users) on the network. Services provided can include printing and faxing, software hosting, file storage and sharing, messaging, data storage and retrieval, complete access control (security) for the network's resources, and many others.

Workstations are called such because they typically do have a human user that interacts with the network through them. Workstations were traditionally considered a desktop, consisting of a computer, keyboard, display, and mouse, or a laptop, with integrated keyboard, display, and touchpad. With the advent of the tablet computer, and the touch screen devices such as iPad and iPhone, our definition of workstation is quickly evolving to include those devices, because of their ability to interact with the network and utilize network services.

Servers tend to be more powerful than workstations, although configurations are guided by needs. For example, a group of servers might be located in a secure area, away from humans, and only accessed through the network. In such cases, it would be common for the servers to operate without a dedicated display or keyboard. However, the size and speed of the server's processor(s), hard drive, and main memory might add dramatically to the cost of the system. On the other hand, a workstation might not need as much storage or working memory, but might require an expensive display to accommodate the needs of its user. Every computer on a network should be appropriately configured for its use.

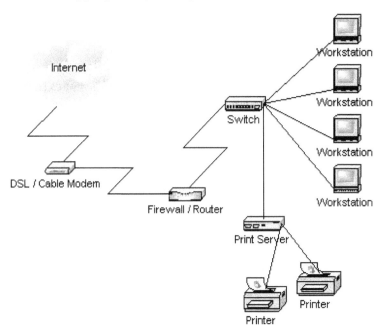

Figure 16 Example of a LAN Diagram

On a single LAN, computers and servers may be connected by cables or wirelessly. Wireless access to a wired network is made possible by wireless access points (WAPs). These WAP devices provide a bridge between computers and networks. A typical WAP might have the theoretical capacity to connect hundreds or even thousands of wireless users to a network, although practical capacity might be far less.

Nearly always servers will be connected by cables to the network, because the cable connections remain the fastest. Workstations which are stationary (desktops) are also usually connected by a cable to the network, although the cost of wireless adapters has dropped to the point that, when installing workstations in an existing facility with inadequate wiring, it can be easier and less expensive to use wireless for a desktop.

Today, Local Area Networks are defined as a single broadcast domain. This means that if a user broadcasts information on his/her LAN, the broadcast will be received by every other user on the LAN. Broadcasts are prevented from leaving a LAN by using a router. The disadvantage of this method is routers usually take more time to process incoming data compared to a bridge or a switch. More importantly, the formation of broadcast domains depends on the physical connection of the devices in the network. Virtual Local Area Networks (VLAN's) were developed as an alternative solution to using routers to contain broadcast traffic.

In this section, we define VLAN's and examine the difference between a LAN and a VLAN. This is followed by a discussion on the advantages VLAN's introduce to a network in next section.

WHAT IS A VLAN

In a traditional LAN, workstations are connected to each other by means of a hub or a repeater. These devices propagate any incoming data throughout the network. However, if two people attempt to send information at the same time, a collision will occur and all the transmitted data will be lost. Once the collision has occurred, it will continue to be propagated throughout the network by hubs and repeaters. The original information will therefore need to be resent after waiting for the collision to be resolved, thereby incurring a significant wastage of time and resources. To prevent collisions from traveling through all the workstations in the network, a bridge or a switch can be used. These devices will not forward collisions, but will allow broadcasts (to every user in the network) and multicasts (to a pre-specified group of users) to pass through. A router may be used to prevent broadcasts and multicasts from traveling through the network.

The workstations, hubs, and repeaters together form a LAN segment. A LAN segment is also known as a collision domain since collisions remain within the segment. The area within which broadcasts and multicasts are confined is called a broadcast domain or LAN. Thus, a LAN can consist of one or more LAN segments. Defining broadcast and collision domains in a LAN depends on how the workstations, hubs, switches, and routers are physically connected together. This means that everyone on a LAN must be located in the same area (see *Figure*1).

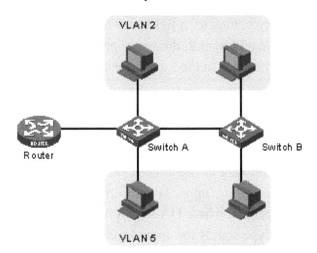

Figure 17 Physical View of VLAN

Ethernet is a network technology based on the Carrier Sense Multiple Access/Collision Detect (CSMA/CD) mechanism. As the medium is shared in an Ethernet, network performance may degrade as the number of hosts on the network is increasing. If the number of the hosts in the network reaches a certain level, problems caused by collisions, broadcasts, and so on emerge, which may cause the network operating improperly. In addition to the function that suppresses collisions (which can also be achieved by interconnecting LANs), virtual LAN (virtual LAN) can also isolate broadcast packets. VLAN divides a LAN into multiple logical LANs with each being a broadcast domain. Hosts in the same VLAN can communicate with each other like in a LAN.

However, hosts from different VLANs cannot communicate directly. In this way, broadcast packets are confined to a single VLAN, as illustrated above in the diagram.

A VLAN is not restricted by physical factors, that is to say, hosts that reside in different network segments may belong to the same VLAN, users in a VLAN can be connected to the same switch, or span across multiple switches or routers.

VLAN technology has the following advantages:

1)   Broadcast traffic is confined to each VLAN, reducing bandwidth utilization and improving network performance.

2)   LAN security is improved. Packets in different VLANs cannot communicate with each other directly. That is, users in a VLAN cannot interact directly with users in other VLANs, unless routers or Layer 3 switches are used.

3)   A more flexible way to establish virtual working groups. With VLAN technology, clients can be allocated to different working groups, and users from the same group do not have to be within the same physical area, making network construction and maintenance much easier and more flexible.

VLAN Fundamental

To enable packets being distinguished by the VLANs they belong to, a field used to identifying VLANs is added to packets. As common switches operate on Layer 2, they only process Layer 2 encapsulation information and the field thus needs to be inserted to the Layer 2 encapsulation information of packets.

The format of the packets carrying the fields identifying VLANs is defined in IEEE 802.1Q, which is issued in 1999.

In the header of a traditional Ethernet packet, the field following the destination MAC address and the source MAC address is protocol type, which indicates the upper layer protocol type. Figure 13 illustrates the format of a traditional Ethernet packet, where DA stands for destination MAC address, SA stands for source MAC address, and Type stands for upper layer protocol type.

DA&SA	Type	DATA

Figure 18 The format of a triditional Ethernet package

IEEE802.1Q defines a four-byte VLAN Tag field between the DA&SA field and the Type field to carry VLAN-related information, as shown in Figure14.

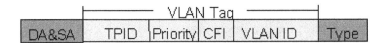

Figure 19 The position and format of the VLAN Tag Field

The VLAN Tag field comprises four sub-fields: the TPID field, the Priority field, the CFI field, and the VLAN ID field.

- The TPID field, 16 bits in length and with a value of 0x8100, indicates that a packet carries a VLAN tag with it.

- The Priority field, three bits in length, indicates the priority of a packet. For information about packet priority, refer to *QoS Configuration* in *QoS Volume*.

- The CFI field, one bit in length, specifies whether or not the MAC addresses are encapsulated in standard format when packets are transmitted across different medium. This field is not described here.

- The VLAN ID field, 12 bits in length and with its value ranging from 0 to 4095, identifies the ID of the VLAN a packet belongs to. As VLAN IDs of 0 and 4095 are reserved by the protocol, the actual value of this field ranges from 1 to 4094.

A network device determines the VLAN to which a packet belongs to by the VLAN ID field the packet carries. The VLAN Tag determines the way a packet is processed.

VLAN Classification

Based on different criteria, VLANs can be classified into different categories. The following types are the most commonly used:

- Port-based

- MAC address-based

- Protocol-based

- IP-subnet-based

- Policy-based

- Other types

Let us look at the port-based VLANs, protocol-based VLANs, and IP-subnet-based VLANs.

VLAN Interface

VLAN interfaces are virtual interfaces used for communications between different VLANs. Each VLAN can have one VLAN interface. Packets of a VLAN can be forwarded on network layer through the corresponding VLAN interface. As each VLAN forms a broadcast domain, a VLAN can be an IP network segment and the VLAN interface can be the gateway to enable IP address-based Layer 3 forwarding.

Port-Based VLAN

This is the simplest yet the most effective way of classifying VLANs. It groups VLAN members by port. After added to a VLAN, a port can forward the packets of the VLAN.

I. Port link type

Based on the tag-handling mode, a port's link type can be one of the following three:

- Access port: the port only belongs to one VLAN, normally used to connect user device;

- Trunk port: the port can belong to multiple VLANs, can receive/send packets for multiple VLANs, normally used to connect network devices;

- Hybrid port: the port can belong to multiple VLANs, can receive or send packets for multiple VLANs, used to connect either user or network devices;

- The differences between Hybrid and Trunk port:

- A Hybrid port allows packets of multiple VLANs to be sent without the Tag label;

- A Trunk port only allows packets from the default VLAN to be sent without the Tag label.

II. Default VLAN

You can configure the default VLAN for a port. By default, VLAN 1 is the default VLAN for all ports. However, this can be changed as needed.

- An Access port only belongs to one VLAN. Therefore, its default VLAN is the VLAN it resides in and cannot be configured.

- You can configure the default VLAN for the Trunk port or the Hybrid port as they can both belong to multiple VLANs.

Protocol-Based VLAN

In this approach, inbound packets are assigned with different VLAN IDs based on their protocol type and encapsulation format. The protocols that can be used to categorize VLANs include IP, IPX, and AppleTalk (AT). The encapsulation formats include Ethernet II, 802.3, 802.3/802.2 LLC, and 802.3/802.2 SNAP.

A protocol-based VLAN can be defined by a protocol template, which is determined by encapsulation format and protocol type. A port can be associated to multiple protocol templates.

An untagged packet (that is, packet carrying no VLAN tag) reaching a port associated with a protocol-based VLAN will be processed as follows.

- If the packet matches a protocol template, the packet will be tagged with the VLAN ID of the protocol-based VLAN defined by the protocol template.

- If the packet matches no protocol template, the packet will be tagged with the default VLAN ID of the port.

A tagged packet (that is, a packet carrying VLAN tags) reaching the port is processed in the same way as that of port-based VLAN.

- If the port is configured to permit packets with the VLAN tag, the packet is forwarded.

- If the port is configured to deny packets with the VLAN tag, the packet is dropped.

- This feature is mainly used to bind the service type with VLAN for ease of management and maintenance.

IP-Subnet-Based VLAN

In this approach, VLANs are categorized based on the source IP addresses and the subnet masks of packets. After receiving an untagged packet from a port, the device finds its association with the current VLAN based on the source address contained in the packet, and then forwards the packet in the corresponding VLAN. This allows packets from a certain network segment or with certain IP addresses to be forwarded in a VLAN.

Super VLAN

With the development of networks, network address resource has become more and more scarce. The concept of Super VLAN was introduced to save the IP address space. Super VLAN is also named as VLAN aggregation. A super VLAN involves multiple sub-VLANs. It has a VLAN interface with an IP address, but no physical ports can be added to the super VLAN. A sub-VLAN can has physical ports added but has no IP address and VLAN interface. All ports of sub-VLANs use the VLAN interface's IP address of the super VLAN. Packets cannot be forwarded between sub-VLANs at Layer 2.

If Layer 3 communication is needed from a sub-VLAN, it will use the IP address of the super VLAN as the gateway IP address. Thus, multiple sub-VLANs share the same gateway address and thereby save IP address resource.

The local Address Resolution Protocol (ARP) proxy function is used to realize Layer 3 communications between sub-VLANs and between sub-VLANs and other networks. It works as follows: after creating the super VLAN and the VLAN interface, enable the local ARP proxy function to forward ARP response and request packets.

Isolate-User-VLAN

The isolate-user-VLAN adopts a two-tier VLAN structure. In this approach, two types of VLANs, isolate-user-VLAN and secondary VLAN, are configured on the same device.

- The isolate-user-VLAN is mainly used for upstream data exchange. An isolate-user-VLAN can have multiple secondary VLANs associated to it. The upstream device only knows the isolate-user-VLAN, how the secondary VLANs are working is not its concern. In this way, network configurations are simplified and VLAN resources are saved.

- Secondary VLANs are used for connecting users. Secondary VLANs are isolated from each other on Layer 2. To allow users from different secondary VLANs under the same isolate-user-VLAN to communicate with each other, you can enable ARP proxy on the upstream device to realize Layer 3 communication between the secondary VLANs.

- One isolate-user-VLAN can have multiple secondary VLANs, which are invisible to the corresponding upstream device.

As illustrated in the figure 15, the isolate-user-vlan function is enabled on Switch B. VLAN 10 is the isolate-user-VLAN, and VLAN 2, VLAN 5, and VLAN 8 are secondary VLANs that are mapped to VLAN 10 and are invisible to Switch A.

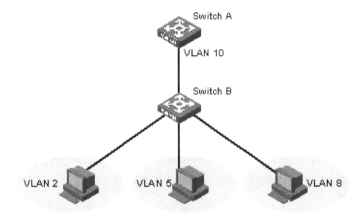

Figure 20 Example of an isolate user VLAN

Voice VLAN

Voice VLANs are configured specially for voice traffic. By adding the ports that connect voice devices to voice VLANs, you can configure quality of service (QOS for short) attributes for the voice traffic, increasing transmission priority and ensuring voice quality. A device determines whether a received packet is a voice packet by checking its source MAC address. Packets containing source MAC addresses that comply with the voice device Organizationally Unique Identifier (OUI for short) addresses are regarded as voice traffic, and are forwarded in the voice VLANs.

You can configure the OUI addresses in advance or use the default OUI addresses, which are listed as follows:

Table 1 The default OUI addresses of different vendors

Number	OUI address	Vendors
1	0001-e300-0000	Siemens phone
2	0003-6b00-0000	Cisco phone
3	0004-0d00-0000	Avaya phone
4	00d0-1e00-0000	Pingtel phone
5	0060-b900-0000	Philips/NEC phone
6	00e0-7500-0000	Polycom phone
7	00e0-bb00-0000	3Com phone

Note:

- As the first 24 bits of a MAC address (in binary format), an OUI address is a globally unique identifier assigned to a vendor by IEEE (Institute of Electrical and Electronics Engineers).

- The default OUI address can be configured/removed manually.

WORKING MODES OF VOICE VLAN

A voice VLAN can operate in two working modes: automatic mode and manual mode.

- In automatic mode, the system identifies the source MAC address contained in the untagged packet sent when the IP phone is powered on and matches it against the OUI addresses. If a match is found, the system will automatically add the port into the Voice VLAN and apply ACL rules to ensure the packet precedence. An aging time can be configured for the voice VLAN. The system will remove a port from the voice VLAN if no voice packet is received from it after the aging time. The adding and deleting of ports are automatically realized by the system.

- In manual mode, administrators add the IP phone access port to the voice VLAN. It then identifies the source MAC address contained in the packet, matches it against the OUI addresses, and decides whether to forward the packet in the voice VLAN. The administrators apply ACL rules while adding or deleting a port from the voice VLAN. In this mode, the adding or deleting of ports is realized by the administrators.

- Both modes forward tagged packets according to their tags.

The above two working modes are configured in interface view. The working modes for different voice VLANs vary and different ports can be configured to work in different modes.

The following table lists the co-relation between the working modes of a voice VLAN, the voice traffic type of an IP phone, and the interface modes of a VLAN interface.

Table 2 Voice VLAN Operating mode and the corresponding voice traffic types

Voice VLAN operating mode	Voice traffic type	Interface link type
Automatic mode	Tagged voice traffic	Access: the traffic type is not supported
		Trunk: supported provided that the default VLAN of the access port exists and is not a voice VLAN and that the access port belongs to the voice VLAN
		Hybrid: supported if the default VLAN of the access port exists and is not a voice VLAN. Besides, the default VLAN need to be in the list of tagged VLANs whose packets can pass through the access port
	Untagged voice traffic	Access, Trunk, Hybrid: not supported

Voice VLAN operating mode	Voice traffic type	Interface link type
Manual mode	Tagged voice traffic	Access: not supported
		Trunk: supported provided that the default VLAN of the access port exists and is not a voice VLAN and that the access port belongs to the default VLAN
		Hybrid: supported provided that the default VLAN of the access port exists and is not the voice VLAN. Besides, the voice VLAN must be in the list of tagged VLANs whose packets can pass through the access port
	Untagged voice traffic	Access: supported provided that the default VLAN of the access port is a voice VLAN
		Trunk: supported provided that the default VLAN of the access port is a voice VLAN and that the access port allows packets from the voice VLAN to pass through
		Hybrid port: supported provided that the default VLAN of the access port is a voice VLAN and that the voice VLAN is in the list of untagged VLANs whose packets are allowed to pass through the access port

Caution:

- If the voice traffic sent by an IP phone is tagged and that the access port has 802.1-x authentication and Guest VLAN enabled, assign different VLAN IDs for the voice VLAN, the default VLAN of the access port, and the 802.1x guest VLAN.

- If the voice traffic sent by an IP phone is untagged, to realize the voice VLAN feature, the default VLAN of the access port can only be configured as the voice VLAN. Note that at this time 802.1 x authentication function cannot be realized.

- Note:

- The default VLANs for all ports is VLAN 1. Using commands, users can either configure the default VLAN of a port, or configure to allow a certain VLAN to pass through the port.

- Use the **display interface** command to display the default VLAN and the VLANs that are allowed to go through a certain port.

Security Mode and Normal Mode of Voice VLAN

Ports that have the voice VLAN feature enabled can be divided into two modes based on their filtering mechanisms applied to inbound packets.

- Security mode: only voice packets with source OUI MAC addresses can pass through the inbound port (with the voice VLAN feature enabled), other non-voice packets will be discarded, including authentication packets, such as 802.1 authentication packet.

- Normal mode: both voice packets and non-voice packets are allowed to pass through an inbound port (with the voice VLAN feature enabled), the former will abide by the voice VLAN forwarding mechanism whereas the latter normal VLAN forwarding mechanism.

It is recommended that you do not mix voice packets with other types of data in a voice VLAN. If necessary, please ensure that the security mode is disabled.

WLAN

A wireless local area network (WLAN) is a local area network (LAN) that doesn't rely on wired Ethernet connections. A WLAN can be either an extension to a current wired network or an alternative to it.

WLANs have data transfer speeds ranging from 1 to 54Mbps, with some manufacturers offering proprietary 108Mbps solutions. The 802.11n standard can reach 300 to 600Mbps.

Because the wireless signal is broadcast so everybody nearby can share it, several security precautions are necessary to ensure only authorized users can access your WLAN.

A WLAN signal can be broadcast to cover an area ranging in size from a small office to a large campus. Most commonly, a WLAN access point provides access within a radius of 65 to 300 feet.

WLAN types

Private home or small business WLAN

Commonly, a home or business WLAN employs one or two access points to broadcast a signal around a 100- to 200-foot radius. You can find equipment for installing a home WLAN in many retail stores.

With few exceptions, hardware in this category subscribes to the 802.11a, b, or g standards (also known as Wi-Fi); some home and office WLANs now adhere to the new 802.11n standard. In addition, because of security concerns, many home and office WLANs adhere to the Wi-Fi Protected Access 2 (WPA2) standard.

ENTERPRISE CLASS WLAN

An enterprise class WLAN employs a large number of individual access points to broadcast the signal to a wide area. The access points have more features than home or small office WLAN equipment, such as better security, authentication, remote management, and tools to help integrate with existing networks. These access points have a larger coverage area than home or small office equipment. They are designed to work together to cover a much larger area. This equipment can adhere to the 802.11a, b, g, or n standard, or to security-refining standards, such as 802.1x and WPA2.

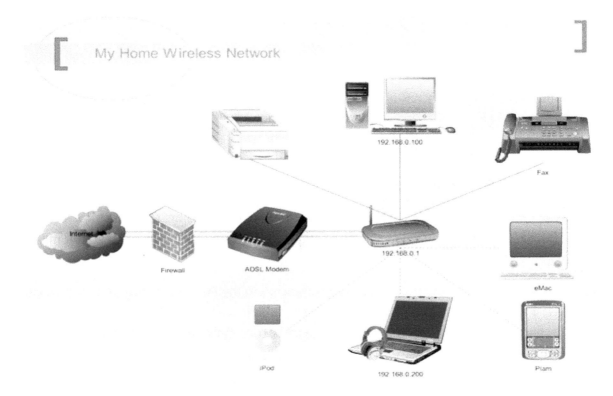

Figure 21 A Home wireless networks

WLAN standards

Several standards for WLAN hardware exist:

Table 3 Standards for WLAN

WLAN standard	Pros	Cons
802.11a	<ul><li>Faster data transfer rates (up to 54Mbps)</li><li>Supports more simultaneous connections</li><li>Less susceptible to interference</li></ul>	<ul><li>Short range (60-100 feet)</li><li>Less able to penetrate physical barriers</li></ul>
812.11b	<ul><li>Better at penetrating physical barriers</li><li>Longest range (70-150 feet)</li></ul>	<ul><li>Slower data transfer rates (up to 11Mbps)</li><li>Doesn't support as many</li></ul>

	• Hardware is usually less expensive	simultaneous connections
		• More susceptible to interference
802.11g	• Faster data transfer rates (up to 54Mbps)	• More susceptible to interference
	• Better range than 802.11b (65-120 feet)	
802.11n	The 802.11n standard was recently ratified by the Institute of Electrical and Electronics Engineers (IEEE), as compared to the previous three standards. Though specifications may change, it is expected to allow data transfer rates up to 600Mbps, and may offer larger ranges.	

Security standards

The 802.11x standards provide some basic security, but are becoming less adequate as use of wireless networking spreads. Following are security standards that extend or replace the basic standard:

WEP (Wired Equivalent Privacy)

WEP encrypts data traffic between the wireless access point and the client computer, but doesn't actually secure either end of the transmission. WEP's encryption level is relatively weak (only 40 to 128 bits). Many analysts consider WEP security to be weak and easy to crack.

WPA (Wi-Fi Protected Access)

WPA implements higher security and addresses the flaws in WEP, but is intended to be only an intermediate measure until further 802.11i security measures are developed.

802.1x

This standard is part of a full WPA security standard. WPA consists of a pair of smaller standards that address different aspects of security:

- TKIP (Temporal Key Integrity Protocol encryption), which encrypts the wireless signal

- 802.1x, which handles the authentication of users to the network

Commonly, wireless systems have you log into individual wireless access points or let you access the wireless network, but then keep you from accessing network data until you provide further authentication (e.g., VPN).

802.1x makes you authenticate to the wireless network itself, not an individual access point, and not to some other level, such as VPN. This boosts security, because unauthorized traffic can be denied right at the wireless access point.

WPA2/802.11i

The Wi-Fi Alliances coined the term "WPA2" for easy use by manufacturers, technicians, and end users. However, the IEEE name of the standard itself is 802.11i. The encryption level is so high that it requires dedicated chips on the hardware to handle it.

In practical use, WPA2 devices have interoperability with WPA devices. When not interfacing with older WPA hardware, WPA2 devices will run strictly by the 802.11i specifications.

WPA2 consists of a pair of smaller standards that address different aspects of security:

- WPA2-Personal, which uses a pre-shared key (similar to a single password available to groups of users, instead of a single individual); the pre-shared key is stored on the access point and the end user's computer

- WPA2-Enterprise, which authenticates users against a centralized authentication service

IU Secure, the new IU wireless network for students, faculty, and staff, uses WPA2 Enterprise for authentication.

MAN

Metropolitan Area Network (MAN) is a computer network usually spanning a campus or a city, which typically connect a few local area networks using high-speed backbone technologies. A MAN often provides efficient connections to a wide area network (WAN). Three important features discriminate MANs from LANs or WANs:

1. The network size falls intermediate between LANs and WANs. A MAN typically covers an area of between two miles or 5 and 50 km range. Many MANs cover an area the size of a city, although in some cases MANs may be as small as a group of buildings.

2. A MAN (like a WAN) is not generally owned by a single organization. The MAN, its communications links, and equipment are generally owned either by a consortium of users or by a network service provider who sells the service to the users.

3. A MAN often acts as a high-speed network to allow sharing of regional resources. It is also frequently used to provide a shared connection to other networks using a link to a WAN.

MAN adopted technologies from both LAN and WAN to serve its purpose. Some legacy technologies used for MAN are ATM, FDDI, DQDB, and SMDS. These older technologies are in the process of being displaced by Gigabit Ethernet and 10 Gigabit Ethernet. At the physical level, MAN links between LANs have been built on fibre optical cables or using wireless technologies such as microwave or radio.

Most widely used technologies to develop a MAN (Metropolitan Area Network) network are FDDI (fiber distribution data interface), **ATM (Asynchronous Transfer Mode)** and SMDS (switched multi megabit data service).**ATM (Asynchronous Transfer Mode)** is the most frequently used of all. ATM (Asynchronous Transfer Mode) is a digital data transfer technology. It was developed in 1980 to improve the transportation of real time data over a single network. ATM (Asynchronous Transfer Mode) works just like cell relay system, where data is separated in the form of fixed equal sized packets and is transferred overtime. The purpose of ATM (Asynchronous Transfer Mode) was to access clear audio and video results during a video conferencing. The attributes of ATM has enabled it to become a base of wide area data networking.

ATM (Asynchronous Transfer Mode) combines the characteristics of circuit switching and packet switching, which allows it to transfer even the real time data. **FDDI** is a standard for data transfer over LAN, which can be extended to the range of approximately 200kms. **FDDI** can help support the data transmission of many thousand users. This is the reason why it is referred to as the MAN (Metropolitan Area Network) technology. **FDDI** uses optical fiber for its basic infrastructure that is why it is referred to as fiber distribution data interface. When data is transferred through a connectionless service, we use the technology named as **SMDS**. Connectionless service implies that data is transferred by storing the information in the header and it reaches its destination independently through any network. When the data is transferred using the technology of **SMDS**, it also forms small data packets just like in ATM. However **SMDS** allows the transmission of data over large geographical areas in the form of datagrams (the data packets of an unreliable data service provider). Nowadays MAN (Metropolitan Area Network) links are established using infrared and microwave signals.

How MAN works

MAN (Metropolitan Area Network) usually falls between LAN and WAN. It is generally applied to connect geographically dispersed LANs. Therefore, the goal of MAN is to develop a communication link between two independent LAN nodes. A MAN (Metropolitan Area Network) is usually established using optical fiber. The network is established using routers and switches. A switch is a port which is active in handling the filtration of data usually coming in the form of frames. Any switch acts as a dual port, at one end it is handling filtration of data and at the other end managing connections. Router is another device for facilitating the netwosrk connection. Router helps the data packets to identify the path to be taken. Hence in other words it keeps an eye on the data transfer. MAN (Metropolitan Area Network) is usually operated over an area of up to 50kms.

ADVANTAGES OF MAN (METROPOLITAN AREA NETWORK)

MAN (Metropolitan Area Network) falls in between the LAN and WAN. It therefore increases the efficiency of handling data while at the same time saves the cost attached to establish a wide area network. MAN (Metropolitan Area Network) offers centralized management of data. It enables you to connect many fast LANs together. Telephone companies worldwide have facilitated the transfer of data with the help of an underground optical fiber network. These optical fibers increase the efficiency and speed of data transfer. The optical fibers enable you to access a speed of almost 1000mbps. If you develop a WAN of 1.45 mbps its cost is more than what it gives you. Whereas when you establish metropolitan area network it offers you the speed of 1000mbps as a whole with the lowest cost involved.

The onslaught of single-mode fiber being installed in virtually every available right-of-way has given much access to fiber between remote locations in most major cities. Commonly referred to as "dark fiber" this installed fiber can be leased for the purpose of effectively extending your LAN (local area network) over distances up to two miles or little more or 80 Kilometers (see diagram below). This metamorphosis of the LAN from a relatively limited geographic location (within a building or a local campus) to a significantly expanded area is referred to as a MAN (metropolitan area network).

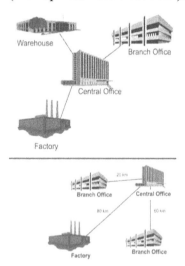

Figure 22 Example of MAN

There are significant advantages to a MAN when compared to the alternative, a WAN (wide area network). MANs allow communication between network equipment using native protocols such as Fast Ethernet, Gigabit Ethernet, or ATM. In contrast, WANs require conversion from native LAN protocol to a protocol offered by a given carrier/service provider. This requires the use of a network router to deal with conversion between the disparate protocols. This is typically more expensive for the service provided and reduces the throughput (100Mbps or Gbps traffic must be transmitted across slower speed WAN protocols like T1/E1 at no more than about 2 Mbps).

Looking at other advantage is that MAN provides far more control of the connection for end to end. With a MAN, you have complete control of the communication process. This includes the ability to remotely manage, monitor, and perform diagnostics yourself in comparison to the WAN connection in which you must rely on your service provider to manage and maintain the link between you and your remote office.

Conversion technology allows common native network protocols to be delivered over distances that can traverse most major metropolitan areas. The two most common network backbone protocols, Fast Ethernet and Gigabit Ethernet, can be transmitted as far as 80 km (65km for Gigabit). Long haul options are also available for T1 DS3, ATM and others. Again, chassis-based conversion technology is capable of handling multiple protocols and multiple interface types in a single modular chassis. The Metropolitan Area Network (MAN) protocols are mostly at the data link level (layer 2 in the OSI model), which are defined by IEEE, ITU-T, etc.

WAN – WIDE AREA NETWORK

METROPOLITAN AREA NETWORK (MAN)-The interprocessor distance is 10 kilometers and the processors are located in a city.

WIDE AREA NETWORKS (WAN)-The interprocessor distance is from 100 kilometers to 1000 kilometers and the processors are located in a country or a continent.

INTERNETWORKS-The interprocessor distance is 10,000 kilometers and a popular example is the INTERNET.

WIDE AREA NETWORK

Wide Area Networks (WANs) connect networks in larger geographic areas, such as Florida, the United States, or the world. Dedicated transoceanic cabling or satellite uplinks may be used to connect this type of global network. A WAN could also be described as a voice, data, or video network that provides connections from one or more computers or networks within an eligible school or library to one or more computers or networks that are *external* to such eligible school or library. Excluded from this definition is a network that provides connections between or among buildings of a single school campus or between or among buildings of a single library outlet or branch, when those connections do not cross a public right of way.

Using a WAN, schools in Florida can communicate with places like Tokyo in a matter of seconds, without paying enormous phone bills. Two users a half-world apart with workstations equipped with microphones and a webcams might teleconference in real time. A WAN is complicated. It uses multiplexers, bridges, and routers to connect local and metropolitan networks to global communications networks like the Internet. To users, however, a WAN will not appear to be much different than a LAN. A wide area network (WAN) is a large telecommunications network that consists of a collection of LANs and other networks. WANs generally span a wide geographical area, and can be used to connect cities, states, or even countries.

Although they appear like an up-scaled version of a LAN, WANs are actually structured and operated quite differently.

Many WANs are built for one particular organization and are private. Others, built by Internet service providers (ISPs), provide connections from an organization's LAN to the Internet." ♦

Several options are available for WAN connectivity: leased line, circuit switching, packet switching, and cell relay. WANs are often built using leased lines. These leased lines involve a direct point-to-point connection between two sites. Point-to-point WAN service may involve either analog dial-up lines or dedicated leased digital private lines.

The Existence of WANs

WANs have existed for decades, but new technologies, services, and applications have developed over the years to increase their effect on business. WANs were originally developed for digital leased-line services carrying only voice (not data).

At first, they connected the private branch exchanges (PBXs) of remote offices of the same

company. WANs are still used for voice services, but today they are used more frequently for data and image transmission (like videoconferencing). These added applications have spurred significant growth in WAN usage, primarily because of the surge in LAN connections to the wider networks.

A wide area network allows companies to make use of common resources in order to operate. Internal functions such as sales, production and development, marketing, and accounting can also be shared with authorized locations through

FIGURE 23 EXAMPLE OF A PBX

this sort of network.

In the event of a problem – say a company facility is damaged from a natural disaster – employees can move to another location and access the network. Productivity is not lost.

IP CLASSIFICATIONS

Internet Protocol, **IP** is an address of a computer or other network device on a network using IP or TCP/IP. For example, the number "166.70.10.23" is an example of such an address. These addresses are similar to an addresses used on a house and is what allows data to reach the appropriate destination on a network and the Internet.

There are five classes of available IP ranges: Class A, Class B, Class C, Class D and Class E, while only A, B, and C are commonly used. Each class allows for a range of valid IP addresses. Below is a listing of these addresses.

Table 4 Address range

Class	Address Range	Supports
Class A	1.0.0.1 to 126.255.255.254	Supports 16 million hosts on each of 127 networks.
Class B	128.1.0.1 to 191.255.255.254	Supports 65,000 hosts on each of 16,000 networks.
Class C	192.0.1.1 to 223.255.254.254	Supports 254 hosts on each of 2 million networks.
Class D	224.0.0.0 to 239.255.255.255	Reserved for multicast groups.
Class E	240.0.0.0 to 254.255.255.254	Reserved for future use, or Research and Development Purposes.

Ranges 127.x.x.x are reserved for the loopback or localhost, for example, **127.0.0.1** is the common loopback address. Range **255.255.255.255** broadcasts to all hosts on the local network.

IP address breakdown

Every IP address is broke down into four sets of octets that break down into binary to represent the actual IP address. The below table is an example of the IP 255.255.255.255. If you are new to binary, we highly recommend reading our binary and hexadecimal conversions section to get a better understanding of what we are doing in the below charts.

Table 5 IP Address Breakdown

IP:	255	255	255	255
Binary value:	11111111	11111111	11111111	11111111
Octet value:	8	8	8	8

If we were to break down the IP "166.70.10.23", you would get the below value. In the below table, the first row is the IP address, the second row is the binary values, and the third row shows how the binary value equals the section of the IP address.

Table 6 IP Address Breakdown

166	70	10	23
10100110	01000110	00001010	00010111
128+32+4+2=166	64+4+2=70	8+2=10	16+4+2+1=23

Automatically assigned addresses

Several IP addresses are automatically assigned when you setup a home network. These default addresses are what allow your computer and other network devices to communicate and broadcast information over your network. Table 8 displays the most commonly assigned network addresses in a home network:

Table 7 commonly assigned IP addresses in a home network

192.168.1.0   0 is the automatically assigned network address.

192.168.1.1   1 is the commonly used address used as the gateway.

192.168.1.2   2 is also a commonly used address used for a gateway.

192.168.1.3 - 254 Addresses beyond 3 are assigned to computers and devices on the network.

192.168.1.255   255 is automatically assigned on most networks as the broadcast address.

If you have ever connected to your home network, you should be familiar with the gateway address or 192.168.1.1, which is the address you use to connect to your home network router and change its settings.

By default, the router you use will assign each of your computers their own IP address, often using NAT to forward the data coming from those computers to outside networks such as the Internet. If you need to register an IP address that can be seen on the Internet, you must register through InterNIC or use a web host that can assign you addresses.

Anyone who connects to the Internet is assigned an IP address by their Internet Service Provider (ISP) who has registered a range of IP addresses. For example, lets assume your ISP is given 100 addresses, 109.145.93.150-250. This means the ISP owns addresses 109.145.93.150 to 109.145.93.250 and is able to assign any address in that range to its customers. Therefore, all these addresses belong to your ISP address until they are assigned to a customer's computer. In the case of a dial-up connection, you are given a new IP address each time you dial into your ISP. With most broadband Internet, service providers because you are always connected to the Internet your address rarely changes and will remain the same until the service provider requires it to be changed.

IP SUBNETTING (IPV4)

Addresses beginning with **01111111**, or **127** decimal, are reserved for loopback and for internal testing on a local machine; [You can test this: you should always be able to ping **127.0.0.1**, which points to yourself] Class D addresses are reserved for multicasting; Class E addresses are reserved for future use. They should not be used for host addresses.

Now we can see how the Class determines, by default, which part of the IP address belongs to the network (N, in blue) and which part belongs to the node (n, in red).

- Class A -- NNNNNNNN.nnnnnnnn.nnnnnnnn.nnnnnnnn
- Class B -- NNNNNNNN.NNNNNNNN.nnnnnnnn.nnnnnnnn
- Class C -- NNNNNNNN.NNNNNNNN.NNNNNNNN.nnnnnnnn

In the example, 140.179.220.200 is a Class B address so by default the Network part of the address (also known as the *Network Address*) is defined by the first two octets (140.179.x.x) and the node part is defined by the last 2 octets (x.x.220.200).

In order to specify the network address for a given IP address, the node section is set to all "0"s. In our example, 140.179.0.0 specifies the network address for 140.179.220.200. When the node section is set to all "1"s, it specifies a broadcast that is sent to all hosts on the network. 140.179.255.255 specifies the example broadcast address. Note that this is true regardless of the length of the node section.

Subnetting an IP Network can be done for a variety of reasons, including organization, use of different physical media (such as Ethernet, FDDI, WAN, etc.), preservation of address space, and security. The most common reason is to control network traffic. In an Ethernet network, all nodes on a segment see all the packets transmitted by all the other nodes on that segment.

Performance can be adversely affected under heavy traffic loads, due to collisions and the resulting retransmissions. A router is used to connect IP networks to minimize the amount of traffic each segment must receive.

Subnet Masking

Applying a subnet mask to an IP address allows you to identify the network and node parts of the address. The network bits are represented by the 1's in the mask, and the node bits are represented by the 0's. Performing a bitwise logical AND operation between the IP address and the subnet mask results in the *Network Address* or Number.

For example, using our test IP address and the default Class B subnet mask, we get:

10001100.10110011.11110000.11001000   140.179.240.200   Class B IP Address

11111111.11111111.00000000.00000000   255.255.000.000   Default Class B Subnet Mask

----

10001100.10110011.00000000.00000000   140.179.000.000   Network Address

Default subnet masks:

- **Class A** - 255.0.0.0 - 11111111.00000000.00000000.00000000

- **Class B** - 255.255.0.0 - 11111111.11111111.00000000.00000000

- **Class C** - 255.255.255.0 - 11111111.11111111.11111111.00000000

Additional bits can be added to the default subnet mask for a given Class to further subnet, or break down, a network. When a bitwise logical AND operation is performed between the subnet mask and IP address, the result defines the *Subnet Address* (also called the *Network Address* or *Network Number*). There are some restrictions on the subnet address. Node addresses of all "0"s and all "1"s are reserved for specifying the local network (when a host does not know its network address) and all hosts on the network (broadcast address), respectively. This also applies to subnets. A subnet address cannot be all "0"s or all "1"s. This also implies that a 1 bit subnet mask is not allowed. This restriction is required because older standards enforced this restriction. Recent standards that allow use of these subnets have superseded these standards, but many "legacy" devices do not support the newer standards. If you are operating in a controlled environment, such as a lab, you can safely use these restricted subnets.

To calculate the number of subnets or nodes, use the formula (2^n-2) where n = number of bits in either field, and 2^n represents 2 raised to the nth power. Multiplying the number of subnets by the number of nodes available per subnet gives you the total number of nodes available for your class and subnet mask. Also, note that although subnet masks with non-contiguous mask bits are allowed, they are not recommended.

Example:

10001100.10110011.11011100.11001000   140.179.220.200 IP Address

11111111.11111111.**111**00000.00000000   255.255.**224**.000 Subnet Mask

----

10001100.10110011.11000000.00000000   140.179.192.000 Subnet Address

10001100.10110011.11011111.11111111   140.179.223.255 Broadcast Address

In this example, a **3-bit subnet mask** was used. There are 6 (2^3-2) subnets available with this size mask (remember that subnets with all 0's and all 1's are not allowed). Each subnet has 8190 (2^{13}-2) nodes. Each subnet can have nodes assigned to any address between the Subnet address and the Broadcast address. This gives a total of 49,140 nodes for the entire class B address subnetted this way. Notice that this is less than the 65,534 nodes an unsubnetted class B address would have.

You can calculate the Subnet Address by performing a bitwise logical AND operation between the IP address and the subnet mask, then setting all the host bits to **0**s. Similarly, you can calculate the *Broadcast Address* for a subnet by performing the same logical AND between the IP address and the subnet mask, then setting all the host bits to **1**s. That is how these numbers are derived in the example above.

Subnetting always reduces the number of possible nodes for a given network. There are complete subnet tables available here for Class A, Class B, and Class C. These tables list all the possible subnet masks for each class, along with calculations of the number of networks, nodes, and total hosts for each subnet.

Here is another, more detailed, example. Say you are assigned a Class C network number of 200.133.175.0 (apologies to anyone who may actually own this domain address). You want to utilize this network across multiple small groups within an organization. You can do this by subnetting that network with a subnet address.

We will break this network into 14 subnets of 14 nodes each. This will limit us to 196 nodes on the network instead of the 254 we would have without subnetting, but gives us the advantages of traffic isolation and security. To accomplish this, we need to use a subnet mask 4 bits long. Recall that the default Class C subnet mask is

255.255.255.0 (11111111.11111111.11111111.00000000 binary)

Extending this by 4 bits yields a mask of

255.255.255.**240** (11111111.11111111.11111111.**1111**0000 binary)

This gives us 16 possible network numbers, two of which cannot be used:

Table 8 Possible network numbers

Subnet bits	Network Number	Node Addresses	Broadcast Address
0000	200.133.175.0	Reserved	None
0001	200.133.175.16	.17 thru .30	200.133.175.31
0010	200.133.175.32	.33 thru .46	200.133.175.47
0011	200.133.175.48	.49 thru .62	200.133.175.63
0100	200.133.175.64	.65 thru .78	200.133.175.79
0101	200.133.175.80	.81 thru .94	200.133.175.95
0110	200.133.175.96	.97 thru .110	200.133.175.111
0111	200.133.175.112	.113 thru .126	200.133.175.127
1000	200.133.175.128	.129 thru .142	200.133.175.143
1001	200.133.175.144	.145 thru .158	200.133.175.159
1010	200.133.175.160	.161 thru .174	200.133.175.175
1011	200.133.175.176	.177 thru .190	200.133.175.191
1100	200.133.175.192	.193 thru .206	200.133.175.207
1101	200.133.175.208	.209 thru .222	200.133.175.223
1110	200.133.175.224	.225 thru .238	200.133.175.239
1111	200.133.175.240	Reserved	None

Now that you understand "classful" IP Subnetting principals, you can forget them. The reason is **CIDR** -- **C**lassless **I**nter**D**omain **R**outing. CIDR was invented several years ago to keep the internet from running out of IP addresses. The "classful" system of allocating IP addresses can be very wasteful; anyone who could reasonably show a need for more that 254 host addresses was given a Class B address block of 65533 host addresses. Even more wasteful were companies and organizations that were allocated Class A address blocks, which contain over 16 Million host addresses! Only a tiny percentage of the allocated Class A and Class B address space has ever been actually assigned to a host computer on the Internet.

People realized that addresses could be conserved if the class system was eliminated. By accurately allocating only the amount of address space that was actually needed, the address space crisis could be avoided for many years. This was first proposed in 1992 as a scheme called **Supernetting**. Under supernetting, the classful subnet masks are extended so that a network address and subnet mask could specify multiple Class C subnets with one address. For example, if I needed about 1000 addresses, I could supernet 4 Class C networks together:

192.60.128.0   (11000000.00111100.10000000.00000000) Class C subnet address

192.60.129.0   (11000000.00111100.10000001.00000000) Class C subnet address

192.60.130.0   (11000000.00111100.10000010.00000000) Class C subnet address

192.60.131.0   (11000000.00111100.10000011.00000000) Class C subnet address

----

192.60.128.0   (11000000.00111100.10000000.00000000) Supernetted Subnet address

255.255.252.0 (11111111.11111111.11111100.00000000) Subnet Mask

192.60.131.255 (11000000.00111100.10000011.11111111) Broadcast address

In this example, the subnet 192.60.128.0 includes all the addresses from 192.60.128.0 to 192.60.131.255. As you can see in the binary representation of the subnet mask, the Network portion of the address is 22 bits long, and the host portion is 10 bits long.

Under CIDR, the subnet mask notation is reduced to simplify shorthand. Instead of spelling out the bits of the subnet mask, it is simply listed as the number of 1's bits that start the mask. In the above example, instead of writing the address and subnet mask as 192.60.128.0, Subnet Mask 255.255.252.0 the network address would be written simply as: 192.60.128.0/22 which indicates starting address of the network, and number of 1s bits (22) in the network portion of the address. If you look at the subnet mask in binary (**11111111.11111111.111111**00.00000000), you can easily see how this notation works.

The use of a CIDR notated address is the same as for a Classful address. Classful addresses can easily be written in CIDR notation (Class A = /8, Class B = /16, and Class C = /24)

It is currently almost impossible for an individual or company to be allocated their own IP address blocks. You will simply be told to get them from your ISP. The reason for this is the ever-growing size of the internet routing table. Just 10 years ago, there were less than 5000 network routes in the entire Internet. Today, there are over 100,000. Using CIDR, the biggest ISPs are allocated large chunks of address space (usually with a subnet mask of /19 or even smaller); the ISP's customers (often other, smaller ISPs) are then allocated networks from the big ISP's pool. That way, all the big ISP's customers (and their customers, and so on) are accessible via 1 network route on the Internet. However, I digress.

It is expected that CIDR will keep the Internet happily in IP addresses for the next few years at least. After that, IPv6, with 128-bit addresses, will be needed. Under IPv6, even sloppy address allocation would comfortably allow a billion unique IP addresses for every person on earth! The complete and gory details of CIDR are documented in RFC1519, which was released in September of 1993.

Table 9 Allowed Class A Subnet and Host IP Addresses

# bits	Subnet Mask	CIDR	# Subnets	# Hosts	Nets * Hosts
2	255.192.0.0	/10	2	4194302	8388604
3	255.224.0.0	/11	6	2097150	12582900
4	255.240.0.0	/12	14	1048574	14680036
5	255.248.0.0	/13	30	524286	15728580
6	255.252.0.0	/14	62	262142	16252804
7	255.254.0.0	/15	126	131070	16514820
8	255.255.0.0	/16	254	65534	16645636
9	255.255.128.0	/17	510	32766	16710660
10	255.255.192.0	/18	1022	16382	16742404
11	255.255.224.0	/19	2046	8190	16756740
12	255.255.240.0	/20	4094	4094	16760836

13	255.255.248.0	/21	8190	2046	16756740
14	255.255.252.0	/22	16382	1022	16742404
15	255.255.254.0	/23	32766	510	16710660
16	255.255.255.0	/24	65534	254	16645636
17	255.255.255.128	/25	131070	126	16514820
18	255.255.255.192	/26	262142	62	16252804
19	255.255.255.224	/27	524286	30	15728580
20	255.255.255.240	/28	1048574	14	14680036
21	255.255.255.248	/29	2097150	6	12582900
22	255.255.255.252	/30	4194302	2	8388604

Table 10 Table Showing Allowed Class B Subnet and Host IP addresses

# bits	Subnet Mask	CIDR	# Subnets	# Hosts	Nets * Hosts
2	255.255.192.0	/18	2	16382	32764
3	255.255.224.0	/19	6	8190	49140
4	255.255.240.0	/20	14	4094	57316
5	255.255.248.0	/21	30	2046	61380
6	255.255.252.0	/22	62	1022	63364
7	255.255.254.0	/23	126	510	64260

8	255.255.255.0	/24	254	254	64516
9	255.255.255.128	/25	510	126	64260
10	255.255.255.192	/26	1022	62	63364
11	255.255.255.224	/27	2046	30	61380
12	255.255.255.240	/28	4094	14	57316
13	255.255.255.248	/29	8190	6	49140
14	255.255.255.252	/30	16382	2	32764

Table 11 Class C Subnet and Host IP Addresses

# bits	Subnet Mask	CIDR	# Subnets	# Hosts	Nets * Hosts
2	255.255.255.192	/26	2	62	124
3	255.255.255.224	/27	6	30	180
4	255.255.255.240	/28	14	14	196
5	255.255.255.248	/29	30	6	180
6	255.255.255.252	/30	62	2	124

HOW TO DETERMINE IP ADDRESS (PART OF ASSIGNMENT)

Issue

How to determine an IP address.

Solution

Note: This document contains information about determining your own **local** IP address and not obtaining obtaining an IP address of another computer or a website. If you want to know how the Internet sees your IP address use the system information tool.

- Microsoft Windows users

- Linux and Unix users

- Apple computer users

Microsoft Windows Users

1. Click Start, Run, and type **cmd** or **command** to open a Windows command line.

From the prompt, type **ipconfig** and press enter. This should give you information similar to what is shown below.

WINDOWS 2000 IP CONFIGURATION

Ethernet adapter Local Area Connection:

Connection-specific DNS Suffix:
IP Address . . .: 192.168.1.101
Subnet Mask . . .: 255.255.255.0
Default Gateway . . .: 192.168.1.1

As seen in the above example, the IP address as well as other important network information is listed when using the "ipconfig" command. If you have more than one network adapter, e.g. a wireless adapter and network adapter you will see each adapter listed when using this command.

Home network and corporate network users

This information is the IP address of your computer in your network. If your computer is connected to the Internet the IP address shown in this screen will more than likely **not** be the IP address other people and web pages see. Use our System Information tool to see your online IP address.

Graphical representation of network settings

Microsoft Windows XP users may get a GUI representation of their network by right clicking the network icon in their windows notification area and selecting "Status." Within the "Local Area Connection Status" window, click the "Support" tab.

Microsoft Windows 98 users may also get a GUI representation of their network settings by clicking Start, Run, and typing **ipconfig** in the run line. Unfortunately, not all versions of Windows have this feature.

Linux and UNIX, BSD 4.2+, and Apple OS X, Operating System Users

For Linux or UNIX users, to view their IP address or network information, users must have administrator or root privileges.

1. Open the Linux or UNIX shell if you are utilizing a GUI interface for your Linux or Unix machine.

2. From the prompt, type "ifconfig eth0" (without the quotes) and press enter. This should give you a listing of network information similar to what is seen below.

eth0 Link encap:Ethernet HWaddr 00:A0:24:72:EB:0A inet addr:10.10.10.2 Bcast:10.0.0.255 Mask:255.255.255.0 UP BROADCAST RUNNING MULTICAST MTU:1500 Metric:1 RX packets:5569799 errors:32 dropped:32 overruns:0 frame:6 TX packets:3548292 errors:0 dropped:0 overruns:0 carrier:3 Collisions:14 Interrupt:18 Base address:0xda00

As seen from the above example, users will commonly see the network settings for all their network devices when running the "ifconfig" command. First in the above example we have the network settings for the "lo" or "local loopback", next is the actual network settings of your network adapter.

Apple Macintosh Users

1. From the Apple menu, select the "Apple System Profiler"

2. Open the "Network overview"

3. Open "TCP/IP"

Within this window, the user will be able to see the computer's network information including the IP address.

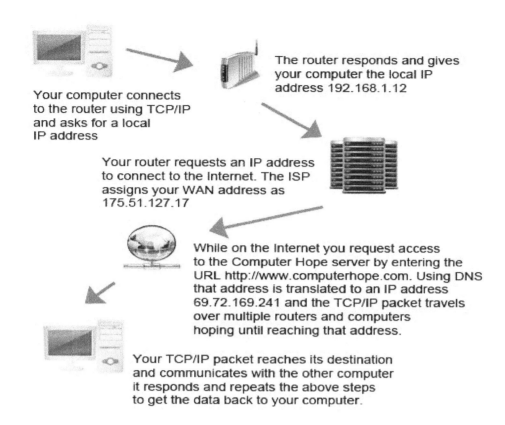

Figure 24 Finding Network address in Apple

ANOTHER ASSIGNMENT

Objectives

1. Understand methods of network design unique to TCP/IP networks, including subnetting, CIDR, and address translation

2. Explain the differences between public and private TCP/IP networks

3. Describe protocols used between mail clients and mail servers, including SMTP, POP3, and IMAP4

4. Employ multiple TCP/IP utilities for network discovery and troubleshooting

- Designing TCP/IP-Based Networks

- TCP/IP protocol suite use

- Public Internet connectivity

- Private connection data transmission

- TCP/IP fundamentals

- IP: routable protocol

Interfaces requires unique IP address

Node may use multiple IP addresses

- Two IP versions: IPv4 and IPv6

IPv4: older; more common

IPv4 addresses

- Four 8-bit octets

- *Binary or dotted decimal*

- Network host name assignment

- Dynamic using DHCP

- Static

- Network classes: A, B, C, D, E

- Class D, E addresses reserved

- Node's network class provides information about segment network node belongs to Subnetting

- Separates network

- Multiple logically defined segments (subnets)

- *Geographic locations, departmental boundaries, technology types*

- Subnet traffic separated from other subnet traffic

Reasons to separate traffic

  Enhance security

  Improve performance

- Simplify troubleshooting

- Classful Addressing in IPv4

- First, simplest IPv4 addressing type

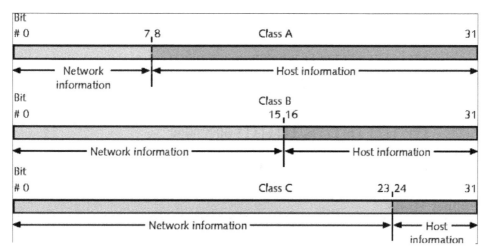

FIGURE 25 BIT ADDRESS RECOGNIZING

- Adheres to network class distinctions

- Recognizes Class A, B, C addresses

- Network information (network ID)

- First 8 bits in Class A address

- First 16 bits in Class B address

- First 24 bits in a Class C address

- Host information

- Last 24 bits in Class A address

- Last 16 bits in Class B address

- Last 8 bits in Class C address

- Drawbacks

- Fixed network ID size limits number of network hosts

- Difficult to separate traffic from various parts of a network

Class	Subnet Mask in Binary	#	CIDR
	Subnet Mask in Decimal	Network	Notation

		Bits	
A	11111111 00000000 00000000 00000000	8	/8
	255 0 0 0		
B	11111111 11111111 00000000 00000000	16	/16
	255 255 0 0		
C	11111111 11111111 11111111 00000000	24	/24
	255 255 255 0		

Figure 26 Subnet Masks

IPv4 Subnet Masks

Identifies how network subdivided

Indicates where network information located

Subnet mask bits

1: corresponding IPv4 address bits contain network information

- 0: corresponding IPv4 address bits contain host information
- Network class
- Associated with subnet mask
- ANDing
- Combining bits

IP address bit	1	1	0	0
Subnet mask bit	1	0	1	0
Resulting bit	1	0	0	0

- *Bit value of 1 AND another bit value of 1 results in 1 Bit value of 0 AND any other bit results in 0*
- ANDing logic
- *1: "true", 0: "false*
- ANDing example

	IP address:	11000111	01000100	01011001	01111111	199.34.89.127
and	Subnet mask:	11111111	11111111	11111100	00000000	255.255.252.0
Equals	Network ID:	11000111	01000100	01011000	00000000	199.34.88.0

FIGURE 27 CALCULATING A HOST NETWORK ID ON SUPERNETTED NETWORK

Address's fourth octet

- *Any combination of 1s and 0s Results in network ID fourth octet of 0s*

Reserved Addresses

- Cannot be assigned to node network interface; used as subnet masks Network ID

- Bits available for host information set to 0

- Classful IPv4 addressing network ID ends with 0 octet

- Subnetting allows network ID with other decimal values in last octet(s)

- Broadcast address

- Octet(s) representing host information equal all 1s

- Decimal notation: 255 (for class C)

- IPv4 Subnetting Techniques

- Subnetting breaks classful IPv4 addressing rules

- IP address bits representing host information change to represent network information

Reduce usable host addresses per subnet Hosts, subnets available after subnetting related to host information bits borrowed

Subnetting a Class C Address

Table 12 Calculating IP v 4 subnet addresses

Subnet Mask in Binary Subnet Mask in Decimal	# Usable Addr	CIDR Notation

11111111 11111111 11111111 10000000	254	/25
255 255 255 128		
11111111 11111111 11111111 11000000	62	/26
255 255 255 192		
11111111 11111111 11111111 11100000	30	/27
255 255 255 224		
11111111 11111111 11111111 11110000	14	/28
255 255 255 240		
11111111 11111111 11111111 11111000	6	/29
255 255 255 248		
11111111 11111111 11111111 11111100	2	/30
255 255 255 252		

Formula: # Usable Addresses = $2^n - 2$ n: number of subnet mask bits that are zero

Example

Class C network

Network ID: 199.34.89.0 Want to divide into six subnets

Class A, Class B, and Class C networks Can be subnetted

Each class has different number of host information bits usable for subnet information Varies depending on network class and the way subnetting is used

LAN subnetting

LAN's devices interpret device subnetting information

External routers

Need network portion of device IP address

Subnet number	Extended network prefix	Broadcast address	Usable host addresses
1	199.34.89.32 or 11000111 00100010 01011001 00100000	199.34.89.63 or 11000111 00100010 01011001 00111111	199.34.89.33 through 199.34.89.62
2	199.34.89.64 or 11000111 00100010 01011001 01000000	199.34.89.95 or 11000111 00100010 01011001 01011111	199.34.89.65 through 199.34.89.94
3	199.34.89.96 or 11000111 00100010 01011001 01100000	199.34.89.127 or 11000111 00100010 01011001 01111111	199.34.89.97 through 199.34.89.126
4	199.34.89.128 or 11000111 00100010 01011001 10000000	199.34.89.159 or 11000111 00100010 01011001 10011111	199.34.89.129 through 199.34.89.158
5	199.34.89.160 or 11000111 00100010 01011001 10100000	199.34.89.191 or 11000111 00100010 01011001 10111111	199.34.89.161 through 199.34.89.190
6	199.34.89.192 or 11000111 00100010 01011001 11000000	199.34.89.223 or 11000111 00100010 01011001 11011111	199.34.89.193 through 199.34.89.222

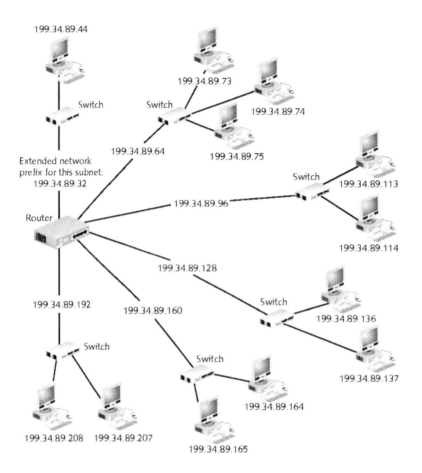

FIGURE 28 ROUTER CONNECTING SEVERAL SUBNETS

CIDR (Classless Interdomain Routing)

- Also called classless routing or supernetting. Not exclusive of subnetting.

- Provides additional ways of arranging network and host information in an IP address

- Conventional network class distinctions do not exist

- Example: subdividing Class C network into six subnets of 30 addressable hosts each Supernet

- Subnet created by moving subnet boundary left

- Subnet and Supernet Masks

Suppose you are starting with a class C address like 192.168.0.0/24

This would be a subnet:

Subnet Address: 192.168.0.0 / 26

Subnet Mask: 11111111 11111111 11111111 11000000

                        255   255   255   192

Usable address range: 192.168.0.1 - 192.168.0.62

This would be a supernet:

Subnet Address: 192.168.0.0 / 22

Subnet Mask: 11111111 11111111 11111100 00000000

                        255   255   252   0

Usable address range: 192.168.0.1 - 192.168.3.254

Example: class C range of IPv4 addresses sharing network ID 199.34.89.0

Need to increase number of default host addresses

CIDR notation (or slash notation)

Shorthand denoting subnet boundary position Form

Network ID followed by forward slash (/), followed by number of bits used for network portion of the address

Like 147.144.51.0/24

Internet Gateways

Gateway

A device that connects two networks or subnets

Default gateway

Sends LAN traffic to other subnets, such as the Internet

Usually a router

Network nodes

Have one default gateway address

Assigned manually or automatically (DHCP)

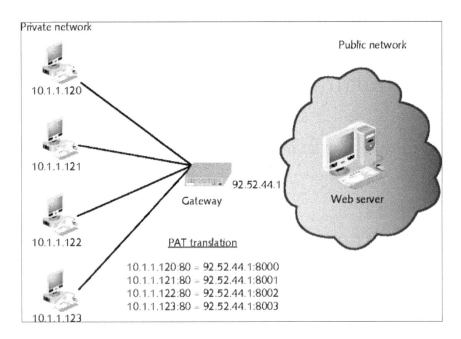

FIGURE 29 PAT TRANSLATION

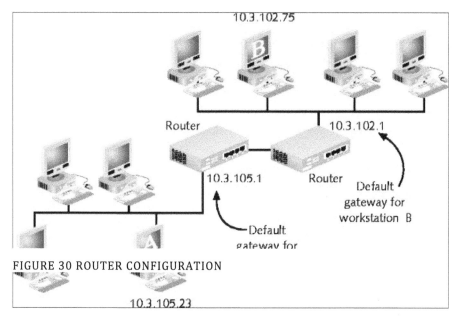

FIGURE 30 ROUTER CONFIGURATION

Address Translation

Public network

Any user may access

Little or no restrictions

Private network

Access restricted

Clients, machines with proper credentials

Hiding IP addresses

Provides more flexibility in assigning addresses

NAT (Network Address Translation)

Gateway replaces client's private IP address with Internet-recognized IP address

Reasons for using address translation

Overcome IPv4 address quantity limitations

Add marginal security to private network when connected to public network

Develop network addressing scheme

SNAT (Static Network Address Translation)

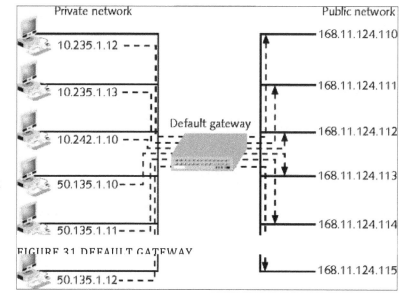

FIGURE 31 DEFAULT GATEWAY

Client associated with one private IP address, one public IP address

Never changes

Useful when operating mail server

DNAT (Dynamic Network Address Translation)

Also called IP masquerading

Internet-valid IP address might be assigned to any clients' outgoing transmission

PAT (Port Address Translation)

>Each client session with server on Internet assigned separate TCP port number

>*Client server request datagram contains port number*

>Internet server responds with datagram's destination address including same port number

NAT

>Separates private, public transmissions on TCP/IP network

>Gateways conduct network translation

>Most networks use router

>Gateway might operate on network host

Windows operating systems

>*ICS (Internet Connection Sharing)*

>TCP/IP Mail Services

>E-mail

>Most frequently used Internet services

Functions

>*Mail delivery, storage, pickup*

>Mail servers

>Communicate with other mail servers

>Deliver messages, send, receive, store messages

Mail clients

>Send messages to; retrieve messages from mail servers

SMTP (Simple Mail Transfer Protocol)

>Used to send email from one mail server to another

>Operates at Application layer

>Relies on TCP at Transport layer

>Uses TCP port 25

Email client software

Administrator must specify SMTP server name

Such as smtp.gmail.com

MIME (Multipurpose Internet Mail Extensions)

SMPT drawback: ASCII characters only

MIME standard encodes, interprets binary files, images, video, non-ASCII character sets within e-mail message identifies each mail message element according to content type

Text, graphics, audio, video, multipart

Does not replace SMTP

Works in conjunction with it

Encodes different content types

Fools SMTP

POP (Post Office Protocol)

Application layer protocol

Retrieve messages from mail server

POP3 (Post Office Protocol, version 3)

Current, popular version

Relies on TCP, operates over port 110

Store-and-forward type of service

Advantages

Minimizes server resources

Mail deleted from server after retrieval

Disadvantage for mobile users

Mail server, client applications support POP3

IMAP (Internet Message Access Protocol)

More sophisticated alternative to POP3

IMAP4: current version

Advantages

Replace POP3 without having to change e-mail programs

E-mail stays on server after retrieval

Good for mobile users

Features

Users can retrieve all or portion of mail message

Users can review messages and delete them while messages remain on server

Users can create sophisticated methods of organizing messages on server

Users can share mailbox in central location

Disadvantages

Requires more storage space, processing resources than POP servers

Network managers must watch user allocations closely

If the IMAP4 server fails, users cannot access mail

Additional TCP/IP Utilities

TCP/IP transmission process

Many points of failure

Increase with network size, distance

Utilities

Help track down most TCP/IP-related problems

Help discover information about node, network

Nearly all TCP/IP utilities

Accessible from command prompt

Syntax differs per operating system

Ipconfig

Command-line utility providing network adapter information

IP address, subnet mask, default gateway

Windows operating system tool

Command prompt window

Type ipconfig and press Enter

Switches manage TCP/IP settings

Forward slash (/) precedes command switches

Requires administrator rights to change workstation's IP configuration

Useful in
Vista and
Windows 7
because they
have a lot of
extra virtual
network adapters

```
Administrator: Command Prompt

C:\Windows\system32>ipconfig | more

Windows IP Configuration

Wireless LAN adapter Wireless Network Connection:

    Connection-specific DNS Suffix  . : sbx06440.dalycca.wayport.net
    Link-local IPv6 Address . . . . . : fe80::980:f6f3:ca2a:20d0%12
    Link-local IPv6 Address . . . . . : fe80:eeee:dddd:cccc:0:1111:2222:3333%12
    IPv4 Address. . . . . . . . . . . : 192.168.5.16
    Subnet Mask . . . . . . . . . . . : 255.255.255.0
    Default Gateway . . . . . . . . . : 192.168.5.1
```

FIGURE 32 EXAMPLE OF IPCONFIG

Renewing a IP Address

IPCONFIG /RELEASE

Ends the current IP address lease

IPCONFIG /RENEW

Asks DHCP for a new IP address

These commands are often required when moving from one LAN to another

Ifconfig

Utility used on UNIX and Linux systems

Modify TCP/IP network interface settings, release and renew DHCP-assigned addresses, check TCP/IP setting status

```
Administrator: Command Prompt

C:\Windows\system32>netstat

Active Connections

  Proto  Local Address          Foreign Address        State
  TCP    127.0.0.1:2198         SamEee:2199            ESTABLISHED
  TCP    127.0.0.1:2199         SamEee:2198            ESTABLISHED
  TCP    127.0.0.1:2200         SamEee:2201            ESTABLISHED
  TCP    127.0.0.1:2201         SamEee:2200            ESTABLISHED
  TCP    192.168.5.16:4133      nmd:http               CLOSE_WAIT
  TCP    192.168.5.16:4237      12.120.15.171:http     ESTABLISHED
  TCP    192.168.5.16:4238      12.120.15.171:http     ESTABLISHED
  TCP    192.168.5.16:4239      174:https              CLOSE_WAIT
  TCP    192.168.5.16:4240      208:http               ESTABLISHED
  TCP    192.168.5.16:4417      px-in-f18:https        ESTABLISHED
  TCP    192.168.5.16:4419      px-in-f19:https        ESTABLISHED
```

Runs at
UNIX, Linux
system starts

*Establishes
computer
TCP/IP
configuration*

Used alone or with switches

FIGURE 33 EXAMPLE OF NETSTAT

Uses hyphen (-) before some switches

No preceding character for other switches

Netstat

Displays TCP/IP statistics, component details, host connections

Used without switches

Displays active TCP/IP connections on machine

Can be used with switches

-a   shows all connections including listening ones

-n   display raw port numbers instead of letters like http

For help, use NETSTAT /?

Nbtstat

NetBIOS

Used on Windows LANs

Protocol runs in Session and Transport layers

Associates NetBIOS names with workstations

Not routable

Can be made routable by encapsulation

Nbtstat utility

Provides information about NetBIOS statistics

Resolves NetBIOS names to IP addresses

Limited use as TCP/IP diagnostic utility

Hostname and Nslookup

Hostname utility

Provides client's host name

Administrator may change

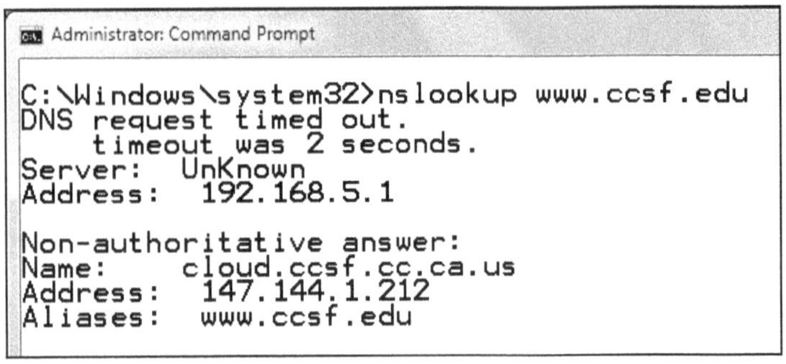

```
Administrator: Command Prompt

C:\Windows\system32>nslookup www.ccsf.edu
DNS request timed out.
      timeout was 2 seconds.
Server:   UnKnown
Address:  192.168.5.1

Non-authoritative answer:
Name:     cloud.ccsf.cc.ca.us
Address:  147.144.1.212
Aliases:  www.ccsf.edu
```

FIGURE 34 EXAMPLE OF NSLOOKUP

Nslookup

Query DNS database from any network computer

Find the device host name by specifying its IP address

Verify host configured correctly; troubleshoot DNS resolution problems

Dig

Domain information groper

Similar to nslookup

Query DNS database

Find specific IP address host name

Useful for diagnosing DNS problems

Dig utility provides more detailed information than nslookup

Flexible: two dozen switches

Included with UNIX, Linux operating systems

Windows system: must obtain third party code

```
Administrator: Command Prompt

D:\tools>dig @208.67.222.222 ftp.ccsf.edu |more

; <<>> DiG 9.3.2 <<>> @208.67.222.222 ftp.ccsf.edu
; (1 server found)
;; global options:  printcmd
;; Got answer:
;; ->>HEADER<<- opcode: QUERY, status: NOERROR, id: 412
;; flags: qr rd ra; QUERY: 1, ANSWER: 2, AUTHORITY: 3, ADDITIONAL: 3

;; QUESTION SECTION:
;ftp.ccsf.edu.                  IN      A

;; ANSWER SECTION:
ftp.ccsf.edu.           10596   IN      CNAME   sol.ccsf.cc.ca.us.
sol.ccsf.cc.ca.us.      21396   IN      A       147.144.1.211
```

Whois

Query DNS registration database

Obtain domain information

Troubleshoot network problems

Syntax on Linux or Unix

whois xxx.yy

xxx.yy is second-level domain name

Windows system

Requires additional utilities

Web sites provide simple, Web-based interfaces

Traceroute

Windows-based systems: tracert

Linux systems: tracepath

ICMP ECHO requests

Trace path from one networked node to another

Identifying all intermediate hops between two nodes

Transmits UDP datagrams to specified destination

Using either IP address or host name

To identify destination

Command used a number of switches

```
Administrator: Command Prompt
^C
D:\tools>tracert yahoo.com

Tracing route to yahoo.com [69.147.114.224]
over a maximum of 30 hops:

  1     1 ms     1 ms     1 ms  192.168.5.1
  2     4 ms     3 ms     2 ms  98-96-53-69.sbx06440.dalycca.wayport.net [98.96.
53.69]
  3     5 ms     4 ms     7 ms  12.88.110.125
  4    76 ms    78 ms    78 ms  cr1.sffca.ip.att.net [12.122.137.138]
  5    77 ms    81 ms    76 ms  cr1.cgcil.ip.att.net [12.122.4.122]
  6    83 ms    76 ms    80 ms  cr1.cl2oh.ip.att.net [12.122.2.206]
  7    77 ms    79 ms    76 ms  cr2.cl2oh.ip.att.net [12.122.2.126]
  8    78 ms    82 ms    76 ms  cr2.phlpa.ip.att.net [12.122.2.210]
  9    76 ms    78 ms    79 ms  cr1.wswdc.ip.att.net [12.122.4.54]
 10    76 ms    75 ms    75 ms  12.122.135.45
 11    75 ms    76 ms    76 ms  12.86.111.22
 12    76 ms    78 ms    76 ms  ae2-p170.msr2.re1.yahoo.com [216.115.108.69]
 13    76 ms    75 ms    77 ms  te-9-2.bas-a2.re3.yahoo.com [66.196.112.55]
 14    77 ms    76 ms    76 ms  b1.www.vip.re3.yahoo.com [69.147.114.224]

Trace complete.

D:\tools>
```

Mtr (my traceroute)

UNIX, Linux operating systems

Route discovery, analysis utility

Combines ping, traceroute functions

Output: easy-to-read chart

Simplest form

mtr ip_address or mtr host_name

Run continuously

Stop with Ctrl+C or add limiting option to command

Number of switches refine functioning, output

Results misleading

If devices prevented from responding to ICMP traffic

Windows XP, Vista, Server 2003, Server 2008

Pathping program as command-line utility

Similar switches as mtr

Pathping output differs slightly

Displays path first

Then issues hundreds of ICMP ECHO requests before revealing reply, packet loss statistics

Route

Route utility

Allows viewing of host's routing table

UNIX or Linux system

Type route and press Enter

Windows-based system

Type route print and press Enter

Cisco-brand router

Type show ip route and press Enter

Route command

Add, delete, modify routes

Route command help

UNIX or Linux system

Type man route and press Enter

Windows system

```
Kernel IP routing table
Destination     Gateway        Genmask         Flags Metric Ref  Use   Iface
223.37.128.0    0.0.0.0        255.255.255.0    U     0      0    4580  eth0
127.0.0.1       0.0.0.0        255.0.0.0        U     0      0    1360  lo
0.0.0.0         223.37.128.1   0.0.0.0          UG    0      0    3780  eth0
```

Type route ? and press Enter

Field	Explanation
Destination	The destination host's identity
Gateway	The destination host's gateway
Genmask	The destination host's netmask number
Flags	Additional information about the route, including whether it's usable (U), whether it's a gateway (G), and whether, as is the case with the loopback entry, only a single host can be reached via that route (H)
Metric	The cost of the route—that is, how efficiently it carries traffic
Ref	The number of references to the route that exist—that is, the number of routes that rely on this route
Use	The number of packets that have traversed the route
Iface	The type of interface the route uses

	IP address:	11000111	01000100	00100010	01111111	199.34.89.127
and	Subnet mask:	11111111	11111111	11111111	00000000	255.255.255.0
Equals	Network ID:	11000111	01000100	00100010	00000000	199.34.89.0

COMMON LOGICAL OPERATIONS

The common logical bitwise operations AND, OR, XOR (Exclusive OR) and NOT. Logical operations are performed between two data bits (except for NOT). Bits can be either "1" or "0", and these operations are essential to performing digital math operations.

In the "truth tables" below, the input bits are in **bold**, and the results are plain.

AND

The logical AND operation compares 2 bits and if they are both "1", then the result is "1", otherwise, the result is "0".

Table 13 Logical AND Operation

	0	**1**
0	0	0
1	0	1

OR

The logical OR operation compares 2 bits and if either or both bits are "1", then the result is "1", otherwise, the result is "0".

Table 14 Logical OR Operation

	0	**1**
0	0	1
1	1	1

XOR

The logical XOR (Exclusive OR) operation compares 2 bits and if exactly one of them is "1" (i.e., if they are different values), then the result is "1"; otherwise (if the bits are the same), the result is "0".

Table 15 Logical XOR Operation

	0	1
0	0	1
1	1	0

NOT

The logical NOT operation simply changes the value of a single bit. If it is a "1", the result is "0"; if it is a "0", the result is "1". Note that this operation is different in that instead of comparing two bits, it is acting on a single bit.

Table 16 Logical NOT Operation

0	1
1	0

Identifing and analyzing customer/organizational network system needs and requirements.

Identify customer/organizational requirements.

Network requirements can vary from organization to organization; designing a network can be a challenging task. Your first step is to understand your networking requirements. The rest of this lesson explains how to determine these requirements.

Networking devices must reflect the goals, characteristics, and policies of the organizations in which they operate. Two primary goals drive networking design and implementation:

- **Application availability**: Networks carry application information between computers. If the applications are not available to network users, the network is not doing its job.

- **Cost of ownership**: Information system (IS) budgets today often run in the millions of dollars. As large organizations increasingly rely on electronic data for managing business activities, the associated costs of computing resources will continue to rise.

A well-designed network can help balance these objectives. When properly implemented, the network infrastructure can optimize application availability and allow the cost-effective use of existing network resources.

As Figure 1-1 shows, designing your network is an iterative activity. The discussions that follow outline several areas that you should carefully consider when planning your networking implementation.

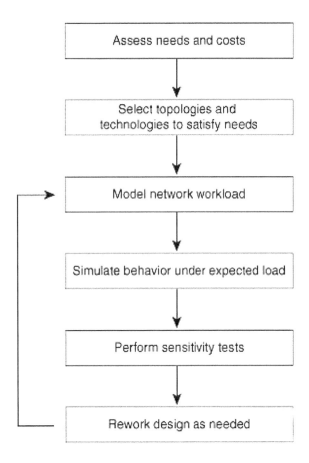

Figure 1-1 General Network Design Process

Assessing User Requirements

In general, users primarily want application availability in their networks. The chief components of application availability are response time, performance, and reliability:

- Response time is the time between entry of a command or keystroke and the host system's execution of the command or delivery of a response. User satisfaction about response time is generally considered a monotonic function up to some limit, at which point user satisfaction falls off to nearly zero. Applications in which fast response time is considered critical include interactive online services, such as automated tellers and point-of-sale machines.

- Applications that put high-volume traffic onto the network have more effect on performance than end-to-end connections. Throughput-intensive applications generally involve file-transfer activities. However, throughput-intensive applications also usually have low response-time requirements. Indeed, they can often be scheduled at times when response-time–sensitive traffic is low (for example, after normal work hours).

- Although reliability is always important, some applications have genuine requirements that exceed typical needs. Organizations that require nearly 100% uptime conduct all activities online or over the telephone. Financial services, securities exchanges, and emergency/police/military operations are a few examples. These situations imply a requirement for a high level of hardware and topological redundancy. Determining the cost of any downtime is essential in determining the relative importance of reliability to your network.

You can assess user requirements in a number of ways. The more involved your users are in the process, the more likely that your evaluation will be accurate. In general, you can use the following methods to obtain this information:

- **User community profiles**: Outline what different user groups require. This is the first step in determining network requirements. Although many users have roughly the same requirements for an electronic mail system, engineering groups using X Windows terminals and Sun workstations in an NFS environment have different needs than PC users sharing print servers in a finance department.

- **Interviews, focus groups, and surveys**: Build a baseline for implementing a network. Understand that some groups might require access to common servers. Others might want to allow external access to specific internal computing resources. Certain organizations might require IS support systems to be managed in a particular way according to some external standard. The least formal method of obtaining information is to conduct interviews with key user groups. Focus groups can also be used to gather information and generate discussion among different organizations with similar (or dissimilar) interests. Finally, formal surveys can be used to get a statistically valid reading of user sentiment regarding a particular service level or proposed networking architecture.

- **Human factors tests**: The most expensive, time-consuming, and possibly revealing method is to conduct a test involving representative users in a lab environment. This is most applicable when evaluating response-time requirements. You might set up working systems and have users perform normal remote host activities from the lab network, for example. By evaluating user reactions to variations in host responsiveness, you can create benchmark thresholds for acceptable performance.

Assessing Proprietary and Nonproprietary Solutions

Compatibility, conformance, and interoperability are related to the problem of balancing proprietary functionality and open networking flexibility. As a network designer, you might be forced to choose between implementing a multivendor environment and implementing a specific, proprietary capability. For example, the Interior Gateway Routing Protocol (IGRP) provides many useful capabilities, such as a number of features designed to enhance its stability. These include hold downs, split horizons, and poison reverse updates.

The negative side is that IGRP is a proprietary routing protocol. In contrast, the integrated Intermediate System-to-Intermediate System (IS-IS) protocol is an open networking alternative that also provides a fast converging routing environment; however, implementing an open routing protocol can potentially result in greater multivendor configuration complexity.

The decisions that you make have far-ranging effects on your overall network design. Assume that you decide to implement integrated IS-IS rather than IGRP. In doing this, you gain a measure of interoperability; however, you lose some functionality. For instance, you cannot load balance traffic over unequal parallel paths. Similarly, some modems provide a high level of proprietary diagnostic capabilities but require that all modems throughout a network be of the same vendor type to fully exploit proprietary diagnostics.

Previous networking investments and expectations for future requirements have considerable influence over your choice of implementations. You need to consider installed networking equipment; applications running (or to be run) on the network; traffic patterns; physical location of sites, hosts, and users; rate of growth of the user community; and both physical and logical network layout.

Assessing Costs

The network is a strategic element in your overall information system design. As such, the cost of your network is much more than the sum of your equipment purchase orders. View it as a total-cost-of-ownership issue. You must consider the entire life cycle of your networking environment. A brief list of costs associated with networks follows:

- **Equipment hardware and software costs**: Consider what is really being bought when you purchase your systems; costs should include initial purchase and installation, maintenance, and projected upgrade costs.

- **Performance trade-off costs**: Consider the cost of going from a 5-second response time to a half-second response time. Such improvements can cost quite a bit in terms of media selection, network interfaces, networking nodes, modems, and WAN services.

- **Installation costs**: Installing a site's physical cable plant can be the most expensive element of a large network. The costs include installation labor, site modification, fees associated with local code conformance, and costs incurred to ensure compliance with environmental restrictions (such as asbestos removal). Other important elements in keeping your costs to a minimum include developing a well-planned wiring-closet layout and implementing color-codes conventions for cable runs.

- **Expansion costs**: Calculate the cost of ripping out all thick Ethernet, adding additional functionality, or moving to a new location. Projecting your future requirements and accounting for future needs saves time and money.

- **Support costs**: Complicated networks cost more to monitor, configure, and maintain. Your network should be no more complicated than necessary. Costs include training, direct labor (network managers and administrators), sparing, and replacement costs. Additional costs that should be considered are out-of-band management, SNMP management stations, and power.

- **Cost of downtime**: Evaluate the cost of every minute that a user is unable to access a file server or a centralized database. If this cost is high, you must attribute a high cost to downtime. If the cost is high enough, fully redundant networks might be your best option.

- **Opportunity costs**: Every choice you make has an opposing alternative option. Whether that option is a specific hardware platform, topology solution, level of redundancy, or system integration alternative, there are always options. Opportunity costs are the costs of not picking one of those options. The opportunity costs of not switching to newer technologies and topologies might be lost competitive advantage, lower productivity, and slower overall performance. Any effort to integrate opportunity costs into your analysis can help make accurate comparisons at the beginning of your project.

- **Sunken costs**—Your investment in existing cable plant, routers, concentrators, switches, hosts, and other equipment and software is your sunken costs. If the sunken costs are high, you might need to modify your networks so that your existing network can continue to be utilized. Although comparatively low incremental costs might appear to be more attractive than significant redesign costs, your organization might pay more in the long run by not upgrading systems. Too much reliance on sunken costs can cost your organization sales and market share when calculating the cost of network modifications and additions.

After you have determined your network requirements, you must identify and then select the specific capability that fits your computing environment.

QUIZ

1. Two primary goals drive networking design and implementation:

- Application availability

- Cost of ownership

2. The network design problem consists of the following three general elements:

- Environmental givens

- Performance constraints

- Networking variables

3. Define for network systems what time is:

Response time is the time between entry of a command or keystroke and the host system's execution of the command or delivery of a response

4. Financial services, securities exchanges, and emergency/police/military operations are a few examples of situations that imply:

A requirement for a high level of hardware and topological redundancy

5. These are some of common network requirements:

- An electronic mail system

- X Windows terminals and Sun workstations

- Users sharing print servers in a finance department

6. Name at least two kinds of costs associated with networks:

- Equipment hardware and software costs

- Performance trade-off costs

- Installation costs

- Expansion costs

- Support costs

- Cost of downtime

- Opportunity costs

- Sunken costs

Computer network needs analysis.

As Figure 1-2 shows, there are some hardware components that could be taken into account for the network needs analysis:

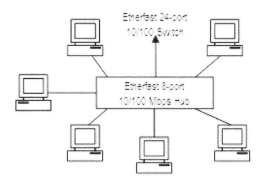

Figure 1-2 Six PC Ethernet 10/100 Network

In the earlier figure we observed a six PC network attached to a so-called eight port Hub, they exist with different number of ports according with the quantity of users, the Hubs were named before in legacy networks as concentrators and helped to allow communicate a certain quantity of computers between them. Next observe there is an arrow pointing to a hardware so-called Switch, it help to segment the network in order to avoid overload the network traffic, the switches were meant to separate two or more networks that in global are part of the same organization, for example, the Human Resources department commonly needs to interact only within the department system server and users but the Finance department, in contrast, needs to get interact only within its Finance system server and users but in some cases one of them needs to access across their systems, servers, or PC's and there is where the Switches take place, they only work to join one network to another. All these components are joined by network cables commonly used as category number five, this is how they are known and are represented as CAT5.

Now will have a look to Figure 1-3, it will present a more complex network needs:

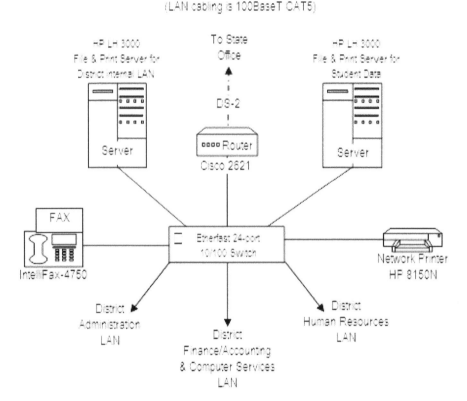

Figure 1-3 Six PC Ethernet 10/100 Network

In the Figure before we observe more hardware that we didn't saw in the 1-2 figure. They could or not be needed into a network structure, there you can see servers, at a later stage it will be explained one by one of this components but now we will learn briefly what for they are made. The servers help commonly to share, save, and maintain files that could be read and modified by all the members of one or more departments. It helped also to share printers, to manage the security, i.e. to manage all users accounts and control how, who, and when each user can access that resources, also if they can read, modify, or delete files, also act as a system server, i.e. a payroll or account software. We also observe a Printer and a Fax.

Now let us have a more clear and technical definition of each of all those components that could take place into a network organization.

HUB

An Ethernet hub, active hub, network hub, repeater hub, multiport repeater or hub is a device for connecting multiple Ethernet devices together and making them act as a single network segment. It has multiple input/output (I/O) ports, in which a signal introduced at the input of any port appears at the output of every port except the original incoming. A hub works at the physical layer (layer 1) of the OSI model.

4-port Ethernet hub

ROUTER

A router is a device that forwards data packets between computer networks, creating an overlay internetwork. A router is connected to two or more data lines from different networks. When a data packet comes in one of the lines, the router reads the address information in the packet to determine its ultimate destination. Then, using information in its routing table or routing policy, it directs the packet to the next network on its journey.   A router is also known as a hardware device designed to take incoming packets, analyzing the packets and then directing them to the appropriate locations, moving the packets to another network, converting the packets to be moved across a different network interface, dropping the packets, or performing any other number of other actions. A **router** has a lot more capabilities than other network devices such as a hub or a switch that are only able to perform basic network functions. For example, a hub is often used to transfer data between computers or network devices, but does not analyze or do anything with the data it is transferring. Routers however can analyze the data being sent over a network, change how it is packaged and send it to another network or over a different network. For example, routers are commonly used in home networks to share a single Internet connection with multiple computers.

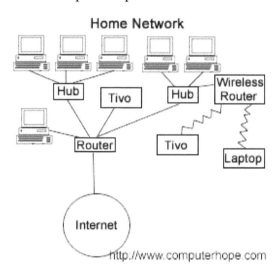

Figure 35 eXAMPLE OF A hOME nETWORK

In the above example of a home network, there are two different examples of a router, the router and the wireless router. As can be seen in the example the router is what allows all the computers and other network devices access the Internet. Below are some additional examples of different types of routers used in a large network.

BROUTER

Short for Bridge Router, a "**brouter**" is a networking device that serves as both a bridge and a router.

Core router

A core router is a router in a computer network that routes data within a network, but not between networks.

Edge router

An edge Router is a router in a computer network that routes data between one or more networks.

VIRTUAL ROUTER

A Virtual Router is a backup router used in a "VRRP" setup. VRRP is short for **Virtual Router Redundancy Protocol, VRRP** and is defined by RFC 2338 and also a protocol used with routers that helps prevent network downtime. In the event of a router failing, the backup or virtual router would become the master router.

Wireless router

Alternatively referred to as a **base station** and **wireless router**, an **access point** is the location of a wireless receiver that enables a user with wireless access to connect to a network or the Internet. This term can refer to both Wi-Fi and Bluetooth devices. Unlike a traditional router, this router will have one or more antennas on it to help get the wireless signal.

A typical home or small office router showing the ADSL telephone line and Ethernet network cable connections.

NETWORK SWITCH

A network switch is a computer networking device that links network segments or network devices. The term commonly refers to a multi-port network bridge that processes and routes data at the data link layer (layer 2) of the OSI model. Switches that additionally process data at the network layer (layer 3) and above are often called layer-3 switches or multilayer switches.

Avaya ERS 2550T-PWR 50-port network switch.

A *network switch* is a device that manages the sharing of multiple computers or networks on the same data connection. Another name for a network switch is a *network bridge*, which is a physical device responsible for routing and processing data within the open systems interconnection model. A network switch does not include hubs or repeaters, as these devices do not include any type of logical processors.

A network switch can support 10/100 Mbit/s (Megabits per second) or 10/100/1000 Mbit/s port transfer rates. It is possible to have multiple network switches operating at different speeds on the same network. However, this type of setup lends itself to bottlenecks and restricts the possible routes available for the flow of data.

A network switch is critical in the management of a computer network. The network switch functions as the traffic management system within the network, directing data packets to the correct destination. These devices are used to connect peripheral devices to the network and ensure maximum cost effectiveness and the ability to share resources.

A typical setup of a network switch is two computers, one printer, and a wireless router. All the devices are connected to the network switch, and each item must be clearly identified and connection rules created.

Once the setup is done, any computer on the network can use the same printer. All computers can transfer files to each other and anyone with a wireless card can access the network, print and transfer files. The network switch is designed to allow the resources to be shared without reducing performance.

A simple analogy for a network switch is a policeman at a four-way stop. The cars are the data packets that are sent from each device as it attempts to communicate with the other devices in the network. The policeman, or network switch, directs traffic, sending the data to the right location, without having any collisions. Switches can be a valuable asset to networking. Overall, they can increase the capacity and speed of your network. However, switching should not be seen as a cure-all for network issues. Before incorporating network switching, you must first ask yourself two important questions: First, how can you tell if your network will benefit from switching? Second, how do you add switches to your network design to provide the most benefit?

There are four main types of network switches. The four types are unmanaged switches, managed switches, smart switches, and enterprise managed switches. Each different types has its own strengths and weaknesses that need to be considered.

An unmanaged switch is the cheapest option and is typically used in a small office or business. These network switches perform the basic functions of managing the data flow between a shared printer and multiple computers. They can either be desktop models or rack mounted.

A managed switch has a user interface or software offering that allows users to modify the settings of the switch. There are multiple methods for updating the network switch, ranging from a serial console to an Internet based application. This type of network switch requires a knowledgeable user to adjust the settings as needed.

A smart switch is the middle product offering between a unmanaged and managed switch. The user interface is web-based and set with the most popular default settings. Adjustments to one setting result in an automatic adjustment to the related setting.

An enterprise-managed network switch has a wide range of adjustable settings to allow use within a large company or organization. These types of network switches are usually managed by network specialists and are constantly monitored, due to the size and complexity of the network.

Switches occupy the same place in the network as hubs. Unlike hubs, switches examine each packet and process it accordingly rather than simply repeating the signal to all ports. Switches map the Ethernet addresses of the nodes residing on each network segment and then allow only the necessary traffic to pass through the switch. When a packet is received by the switch, the switch examines the destination and source hardware addresses and compares them to a table of network segments and addresses. If the segments are the same, the packet is dropped or "filtered"; if the segments are different, then the packet is "forwarded" to the proper segment. Additionally, switches prevent bad or misaligned packets from spreading by not forwarding them.

Filtering packets and regenerating forwarded packets enables switching technology to split a network into separate collision domains. The regeneration of packets allows for greater distances and more nodes to be used in the total network design, and dramatically lowers the overall collision rates. In switched networks, each segment is an independent collision domain. This also allows for parallelism, meaning up to one-half of the computers connected to a switch can send data at the same time. In shared networks, all nodes reside in a single shared collision domain.

Easy to install, most switches are self-learning. They determine the Ethernet addresses in use on each segment, building a table as packets are passed through the switch. This "plug and play" element makes switches an attractive alternative to hubs.

Switches can connect different network types (such as Ethernet and Fast Ethernet) or networks of the same type. Many switches today offer high-speed links, like Fast Ethernet, which can be used to link the switches together or to give added bandwidth to important servers that get a lot of traffic. A network composed of a number of switches linked together via these fast uplinks is called a "collapsed backbone" network.

Dedicating ports on switches to individual nodes is another way to speed access for critical computers. Servers and power users can take advantage of a full segment for one node, so some networks connect high traffic nodes to a dedicated switch port.

Full duplex is another method to increase bandwidth to dedicated workstations or servers. To use full duplex, both network interface cards used in the server or workstation and the switch must support full duplex operation. Full duplex doubles the potential bandwidth on that link.

General Benefits of Network Switching

Switches replace hubs in networking designs, and they are more expensive. So why is the desktop switching market doubling every year with huge numbers sold? The price of switches is declining precipitously, while hubs are a mature technology with small price declines. This means that there is far less difference between switch costs and hub costs than there used to be, and the gap is narrowing.

Since switches are self learning, they are as easy to install as a hub. Just plug them in and go. And they operate on the same hardware layer as a hub, so there are no protocol issues.

There are two reasons for switches being included in network designs. First, a switch breaks one network into many small networks so the distance and repeater limitations are restarted. Second, this same segmentation isolates traffic and reduces collisions relieving network congestion. It is very easy to identify the need for distance and repeater extension, and to understand this benefit of network switching. But the second benefit, relieving network congestion, is hard to identify and harder to understand the degree by which switches will help performance. Since all switches add small latency delays to packet processing, deploying switches unnecessarily can actually slow down network performance. So the next section pertains to the factors affecting the impact of switching to congested networks.

Network Switching

The benefits of switching vary from network to network. Adding a switch for the first time has different implications than increasing the number of switched ports already installed. Understanding traffic patterns is very important to network switching - the goal being to eliminate (or filter) as much traffic as possible. A switch installed in a location where it forwards almost all the traffic it receives will help much less than one that filters most of the traffic.

Networks that are not congested can actually be negatively impacted by adding switches. Packet processing delays, switch buffer limitations, and the retransmissions that can result sometimes slows performance compared with the hub based alternative. If your network is not congested, don't replace hubs with switches. How can you tell if performance problems are the result of network congestion? Measure utilization factors and collision rates.

Table 17 Candidates for Network Switching

**Good Candidates for Performance Boosts
from Switching**

- Utilization more than 35%

- Collision rates more than 10%

Utilization load is the amount of total traffic as a percent of the theoretical maximum for the network type, 10 Mbps in Ethernet, 100 Mbps in Fast Ethernet. The collision rate is the number of packets with collisions as a percentage of total packages

Network response times (the user-visible part of network performance) suffers as the load on the network increases, and under heavy loads small increases in user traffic often results in significant decreases in performance. This is similar to automobile freeway dynamics, in that increasing loads results in increasing throughput up to a point, then further increases in demand results in rapid deterioration of true throughput. In Ethernet, collisions increase as the network is loaded, and this causes retransmissions and increases in load which cause even more collisions. The resulting network overload slows traffic considerably.

Using network utilities found on most server operating systems network managers can determine utilization and collision rates. Both peak and average statistics should be considered.

Replacing a Central Hub with a Switch

This switching opportunity is typified by a fully shared network, where many users are connected in a cascading hub architecture. The two main impacts of switching will be faster network connection to the server(s) and the isolation of non-relevant traffic from each segment.

As the network bottleneck is eliminated performance grows until a new system bottleneck is encountered - such as maximum server performance.

Adding Switches to a Backbone Switched Network

Congestion on a switched network can usually be relieved by adding more switched ports, and increasing the speed of these ports. Segments experiencing congestion are identified by their utilization and collision rates, and the solution is either further segmentation or faster connections. Both Fast Ethernet and Ethernet switch ports are added further down the tree structure of the network to increase performance.

Designing for Maximum Benefit

Changes in network design tend to be evolutionary rather than revolutionary-rarely is a network manager able to design a network completely from scratch. Usually, changes are made slowly with an eye toward preserving as much of the usable capital investment as possible while replacing obsolete or outdated technology with new equipment.

Fast Ethernet is very easy to add to most networks. A switch or bridge allows Fast Ethernet to connect to existing Ethernet infrastructures to bring speed to critical links. The faster technology is used to connect switches to each other, and to switched or shared servers to ensure the avoidance of bottlenecks.

Many client/server networks suffer from too many clients trying to access the same server which creates a bottleneck where the server attaches to the LAN. Fast Ethernet, in combination with switched Ethernet, creates the perfect cost-effective solution for avoiding slow client server networks by allowing the server to be placed on a fast port.

Advanced Switching Technology Issues

There are some technology issues with switching that do not affect 95% of all networks. Major switch vendors and the trade publications are promoting new competitive technologies, so some of these concepts are discussed here.

Managed or Unmanaged

Management provides benefits in many networks. Large networks with mission critical applications are managed with many sophisticated tools, using SNMP to monitor the health of devices on the network. Networks using SNMP or RMON (an extension to SNMP that provides much more data while using less network bandwidth to do so) will either manage every device, or just the more critical areas. VLANs are another benefit to management in a switch. A VLAN allows the network to group nodes into logical LANs that behave as one network, regardless of physical connections. The main benefit is managing broadcast and multicast traffic. An unmanaged switch will pass broadcast and multicast packets through to all ports. If the network has logical grouping that are different from physical groupings then a VLAN-based switch may be the best bet for traffic optimization.

Another benefit to management in the switches is Spanning Tree Algorithm. Spanning Tree allows the network manager to design in redundant links, with switches attached in loops. This would defeat the self-learning aspect of switches, since traffic from one node would appear to originate on different ports. Spanning Tree is a protocol that allows the switches to coordinate with each other so that traffic is only carried on one of the redundant links (unless there is a failure, then the backup link is automatically activated). Network managers with switches deployed in critical applications may want to have redundant links. In this case management is necessary. However, for the rest of the networks an unmanaged switch would do quite well, and is much less expensive.

Store-and-Forward vs. Cut-Through

LAN switches come in two basic architectures, cut-through and store-and-forward. Cut-through switches only examine the destination address before forwarding it on to its destination segment. A store-and-forward switch, on the other hand, accepts and analyzes the entire packet before forwarding it to its destination. It takes more time to examine the entire packet, but it allows the switch to catch certain packet errors and collisions and keep them from propagating bad packets through the network.

Today, the speed of store-and-forward switches has caught up with cut-through switches to the point where the difference between the two is minimal. Also, there are a large number of hybrid switches available that mix both cut-through and store-and-forward architectures.

Blocking vs. Non-Blocking Switches

Take a switch's specifications and add up all the ports at theoretical maximum speed, then you have the theoretical sum total of a switch's throughput. If the switching bus, or switching components cannot handle the theoretical total of all ports the switch is considered a "blocking switch". There is debate whether all switches should be designed non-blocking, but the added costs of doing so are only reasonable on switches designed to work in the largest network backbones. For almost all applications, a blocking switch that has an acceptable and reasonable throughput level will work just fine.

Consider an eight port 10/100 switch. Since each port can theoretically handle 200 Mbps (full duplex) there is a theoretical need for 1600 Mbps, or 1.6 Gbps. But in the real world each port will not exceed 50% utilization, so a 800 Mbps switching bus is adequate. Consideration of total throughput versus total ports demand in the real world loads provides validation that the switch can handle the loads of your network.

Switch Buffer Limitations

As packets are processed in the switch, they are held in buffers. If the destination segment is congested, the switch holds on to the packet as it waits for bandwidth to become available on the crowded segment. Buffers that are full present a problem. So some analysis of the buffer sizes and strategies for handling overflows is of interest for the technically inclined network designer.

In real world networks, crowded segments cause many problems, so their impact on switch consideration is not important for most users, since networks should be designed to eliminate crowded, congested segments. There are two strategies for handling full buffers. One is "backpressure flow control" which sends packets back upstream to the source nodes of packets that find a full buffer. This compares to the strategy of simply dropping the packet, and relying on the integrity features in networks to retransmit automatically. One solution spreads the problem in one segment to other segments, propagating the problem. The other solution causes retransmissions, and that resulting increase in load is not optimal. Neither strategy solves the problem, so switch vendors use large buffers and advise network managers to design switched network topologies to eliminate the source of the problem - congested segments.

Layer 3 Switching

A hybrid device is the latest improvement in internetworking technology. Combining the packet handling of routers and the speed of switching, these multilayer switches operate on both layer 2 and layer 3 of the OSI network model. The performance of this class of switch is aimed at the core of large enterprise networks. Sometimes called routing switches or IP switches, multilayer switches look for common traffic flows, and switch these flows on the hardware layer for speed. For traffic outside the normal flows, the multilayer switch uses routing functions. This keeps the higher overhead routing functions only where it is needed, and strives for the best handling strategy for each network packet.

Many vendors are working on high end multilayer switches, and the technology is definitely a "work in process". As networking technology evolves, multilayer switches are likely to replace routers in most large networks.

Distributed processing also benefits from Fast Ethernet and switching. Segmentation of the network via switches brings big performance boosts to distributed traffic networks, and the switches are commonly connected via a Fast Ethernet backbone.

FIGURE 36 A NETWORK SERVER

Server

In most common use, a server is a physical computer (a computer hardware system) dedicated to run one or more services (as a host), to serve the needs of the users of other computers on a network. Depending on the computing service that it offers it could be a database server, file server, mail server, print server, web server, gaming server, or some other kind of server.

In the context of client-server architecture, a server is a computer program running to serve the requests of other programs, the "clients". Thus, the "server" performs some computational task on behalf of "clients". The clients either run on the same computer or connect through the network.

Servers in a data center: Several servers are mounted on a rack and connected to a KVM switch.

A network server is a computer that provides various shared resources to workstations and other servers on a computer network. The shared resources can include disk space, hardware access, and email services. Any computer can be a "network server." What separates a server from a workstation is not the hardware, but rather the function performed by the computer. In general, a workstation is any computer used by an individual person to perform his or her job duties, while a network server is any computer that provides users with access to shared software or hardware resources.

That said, servers are usually built with more powerful components than individual workstations. For example, a server will usually have more random access memory (RAM) installed than a workstation, or use a more robust operating system (OS). While this may increase the price of the server relative to a single workstation, the overall cost can be significantly lower to an organization.

In addition to the shared services these computers provide, network servers also help simplify the management tasks for network and systems administrators. By centrally locating these services on a single computer rather than on each workstation, configuration changes and security updates need only be applied to the network server rather than to hundreds of individual workstations. For example, one common function of network servers is to provide access to printers across the network. Workstations accessing these printers obtain the necessary software from the network server. If an updated version of that software becomes available, network administrators only need to apply the update to the server.

One network server may also serve different roles. The print server mentioned above may also be a file server and a domain name service (DNS) server. Other typical roles include mail server and authentication server.

File servers provide a centrally located pool of disk space for network users to store and share various documents. These servers help organizations maintain single versions of files across departments and simplify administration. Because all the data is stored in one location, administrators need only backup files from one computer.

Print servers allow organizations to share a single printer, preventing the need for each individual workstation to have its own printer. A mail server provides email services to computers on the network. Authentication servers give networks a centrally located database for storing account and password information, thereby allowing users to logon at any computer on the network.

Types of Servers

There are different **types of servers** according to new era requirements. A **server** is a device or computer on a network that supervise network resources. A file server is a storage device committed to storing files. A server facilitates the user on the network that a user may save files on server. A server cannot carry out any job besides their server task. If you are using multiprocessing operating system than a single system can run lots of program at a time. A server platform is used synonymously by operating system.

Application Servers

Application servers engage a large amount of computing territory among database servers and the end user, and they regularly bond the two. The connection of two dissimilar applications is possible with Middleware software. It facilitate the user to request data from the database using form displayed on a web browser and it make possible the Web server to go back dynamic Web pages based on the user's requirements and profile. Middleware illustrate split products that provided as the super glue among two applications. Middleware also called plumbing since it attach two sides of an application pass out data among them. Generally it consist of TP monitors, DCE environments, RPC systems, Object Request Brokers (ORBs), Database access systems, Message Passing

Audio/Video Servers

Audio/Video Servers make possible multimedia applications that have ability to broadcast streaming multimedia contents on websites. Multimedia streaming is a technique for transporting data. This technology is increasing more rapidly within the growth of internet. Those users have not enough success to download large multimedia files rapidly for them streaming is a best solution. When client side receives data and forwards it as steady stream it processing the data and covert it into sound and pictures so a user receive data immediately in desired format. There are lots of competing streaming technologies rising and for audio the de facto standard is developing Network's RealAudio.

Chat Servers

Through **Chat Servers** a lots of user make conversation and exchange information or data with each other in similar environment and it is possible with real-time discussion capabilities because real time means happening instantly. The real-time offering many features such as navigation, display of moving objects at the same time as text. Real time takes only a minute, or few second to react.

Fax Servers

A **Fax Server** is commonly used in large organization where time is money. **Fax Servers** save the time and decrease incoming and outgoing telephone resources.

FTP Servers

File transfer protocol is an oldest internet service which facilitates the user to move one or more than one files from one location to another location securely. **FTP Servers** also offering file safety, transfer control, and organization of files.

Groupware Servers

The objective behind the design of **Groupware Servers** is to make possible for users to work jointly, in spite of place, through Internet or a mutual Intranet and to work together in a near environment.

IRC Servers

IRC Servers used for seeking real time abilities. IRC is the abbreviation of internet relay chat which consists of numerous split networks of servers that permit users to attach with each other by means of an IRC network.

List Servers

List servers are fantastic method to handle mailing list that bring statement, newsletters, or publicity. **List Servers** are interactive discussions open to the community.

Mail Servers

Mail Servers move about and store up email over mutual networks through LANs and WANs and diagonally the Internet.

News Servers

News Servers used for sharing and delivery towards thousand of news group presently accessible over the USENET news network which is used by the numerous of peoples all over the world.

Proxy Servers

Proxy servers used to filter requirements, get better appearance, and share out connections. Proxy Servers exist among a client programs usually a Web browser and an external server.

Telnet Servers

Through **Telnet Servers,** a user may log on to a computer and perform job.

Web Servers

A **Web server** serves fixed substance to a Web browser by loading a file from any storage device and helping it transversely the network to a user's Web browser. The conversation between browser and server make possible via HTTP mediate this intact exchange.

Strategies and plan to solve the specific network problem.

Network traffic as a specific problem for example, calculate how critical the network is to your organization and then calculate how severely network failure will affect your business. Live monitoring may provide you with enough information and you can let it go at that.

Regardless of the depth of your analysis and planning effort, here are some practices derived in the field:

- Identify your business requirements and how critical the network is to their realization. Can the organization operate without its network? How long? To what degree will operation be curtailed or compromised?

- Identify the key user tasks. If possible, gather data to build a daily task timetable. With some tinkering, you can take into account hours of operation, days of the week, and other factors to get a fairly accurate look at regular network traffic. You may not understand the network's enterprise role accurately until you look at what is done, by whom, when, and how.

- Use Network Monitor to measure the amount of network activity that occurs for each of these tasks and record the results in a spreadsheet.

- Identify network topology and the location of clients and servers. Calculate the basic background traffic client-to-server and server-to-server, then map these onto a spreadsheet by segment (floors in a building, separate buildings, etc.—some segmentation scheme usually, but not necessarily, based on subnets).

- Multiply the total for each task by the number resources completing this task and add these to the spreadsheet.

- If the network is critical, use peak loading figures. Use average loading figures otherwise.

- Look for bottlenecks.

- Calculate how the network will scale and see if you can identify the point at which you will run out of capacity. Scenarios can help with this task. So can Performance Monitor, a tool you can use to observe network load over periods of time and under varying circumstances.

Network Monitor

Capacity planning requires tools. Which tools you need is in part dictated by the approach you plan to take. If your network is business-critical you may need to buy additional packages of analytical tools, for example, Windows NT provides some very good tools for general analysis. Chief among these is Network Monitor. A scaled-down version of NetMon is packaged with Windows NT; a more robust version ships with Systems Management Server.

Network Monitor Interface

The first NetMon window to appear is the Capture window, which presents the UI menus and toolbar, and four panes of statistics you can use to analyze overall network performance:

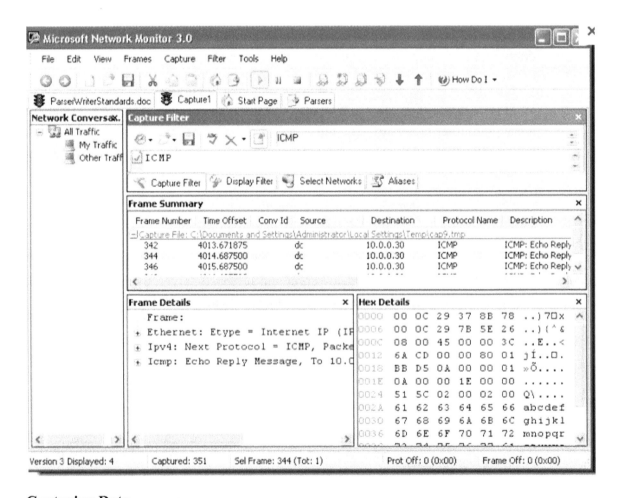

Capturing Data

There are three methods:

- From the Capture menu, click Start.

- Click the Start Capture button on the toolbar.

- Press the F10 function key.

As data is captured, the four panes in the Capture window display current network statistics as well as statistics for the captured data.

To stop the capture, use one of three methods:

- From the Capture menu, click Stop.

- Click the Stop Capture button on the toolbar.

- Press the F11 function key.

In general, there is no one correct way to determine the root cause of a networking problem. Like any troubleshooting of complex systems this is more art than science and the success depends both on your IQ and the level of experience with the environment. However, most networking problems are repetitive and there are a several heuristics that you can follow:

- **Try to correlate the current problem with previous problems**. It might not be 100% match but can steer you at right direction. Keeping detailed log of previous networking problems and method its resolution is easily accessible form is of paramount importance for troubleshooting of complex problems.

- **Collect the logs.** Often the problem unfolds in several hours and the messages from various divides can greatly help what went wrong. That's why simple (and I mean simple) network monitoring tools like the one before presented, are important.

- **Concentrate on the problem in hand and he area that is affected**. Fight distraction and redirection of your efforts even if you discover other serious problems. They can wait. Networks are a lot like cars: You can start out investigating one problem and find 10 other things that may need attention. Make a note of any non-related problems, but focus on investigating the primary problem. Try to narrow the area by eliminating parts and components of network that functioning properly.

- **Focus on one area at a time**. If several users are reporting problems from different areas of the network at the same time, there is a good chance that they are reporting elements of the same problem. It can be overwhelming to have hundreds of users down at once, but the same problem cans simply reoccurring in multiple parts of the network. Select the most vital segment that is affected and work on it. Ignore other no matter what is the level of cries and frequency of phone calls to your boss.

- **Search the web and vendor knowledgebase for error messages**. A pretty common and often very effective approach to tracking down the cause of errors or problems is searching the web. Using search engines like Google or Bing you can find documentation, FAQ's, web forum posts, mailing list archives, Usenet posts, and other useful resources.

After you have determined your network problems, you would like to create a project plan to confront all problems.

QUIZ

1. Most networking problems are repetitive and there are a several heuristics that you can follow, please name at least five:

- Try to correlate the current problem with previous problems.

- Collect the logs.

- Concentrate on the problem in hand and he area that is affected.

- Focus on one area at a time.

- Search the web and vendor knowledgebase for error messages.

2. In general words, what for the network monitor helps?

- Measure the amount of network activity that occurs for each of the tasks.

- Identify network topology and the location of clients and server

Create a project plan.

The key to a successful project is in the planning. Creating a project plan is the first thing you should do when undertaking any kind of project.

Often project planning is ignored in favor of getting on with the work. However, many people fail to realize the value of a project plan in saving time, money and many problems.

This lesson looks at a simple, practical approach to project planning. On completion of this guide, you should have a sound project planning approach that you can use for future projects.

Step 1: Project Goals

A project is successful when the needs of the stakeholders have been met. A stakeholder is anybody directly or indirectly impacted by the project.

As a first step, it is important to identify the stakeholders in your project. It is not always easy to identify the stakeholders of a project, particularly those impacted indirectly. Examples of stakeholders are:

- The project sponsor.

- The customer who receives the deliverables.

- The users of the project outputs.

- The project manager and project team.

Once you understand who the stakeholders are, the next step is to find out their needs. The best way to do this is by conducting stakeholder interviews. Take time during the interviews to draw out the true needs that create real benefits. Often stakeholders will talk about needs that aren't relevant and don't deliver benefits. These can be recorded and set as a low priority.

The next step, once you have conducted all the interviews, and have a comprehensive list of needs is to prioritize them. From the prioritized list, create a set of goals that can be easily measured. A technique for doing this is to review them against the SMART principle (Specific, Measurable, Attainable, Relevant and Time-sensitive). This way it will be easy to know when a goal has been achieved.

Once you have established a clear set of goals, they should be recorded in the project plan. It can be useful to also include the needs and expectations of your stakeholders.

This is the most difficult part of the planning process completed. It's time to move on and look at the project deliverables.

Step 2: Project Deliverables

Using the goals you have defined in step 1, create a list of things the project needs to deliver in order to meet those goals. Specify when and how each item must be delivered.

Add the deliverables to the project plan with an estimated delivery date. More accurate delivery dates will be established during the scheduling phase, which is next.

Step 3: Project Schedule

Create a list of tasks that need to be carried out for each deliverable identified in step 2. For each task identify the following:

- The amount of effort (hours or days) required to complete the task.

- The resource that will carry out the task.

Once you have established the amount of effort for each task, you can work out the effort required for each deliverable, and an accurate delivery date. Update your deliverables section with the more accurate delivery dates.

At this point in the planning, you could choose to use a software package such as **Microsoft Project** to create your project schedule. Alternatively, use one of the many free templates available. Input all of the deliverables, tasks, durations and the resources who will complete each task.

A common problem discovered at this point, is when a project has an imposed delivery deadline from the sponsor that is not realistic based on your estimates. If you discover this is the case, you must contact the sponsor immediately. The options you have in this situation are:

- Renegotiate the deadline (project delay).

- Employ additional resources (increased cost).

- Reduce the scope of the project (less delivered).

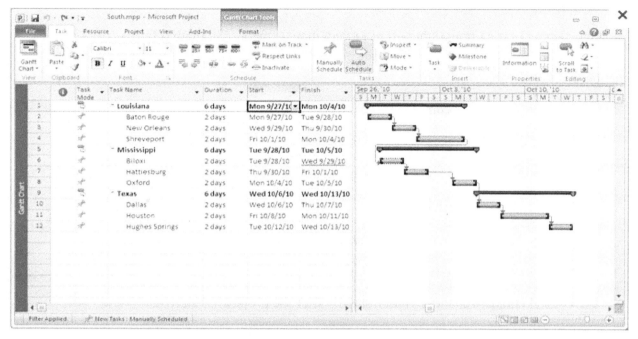

FIGURE 37 EXAMPLE OF A MICROSOFT PROJECT SIGHT PLAN

Use the project schedule to justify pursuing one of these options.

Step 4: Supporting Plans

This section deals with plans you should create as part of the planning process. These can be included directly in the plan.

Human Resource Plan

Identify by name, the individuals and organizations with a leading role in the project. For each, describe their roles and responsibilities on the project.

Next, describe the number and type of people needed to carry out the project. For each resource detail start dates, estimated duration and the method you will use for obtaining them.

Create a single sheet containing this information.

Communications Plan

Create a document showing that needs to be kept informed about the project and how they will receive the information. The most common mechanism is a weekly or monthly progress report, describing how the project is performing, milestones achieved, and work planned for the next period.

Risk Management Plan

Risk management is an important part of project management. Although often overlooked, it is important to identify as many risks to your project as possible, and be prepared if something bad happens.

Here are some examples of common project risks:

- Time and cost estimates too optimistic.

- Customer review and feedback cycle too slow.

- Unexpected budget cuts.

- Unclear roles and responsibilities.

- Stakeholder input is not sought, or their needs are not properly understood.

- Stakeholders changing requirements after the project has started.

- Stakeholders adding new requirements after the project has started.

- Poor communication resulting in misunderstandings, quality problems and rework.

- Lack of resource commitment.

Risks can be tracked using a simple risk log. Add each risk you have identified to your risk log; write down what you will do in the event it occurs, and what you will do to prevent it from occurring. Review your risk log on a regular basis, adding new risks as they occur during the life of the project. Remember, when risks are ignored they don't go away.

After you have created your project plan you would like to know some information system methodologies.

QUIZ

1. Name at least two examples of project risks:

- Unclear roles and responsibilities.

- Lack of resource commitment.

2. Give three examples of project stakeholders:

- The project sponsor.

- The customer who receives the deliverables.

- The project manager and project team.

3. Give a short description of what the project deliverables are:

- List of things the project needs to deliver in order to meet project goals.

Managing information system project methodologies.

In order to achieve goals and planned results within a defined schedule and a budget, a manager uses a project. Regardless of which field or which trade, there are assortments of methodologies to help managers at every stage of a project from the initiation to implementation to the closure. In this lesson, we will try to discuss the most commonly used project management methodologies.

A methodology is a model that project managers employ for the design, planning, implementation, and achievement of their project objectives. There are different project management methodologies to benefit different projects.

For example, there is a specific methodology that NASA uses to build a space station while the Navy employs a different methodology to build submarines. Hence there are different project management methodologies that cater to the needs of different projects, span across different business domains.

Project Methodologies:

Following are the most frequently used project management methodologies in the project management practice.

Adaptive Project Framework:

In this methodology, the project scope is a variable. Additionally, the time and the cost are constants for the project. Therefore, during the project execution, the project scope is adjusted in order to get the maximum business value from the project.

Agile Software Development:

Agile software development methodology is for projects that needs extreme agility in requirements. The key features of agile are its short-termed delivery cycles (sprints), agile requirements, dynamic team culture, less restrictive project control, and emphasis on real-time communication.

Crystal Methods:

In crystal method, the project processes are given a low priority. Instead of the processes, this method focuses more on team communication, team member skills, people, and interaction. Crystal methods come under agile category.

Dynamic Systems Development Model (DSDM):

This is the successor of Rapid Application Development (RAD) methodology. This is also a subset of agile software development methodology and boasts about the training and documents support this methodology has. This method emphasizes more on the active user involvement during the project life cycle.

Extreme Programming (XP):

Lowering the cost of requirements changes is the main objective of extreme programming. XP emphasizes on fine scale feedback, continues process, shared understanding, and programmer welfare. In XP, there is no detailed requirements specification or software architecture built.

Feature Driven Development (FDD):

This methodology is more focused on simple and well defined processes, short iterative, and feature driven delivery cycles. All the planning and execution in this project type take place based on the features.

Information Technology Infrastructure Library (ITIL):

This methodology is a collection of best practices in project management. ITIL covers a broad aspect of project management that starts from the organizational management level.

Joint Application Development (JAD):

Involving the client from the early stages with the project tasks is emphasized by this methodology. The project team and the client hold JAD sessions collaboratively in order to get the contribution from the client. These JAD sessions take place during the entire project lifecycle.

Lean Development (LD):

Lean development focuses on developing change-tolerance software. In this method, satisfying the customer comes as the highest priority. The team is motivated to provide the highest value for the money paid by the customer.

PRINCE2:

PRINCE2 takes a process-based approach to project management. This methodology is based on eight high-level processes.

Rapid Application Development (RAD):

This methodology focuses on developing products faster with higher quality. When it comes to gathering requirements, it uses the workshop method. Prototyping is used for getting clear requirements and re-use the software components to accelerate the development timelines.

In this method, all types of internal communications are considered informal.

Rational Unified Process (RUP):

RUP tries to capture all the positive aspects of modern software development methodologies and offer them in one package. This is one of the first project management methodologies that suggested an iterative approach to software development.

Scrum:

This is an agile methodology. The main goal of this methodology is to improve team productivity dramatically by removing every possible burden. Scrum projects are managed by a Scrum master.

Spiral:

Spiral methodology is the extended waterfall model with prototyping. This method is used instead of using the waterfall model for large projects.

Systems Development Life Cycle (SDLC):

This is a conceptual model used in software development projects. In this method, there is a possibility of combining two or more project management methodologies for the best outcome. SDLC also heavily emphasizes on the use of documentation and has strict guidelines on it.

Waterfall (Traditional):

This is the legacy model for software development projects. This methodology has been in practice for decades before the new methodologies were introduced. In this model, development lifecycle has fixed phases and linear timelines. This model is not capable of addressing the challenges in the modern software development domain.

Let us see a workflow of a **Prince2** methodology extracted from the Leeds Metropolitan University IMTS-Information Systems PDF document as a manner of reference:

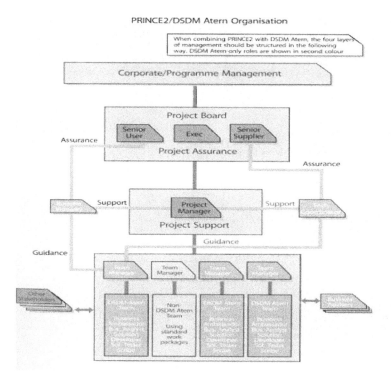

Figure 38 PRINCE2 Methodology

Summary

Selecting the most suitable project management methodology could be a tricky task. When it comes to selecting an appropriate one, there are a few dozens of factors you should consider. Each project management methodology carries its own strengths and weaknesses.

Therefore, there is no good or bad methodology, and what you should follow is the most suitable one for your project management requirements.

QUIZ

1. Give the description of the acronym formed by the letters of ITIL methodology:

- Information Technology Infrastructure Library (ITIL)

2. Name the acronyms of at least two most used in project management methodologies:

- PRINCE2

- Dynamic Systems Development Model (DSDM)

3. In few words tell what for the informatics system project methodologies help us:

- A methodology is a model which project managers employ for the design, planning, implementation and achievement of their project objectives.

Analyze network system interdependencies and constraints.

Analyze the computer site environment.

One of the first things you should do is build a complete picture of the existing physical computers and departments that exist into your organization so you can determine how well the network structure you decide will fit within your needs. Going through this process can help you identify any needs for deploying a LAN or WAN schema. Start with a simple representation of the entire network to identify locations of offices and the connections between them, and then build in more detail, as illustrated by the following figure:

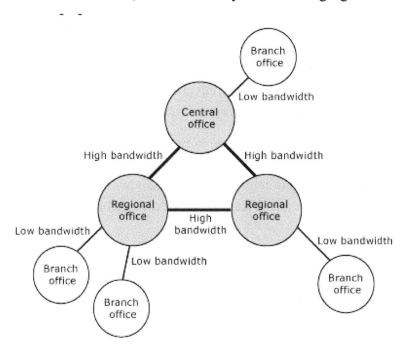

The acronym **LAN** stands for **Local Area Network** and the acronym WAN stands for **Wide Area Network.**

To obtain a detailed picture of the LAN and WAN configuration, it is recommended that you diagram all site locations, connection types, and network topologies (such as bus, token ring, or star). Include the locations of firewalls and perimeter networks. Your assessment should also include a thorough inventory of the hardware that currently makes up your network infrastructure, including stand-alone and clustered servers, routers, and switches. Also note all data center logistics, including rack space, cabling, and power supplies.

In general, you should assess your network infrastructure from the following perspectives:

- Geographical considerations

- Bandwidth and latency

- Current usage

These areas are discussed in the following sections.

Geographical Considerations

After you map the locations of buildings, campuses, and branch offices, determine the types of network connections to each site, as well as the placement of routers and switches.

Bandwidth and Latency

A key consideration for planning the total amount of data that can be transmitted over the network in a given amount of time. This quantity is determined by a combination of bandwidth and latency. Bandwidth is the speed of transmission over a network connection in kilobits per second. Latency refers to the amount of time it takes in milliseconds to transfer data from one point to another. Both of these factors combine to determine the amount of data that can be transmitted in a certain amount of time over the network. The product of these two factors directly affects user perception of how long it takes to process a transaction.

When evaluating your network connections, you need to evaluate bandwidth and latency, recognizing that although some types of network connections can maximize bandwidth, they may increase latency. For example, a satellite connection may offer high bandwidth, but latency may suffer when compared to ground connections such as frame relay or dial-up Integrated Services Digital Network (ISDN).

When mapping site locations and connections, determine the type and speed of network connectivity, and factor for latency introduced due to distances between sites. You may need to recommend network upgrades as part of the project.

Current Usage

The current usage of the network is another key consideration. Examine network usage from all angles, including use by applications and users. Along with identifying the current applications that use the network, consider the impact of future projects or initiatives. You need to plan for the additional impact that future applications will have on the network.

An extremely important consideration is the network load at peak times. To determine user load on the network, look at the number of users in the various sites as well as their patterns of use.

Summary

In general, if a site has more than ten users and is connected by low-bandwidth, high-latency network connections, the site should work in offline mode.

QUIZ

1. What for the acronym LAN stands?

> Local Area Network.

2. What for the acronym WAN stands?

> Wide Area Network.

3. You should assess your network infrastructure from the following perspectives:

- Geographical considerations.
- Bandwidth and latency.
- Current usag

Overview of Wireless Technology.

Wireless Networks

Wireless network is a network set up by using radio signal frequency to communicate among computers and other network devices. Sometimes it's also referred to as WiFi network or WLAN. Wireless networks utilize radio waves and/or microwaves to maintain communication channels between computers. Wireless networking is a more modern alternative to wired networking that relies on copper and/or fiber optic cabling between network devices.

A wireless network offers advantages and disadvantages compared to a wired network. Advantages of wireless include mobility and elimination of unsightly cables. Disadvantages of wireless include the potential for radio interference due to weather, other wireless devices, or obstructions like walls. Wireless is rapidly gaining in popularity for both home and business networking. Wireless technology continues to improve, and the cost of wireless products continues to decrease.

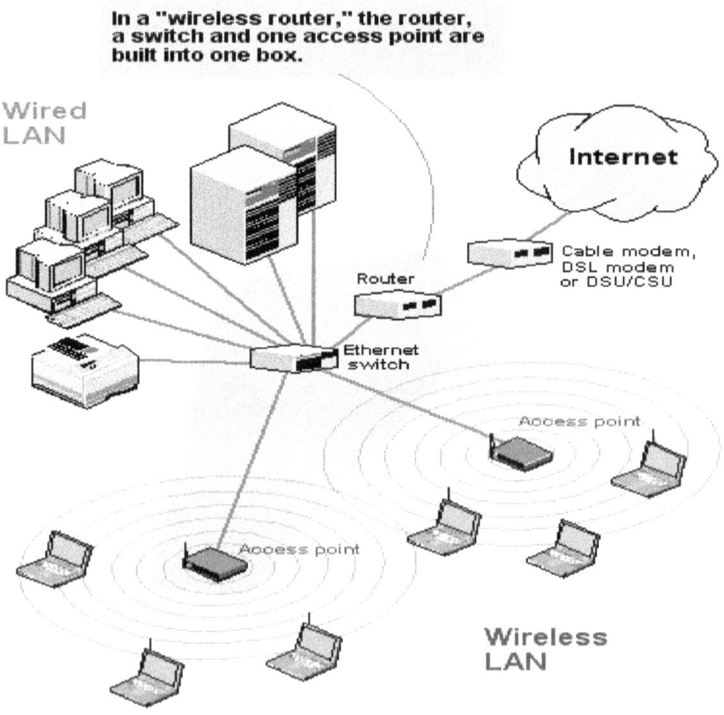

Wireless networks use radio waves to connect devices such as laptops to the Internet, the business network and applications. When laptops are connected to Wi-Fi hot spots in public places, the connection is established to that business's wireless network.

There are four main types of wireless networks:

1. **Wireless Local Area Network (LAN):** Links two or more devices using a wireless distribution method, providing a connection through access points to the wider Internet.

FIGURE 39 EXAMPLE OF WIRELESS LAN

2. **Wireless Metropolitan Area Networks (MAN):** Connects several wireless LANs.

3. **Wireless Wide Area Network (WAN):** Covers large areas such as neighboring towns and cities.

4. **Wireless Personal Area Network (PAN):** Interconnects devices in a short span, generally within a person's reach.

Wireless LANs

Popular wireless local area networking (WLAN) products conform to the 802.11 "Wi-Fi" standards. The gear a person needs to build wireless networks include network adapters (NICs), access points (APs), and routers.

Wireless network getting popular nowadays due to easy to setup feature and no cabling involved. You can connect computers anywhere in your home without the need for wires. Here is simple explanation of how it works, let say you have 2 computers each equipped with wireless adapter and you have set up wireless router. When the computer send out the data, the binary data will be encoded to radio frequency and transmitted via wireless router. The receiving computer will then decode the signal back to binary data. It doesn't matter you are using broadband cable/DSL modem to access internet, both ways will work with wireless network. If you heard about wireless hotspot, that means that location is equipped with wireless devices for you and others to join the network. You can check out the nearest hotspots from your home here.

The two main components are wireless router or access point and wireless clients. If you have not set up any wired network, then just get a wireless router and attach it to cable or DSL modem. You then set up wireless client by adding wireless card to each computer and form a simple wireless network. You can also cable connect computer directly to router if there are switch ports available.

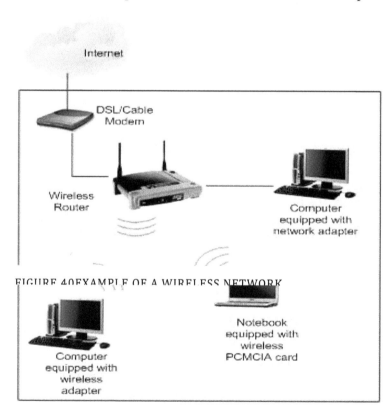

FIGURE 40 EXAMPLE OF A WIRELESS NETWORK

If you already have wired Ethernet network at home, you can attach a wireless access point to existing network router and have wireless access at home. Wireless router or access points should be installed in a way that maximizes coverage as well as throughput. The coverage provided is generally referred to as the coverage cell. Large areas usually require more than one access point in order to have adequate coverage. You can also add access point to your existing wireless router to improve coverage.

Wireless Operating Mode

The IEEE 802.11 standards specify two operating modes: **infrastructure mode** and **ad hoc mode**. **Infrastructure mode** is used to connect computers with wireless network adapters, also known as wireless clients, to an existing wired network with the help from wireless router or access point. The 2 examples which I specified above operate in this mode.

Ad Hoc Networks

Ad hoc mode is used to connect wireless clients directly together, without the need for a wireless router or access point. An ad hoc network consists of up to 9 wireless clients, which send their data directly to each other. Click here to learn more on this ad hoc mode.

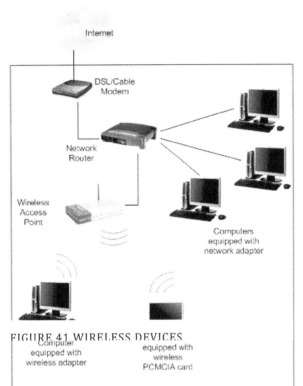

FIGURE 41 WIRELESS DEVICES

Wireless Devices

Devices which use radio frequency transmissions to replace medium-distance wired connections (such as Ethernet cables), to create what is sometimes called a WAN (wireless area network), or employed simply to replace short-distance cabling between digital devices.

Modem

A modem and broadband Internet connection is required if you want to be able to access the Internet. A modem is typically provided by your ISP

FIGURE 42 ROUTER

(Internet Service Provider) when you subscribe for broadband Internet, and is needed for both Cable and DSL Internet service. The modem allows your computer to communicate with the ISP's servers and transfer data back and forth. The modem connects to the phone or cable jack in the wall to receive the Internet data and also connects to the wireless router via an Ethernet cable. The Internet access is then distributed to computers on your network by the wireless router.

Wireless Router

Figure 43 WIRELESS ROUTER

A wireless router is needed to broadcast a wireless signal and allow computers and other wireless devices on the network to communicate with each other. Rather than connecting to each computer with a cable, wireless routers communicate by transmitting and receiving wireless signals. The router should be placed in a location that will provide the best range and signal strength. Walls and metal objects will reduce the signal strength and create connectivity issues. It is important to install the wireless router properly and create a login password. If the router is not password protected, anyone who receives the signal will be able to access your network.

How do wireless routers work?

Wireless routers pass information between devices connected to them as well as to the Internet by putting the information in small "packets". Each time a packet is transferred, the sending and receiving devices (a computer and the router, for example) verify that the packet was sent and received correctly before sending another. These packets can be sent through a wireless or wired connection, or both (for example, from a wireless laptop to a printer connected to the router with an Ethernet cable).

One of the primary functions of a wireless router is to facilitate transfer of these packets within its network. It does this by assigning a unique "IP address" to each device on the network. You can think of an IP address as you would your home address. Your house would be a device on the network and the router would the post office (and postal workers). But unlike your house address, IP addresses can be temporary. As devices come and go from the network they may be assigned a different IP address. The function in a router that performs this task is called aDHCP (Dynamic Host Configuration Protocol) server.

Another primary function of a wireless router is to share one Internet connection with many devices on the network. Your ISP issues your "home" an IP address (from their DHCP server). That IP address is then turned into a set of local IP addresses for your network by your router. The local IP addresses look very similar. They are sets of 4 numbers and look like: 192.168.1.X or 10.0.1.X. The last set of numbers in the series (X) is what DHCP changes for each device on the network. The router usually takes the number ".1" for itself, such as 192.168.0.1. This is referred to as the gateway address. It then issues other devices similar numbers such as 192.168.0.9.

Wireless Adapter

A wireless adapter allows the computer, or other device, to communicate with the wireless router and connect to the network. Every device that you want to have use the wireless network must have a wireless adapter installed. Many laptops come with wireless adapters already installed, but for those computers that don't have one, one must be purchased and installed. There are different types of adapters that can be installed. USB adapters are small and are able to plug directly into the USB port on the outside of the computer. PCI adapters are larger and need to be installed directly to the motherboard inside of the computer's case.

Personal Digital Assistants

PDA (personal digital assistant) is a term for any small mobile hand-held device that provides computing and information storage and retrieval capabilities for personal or business use, often for keeping schedule calendars and address book information handy. The term handheld is a synonym. Many people use the name of one of the popular PDA products as a generic term. These include Hewlett-Packard's Palmtop and 3Com's PalmPilot.

Most PDAs have a small keyboard. Some PDAs have an electronically sensitive pad on which hand writng can be received. Apple's Newton, which has been withdrawn from the market, was the first widely-sold PDA that accepted handwriting. Typical uses include schedule and address book storage and retrieval and note-entering. However, many applications have been written for PDAs. Increasingly, PDAs are combined with telephones and paging systems.

Some PDAs offer a variation of the Microsoft Windows operating system called Windows CE. Other products have their own or another operating system.

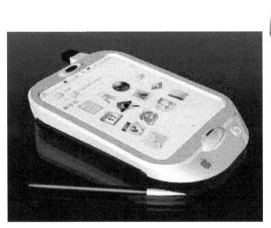

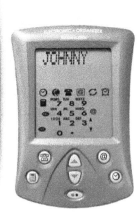

Most PDAs can exchange information with a desktop or laptop computer, although you may have to buy additional accessories.

e-mail and internet access

Most PDAs allow you to download e-mails and some Internet content from a desktop or laptop computer. You can write e-mails with most PDAs and later send them from your computer.

Some PDAs come with software for accessing certain brands of e-mail accounts. Additional software may be available to access other brands of e-mail accounts. Some PDAs also come with Internet browser software, while other PDAs require users to purchase browser software separately.

Many PDAs can access e-mail and the Internet by connecting to a telephone jack, although you may have to purchase a special modem. Other PDAs can provide wireless access to e-mail and the Internet if you buy a wireless modem or connect them to certain types of digital mobile phones. Still other PDAs permit wireless access to e-mail and the Internet without the need for additional hardware or software.

For wireless e-mail and Internet access, you must subscribe to a wireless data network service. You may have to pay a monthly flat fee, connection-time fees, or some other type of fee for that wireless service. Some PDAs may also require you to sign up for a wireless service with a specific ISP, so check before buying. In addition, wireless service may not be available in all areas of the United States or the world, so check with the wireless service provider.

Quality of internet and e-mail access

Currently, the ability to access the content of the Internet through a PDA is more limited than through a desktop computer. Some PDAs permit you to browse any URL on the Web using many Internet service providers (ISPs). Other PDAs require a subscription to a specific ISP. Check before buying if it important for your use.

Be aware that not all content of every Web site may be available on a PDA either because of the limited power relative to a desktop computer or because the PDA does not come with the software necessary to view all content on every Web site. Sometimes, additional software may be purchased and loaded onto the PDA to allow additional Web content to be displayed on a PDA.

Some Internet features that are available to most desktop computer users may not be available to PDA users. For example, PDAs may not allow users to play certain games, use certain audio or video features, or view information in certain formats like PDF (Portable Document Format) files. No currently available PDAs support Real Player, Shockwave, QuickTime, or other multimedia programs available on some Web sites.

Many PDAs allow you to access your e-mail accounts, but some PDAs limit your ability to send, receive, or view e-mail attachments. Not all devices are able to display attachments in popular formats like MS Word and HTML without additional software.

CONNECTING TO A DESKTOP OR NOTEBOOK COMPUTER

Typically, PDAs come with cables or docking stations to connect them to your desktop or notebook computer. Connecting lets you synchronize and update the files on your PDA with your desktop or notebook computer, such as your calendar, address book, and to-do lists. Some PDAs also enable you to synchronize word processing and spreadsheet files as well as e-mail messages, and copy Web site addresses and Web pages for offline viewing on your PDA.

SCREEN DISPLAYS

Some PDAs have monochrome or gray-scale displays, while others can display anywhere from 256 to 64,000 colors.

PDA screen displays are either active matrix or passive matrix. Active matrix displays generally are easier to see, more responsive, faster, and can be viewed at larger angles than passive matrix displays.

Most PDA screens may be seen adequately in many light conditions. Many have gauges for indoor, outdoor, and power-saving modes. Some color PDAs can be set to dim the backlight if the PDA is not in use for a set time - this extends the battery life.

BATTERIES

Some PDAs use permanent rechargeable batteries, while others use either rechargeable batteries that can be replaced or standard alkaline batteries. How long you can go without recharging or changing batteries may vary depending on the PDA. The time it takes for recharging may also vary depending on the battery. You can use the PDA while the battery is recharging.

MEMORY

PDAs in today's market typically have between 2 MB to 32 MB of built-in memory. Two MB of memory is generally sufficient to fill address books, maintain an active calendar, take notes, and load useful programs. More memory may be necessary to store large files like digital photos or audio recordings, or to hold large software programs. You can expand memory of some PDAs with small storage cards that can be inserted into the PDA. Think about your anticipated memory requirements before you buy, so that the PDA you select is capable of addressing your needs.

SIZE AND WEIGHT

Today's PDAs range from the size and thickness of 10 business cards, weighing 1.4 ounces, to the size of a paperback book weighing significantly more. The smallest PDAs have only basic information-organizing functions: they allow you to maintain address books and calendars, and create to-do lists. Complementary hardware -- for example, modems, cradles, and battery chargers -- add to the overall size and weight of PDAs.

ENTERING INFORMATION

You have to use a penlike stylus to enter information into many PDAs. You tap on an on-screen keyboard or enter data by writing on the screen, which may require learning a new way of printing the alphabet. Some PDAs use common alphabet characters, while others use variations. Test the handwriting recognition on several PDAs to make sure you are comfortable with how they work.

Other PDAs have built-in keyboards. Some of these also let you use a stylus; the stylus substitutes for a mouse for navigating through on-screen menus and controls. External keyboards are available as accessories for many smaller PDAs.

ADAPTABILITY

Some PDAs can be upgraded. You may be able to add software from the Web or other sources, and some PDAs offer more software applications than others. You also may be able to add memory or removable storage to a PDA, or connect it to an external monitor, a network, or a modem. Printers and external keyboards can be added to many PDAs as well.

SMART PHONES

Smartphones are mobile phones that can perform a number of different functions, such as playing music, taking pictures, surfing the internet and running applications. Smartphones are quickly replacing 'feature phones', which are lower-priced handsets that can also access the internet and perform similar multimedia tasks.

The difference between the two is that smartphones have much more powerful computer processors and run a complete 'operating system', in the same way your home PC runs an operating system like Windows. So, in many ways, smartphones are more like pocket PCs than mobile phones. Like with PCs, different smartphones can often run the same operating system, even if they are made by different manufacturers. For instance, HTC's Desire HD and Samsung's Galaxy S2 both run Android, an operating system that was developed by Google.

Smartphone features

Not all smartphones offer the same features, but below are the ones that most devices should be capable of.

HIGH-SPEED INTERNET ACCESS

A great deal of a smartphone's functionality relies on it being able to access the internet, allowing you to browse web pages, access email, watch online videos and download apps and music.

MUSIC PLAYER

Nearly all smartphones should be able to play music files in the same way as a dedicated Mp3-player. However, be warned that the sound quality can often be inferior to a dedicated device.

CAMERA

Most smartphones are able to take pictures and record video. If these are features you'll use often, make sure you check the camera quality, as it can vary quite considerably between different smartphones. For instance, despite being the most popular smartphones on the market, the iPhone 3G and 3GS have been criticised for the low resolution of their cameras.

TOUCHSCREEN

Smartphone touchscreens were popularised by Apple's iPhone and have since been used by many other smartphone manufacturers. There are two main types of smartphone touchscreens - resistive and capacitive. Capacitive is the more advanced touchscreen technology and offers more accurate control.

Touchscreens can be divisive when it comes to their usability. Some people find it awkward to type on a touchscreen keypad, while others would never think of going back to regular buttons. So it's a good idea to try out a touchscreen phone before you buy one.Smartphones can download apps - applications that add new functions to your phone. One of the most famous apps is a game called Angry Birds

APPLICATIONS

Applications (or 'apps') are a key feature of smartphones. They broaden the functionality of your phone, in a similar way to the software you buy for your PC. Different smartphone operating systems have access to different online stores where you can buy apps. So not all smartphones have access to the same apps. For instance, the iPhone uses Apple's App Store, whereas Android-based phones access the Android Market.

Tablets Personal Computer (Tablet PCs)

The tablet computer has made enormous strides in the last few years. Thanks to popular tablets like the iPad*, the thin, touch screen-operated computers have become the weapon of choice for many computer users as they offer a great experience when browsing the web or using one of thousands of specialized apps.

Tablets vary by their power and operating systems. Processors like the Intel® Atom™ provide considerable power for the current generation of tablets, and some tablets have dual core processors, including the Motorola Xoom and Asus Eee Transformer.

The most common type of tablet is the slate style, like Apple's iPad or Microsoft's Surface. These devices -- which are what that most people mean when they refer to a tablet -- have electronics integrated into the touch screen unit and lack a hardware keyboard. However, external keyboards are available for slate-style tablets. Some keyboards also function as docks for the devices. The most successful tablet computer is the Apple iPad using the iOS operating system. Its debut in 2010 popularized tablets into mainstream. Samsung's Galaxy Tab and others followed, continuing the now common trends towards multi-touch and other natural user interface features, as well as flash memory solid-state storage drives and "instant on" warm-boot times; in addition, standard external USB and Bluetooth keyboards can often be used. Most frequently, the operating system running on a tablet computer (one not based on the traditional Windows/x86 PC architecture) is a Unix-like OS, such as Darwin, Linux or QNX. Some have 3G mobile telephony capabilities

STYLES OF TABLETS:

- A convertible tablet typically has a display that rotates 180 degrees and can be folded to close, screen up, over the integrated keyboard. Convertible models may allow user input through a variety of methods in addition to the hardware keyboard, including natural handwriting with a stylus or digital pen and typing through a screen-based software keyboard.

- A hybrid tablet, sometimes referred to as a convertible or hybrid notebook, is like a regular notebook but with a removable display that functions independently as a slate.

- A rugged tablet is a slate-like model that is designed to withstand rough handling and extreme conditions. Rugged tablets are usually encased in a protective shell and have shock-protected hard drives.

The idea of tablet computing is generally credited to Alan Kay of Xerox, who sketched out the idea in 1971. The first widely sold tablet computer was Apple Computer's Newton, which was not a commercial success. Technological advances in battery life, display resolution, handwriting recognition software, larger memory, and wireless Internet access have since made tablets a viable computing option.

TABLET OPERATING SYSTEMS.

Most tablets use a special operating system designed to make the most of a touch interface, this gives the tablet the cool interactive feel that makes them fun and useful. A good operating system is an important part of a great tablet computer.

Popular tablet operating systems include the Honeycomb version of Google Android*, mobile versions of Windows 7* and XP*, and Apple's iPad OS. All of these operating systems have distinct advantages and disadvantages and all feature proprietary app stores which expand the capabilities of tablets.

Apps include everything from games to specialized word processors and even instruments. Generally, apps make use of a tablet's touchscreen to deliver an experience that a user couldn't get from a typical computer. A touchscreen is a very intuitive control system, so tablet manufacturers try to deliver the most easily accessible operating systems and apps possible to make sure that tablets offer a different experience from what a user would get from a laptop or netbook.

KEYBOARDS AND DOCKS.

Nevertheless, there are quite a few situations in which a tablet can benefit from the addition of a keyboard or keyboard-equipped docking station. While it's possible to type on the face of a tablet, an attached keyboard can make this process much easier.

Tablets like the Asus Eee Transformer have optional docking stations with built in keyboards which cost extra, but can basically turn a tablet into a full-featured netbook. Apple also sells an optional keyboard for use with its iPad.

CAMERAS.

Most of the current generation tablets also have forward and rear-facing cameras. These cameras are meant to make it easy to use video-conferencing apps and to take a quick high-res photo. It's another way that tablets differ from traditional computers. Since they're flat and portable, an included camera can be a great feature.

Newer tablets have serious power and numerous apps to take advantage of that power. They're an ideal way to browse the web, read an eBook, or to play games. Tablets are a casual type of computer, although they do have professional applications (especially for doctors and lawyers). They can be extremely engaging and useful, especially as prices drop below the $400 mark and the list of features provided by modern tablets continues to grow.

TOUCH USER INTERFACE:

A key and common component among tablet computers is touch input. This allows the user to navigate easily and intuitively and type with a virtual keyboard on the screen. The first tablet to do this was the GRiDPad by GRiD Systems Corporation; the tablet featured both a stylus, a pen-like tool to aid with precision in a touchscreen device as well as an on screen keyboard.

The event processing of the operating system must respond to touches rather than clicks of a keyboard or mouse, which allows integrated hand-eye operation, a natural part of the somatosensory system. Although the device implementation differs from more traditional PCs or laptops, tablets are disrupting the current vendor sales by weakening traditional laptop PC sales in favor of the current tablet computers. This is even more true of the "finger driven multi-touch" interface of the more recent tablet computers, which often emulate the way actual objects behave.

Some tablet personal computers use a stylus. These tablets often implement handwriting recognition. Tablet computers with finger driven screens usually do not. Finger driven screens are potentially better suited for inputting "variable width stroke based" characters, like Chinese/Japanese/Korean writing, due to their built in capability of "pressure sensing". However at the moment not much of this potential is already used, except in digital art applications like Autodesk Sketchbook for the iPad, and as a result even on tablet computers Chinese users often use a (virtual) keyboard for input.

TOUCHSCREEN HARDWARE

Touchscreens are usually one of two forms;

1. Resistive touchscreens are passive and can respond to any kind of pressure on the screen. They allow a high level of precision, useful in emulating a pointer as is common in tablet computers) but may require calibration to be accurate. Because of the high resolution of detection, a stylus or fingernail is often used for resistive screens. Limited possibilities

exist for implementing multi-touch on a resistive touch-screen. As modern tablet computers tend to make heavy use of multi-touch, this technology has faded out on high-end devices where it has been replaced by capacitive touchscreens.

2. Capacitive touchscreens tend to be less accurate, but more responsive than resistive screens. Because they require a conductive material, such as a finger tip, for input, they are not common among (stylus using) Tablet PCs but are more prominent on the smaller scale "tablet computer" devices for ease of use, which generally do not use a stylus, and need multi-touch capabilities.

OTHER TOUCH TECHNOLOGY USED IN TABLETS INCLUDE:

- Palm recognition. It prevents inadvertent palms or other contacts from disrupting the pen's input.

- Multi-touch capabilities, which can recognize multiple simultaneous finger touches, allowing for enhanced manipulation of on-screen objects.

Some professional-grade Tablet PCs use pressure sensitive films that additionally allow pressure sensitivity such as those on graphics tablets.

Concurrently capacitive touch-screens, which use finger tip detection can often detect the size of the touched area, and can make some conclusions to the pressure force used, for a similar result.

OTHER FEATURES OF A TABLET PC

1. Accelerometer: A device that detects the physical movements of the tablet. This allows greater flexibility of use since tablets do not necessarily have a fixed direction of use. The accelerometer can detect the orientation of the tablet relative to the horizontal plane, and movement of the tablet, both of which can be used as an alternative control interface for a tablet's software.

2. Ambient light and proximity sensors are additional "senses", that can provide controlling input for the tablet.

3. Storage drive: Large tablets use storage drives similar to laptops, while smaller ones tend to use drives similar to MP3 players or have on-board flash memory. They also often have ports for removable storage such as Secure Digital cards. Due to the nature of the use of tablets, solid-state memory is often preferable due to its better resistance to damage during movement. Some tablet computers utilize cloud storage in conjunction with local storage to increase storage capacity. Large media files such as videos, photos, eBooks, and music stored on the cloud can be streamed seamlessly into the tablet computer using a wireless Internet connection. This frees up the physical drive to hold less gluttonous data associated with applications and utilities.

4. Wireless: Because tablets by design are mobile computers, wireless connections are less restrictive to motion than wired connections. Wi-Fi connectivity has become ubiquitous among tablets. Bluetooth is commonly used for connecting peripherals and communicating with local devices in place of a wired USB connection.

5. 3D: Following mobile phone, there are also 3D slate tablet with dual lens at the back of the tablet and also provided with blue-red glasses.

6. Docking station: Some newer tablets are offering an optional docking station that has a full size qwerty keyboard and USB port, providing both portability and flexibility.

Wireless Standards

These standards address the need for an organized approach in deploying wireless technologies on the UCSF enterprise network. Adherence to these standards will allow UCSF schools, departments and individuals (including students in residence halls connected to the UCSF network) to deploy wireless networks without compromising the integrity of the campus network. These standards also encourage choices that will result in optimal compatibility between campus wireless local area network (WLAN) installations and will facilitate compatibility with the Medical Center's WLAN. Compatibility will result in better user experiences and lower support requirements. Wireless networking equipment is available that supports varying levels of industry communication standards. At present, the IEEE 802.11b/g standard is widely accepted throughout the industry and provides the necessary balance of range, network throughput, and support for device mobility to effectively serve most needs of the University community. As newer standards emerge, such as IEEE 802.11enhancements they will be evaluated and deployed should they offer security and throughput improvements over 802.11b/g.

FIGURE 44 GLOBAL WIRELESS

Different methods and standards of wireless communication have developed across the world, based on various commercially driven requirements. These technologies can roughly be classified into four individual categories, based on their specific application and transmission range. These categories are summarized in the figure below

WPA

Short for Wi-Fi Protected Access, a Wi-Fi standard that was designed to improve upon the security features of WEP. This technology features improved data encryption through the temporal key integrity protocol (TKIP) and user authentication through the extensible authentication protocol (EAP), PEAP – MSChapV2. Wireless PittNet utilizes the WPA protocol.

802.1X

This standard enhances the security of local area networks by providing an authentication framework allowing users to authenticate to a central authority, such as LDAP or Active Directory. In conjunction with 802.11 access technologies, it provides an effective mechanism for controlling access to the wireless local area network.

802.11A

An extension to the 802.11 standard developed by the IEEE for wireless network technology. 802.11a applies to wireless local area networks and supports a maximum a maximum connect rate of 54 Mbps throughput in the 5GHz band. This specification is not backwardly compatible with 802.11b/g and requires special wireless adapters.

802.11B

An extension to the 802.11 standard developed by the IEEE for wireless network technology. 802.11b applies to wireless local area networks and supports a maximum connect rate of 11 Mbps with fallback to 5.5, 2, and 1 Mbps in the 2.4GHz ISM band. This standard was ratified in 1999.

802.11G

An extension to the 802.11 standard that allows for a maximum connect rate of 54 Mbps while maintaining compatibility with the 802.11b standard in the 2.4Ghz band This specification is compatible and complimentary to the 802.11b standard.

802.11I

An extension to the 802.11 standard to provide improved security over that which is available under 802.11 extensions. This extension provides for improved encryption methods and for the integration of the IEEE 802.1x authentication protocol as well as advanced encryption mechanisms such as AES. (Advanced Encryption Standard) for an optional, fully compliant implementation of 802.11i

802.11N

Uses multiple transmitter and receiver antennas (MIMO) to allow for increased data throughput and range. This is not a ratified standard as of Dec 2006. Pre-standard hardware is commercially available and not compatible with Wireless PittNet.

IEEE 802.11

The standard IEEE 802.11i is designed to provide secured communication of wireless LAN as defined by all the IEEE 802.11 specifications. IEEE 802.11i enhances the WEP (Wireline

Equivalent Privacy), a technologies used for many years for the WLAN security, in the areas of encryption, authentication and key management. IEEE 802.11i is based on the Wi-Fi Protected Access(WPA), which is a quick fix of the WEB weaknesses.

The IEEE 802.11i has the following key components:

FIXING WEP

Although the IEEE 802.11 standard upon which Wi-Fi wireless LAN networks are based addressed security somewhat with the Wired Equivalent Privacy (WEP) protocol in its first instantiation, WEP proved relatively easy to crack. Fortunately, the IEEE 802.11 group became aware of the issues with WEP early on and on June 24 of this year the IEEE Standards Association approved an amendment to the original IEEE 802.11 specification that addresses these issues. The culmination of three and a half years of work by the IEEE 802.11i Task Group, the amendment adds stronger encryption, authentication, and key management strategies that go a long way toward guaranteeing data and system security.

The IEEE 802.11i effort actually started with a task group intended to address both quality of service and security, namely IEEE 802.11e. However, it quickly became apparent that security needed special attention and so that group was split into IEEE 802.11e, which continues to work on quality of service, and IEEE 802.11i, which focused on security.

The resulting IEEE 802.11i amendment has many components, the most obvious of which are the two new data-confidentiality protocols, TKIP and CCMP. IEEE 802.11i also uses IEEE 802.1X's key-distribution system to control access to the network. Because IEEE 802.11 handles unicast and broadcast traffic differently, each traffic type has different security concerns. With several data-confidentiality protocols and the key distribution, IEEE 802.11i includes a negotiation process for selecting the correct confidentiality protocol and key system for each traffic type. Other features introduced include key caching and preauthentication.

WEP has many problems. One of the first papers to reveal WEP's issues came from within the IEEE 802.11i Task Group. In late 2000, Jesse Walker submitted his paper, "Unsafe at any key size; An analysis of the WEP encapsulation" to show that WEP had serious problems and that the Task Group needed to devise an alternative.[1] Another paper demonstrated WEP's biggest shortcomings. "Weaknesses in the Key Scheduling Algorithm of RC4," Scott Fluhrer, Itsik Mantin, and Adi Shamir, made clear that the original WEP key can be obtained from a passive attack.

The IEEE 802.11i Task Group debated if it should attempt to improve the situation with legacy products. At first, the way to improve security with legacy hardware wasn't evident, and it appeared that acknowledging the problem and starting over with a completely different cipher would have been the easiest solution. However, many of the same authors who documented the weaknesses of WEP didn't give up and contributed ideas for an alternative that could be run on legacy products. What they came up with was TKIP.

TKIP

The Temporal Key Integrity Protocol (TKIP) is a data-confidentiality protocol that was designed to improve the security of products that implemented WEP—in other words, legacy products. Among WEP's numerous flaws are its lack of a message integrity code and its insecure data-confidentiality protocol. To get around these limitations, TKIP uses a message integrity code called Michael. Basically, Michael enables devices to authenticate that the packets are coming from the claimed source. This authentication is especially important in a wireless technology where traffic can be easily injected.

TKIP uses a mixing function to defeat weak-key attacks, which enabled attackers to decrypt traffic. Since the decryption could be done passively, it meant that an attacker could watch WEP traffic from a distance, be undetected, and know the original traffic. TKIP fixes this situation by using a mixing function.

CCMP

Although TKIP improves security especially for legacy hardware, a stronger alternative was needed for newer hardware. Many Task Group members wanted the alternative to be acceptable for Federal Information Processing Standards (FIPS) certification, even though it wasn't absolutely necessary. In early drafts, Task Group I included Advanced Encryption Standard-Offset Codebook (AES-OCB). Questions over intellectual property, however, made some members uncomfortable. So, the Task Group switched to the Counter-Mode/CBC-MAC Protocol (CCMP).

CCMP is a data-confidentiality protocol that handles packet authentication as well as encryption. For confidentiality, CCMP uses AES in counter mode. For authentication and integrity, CCMP uses Cipher Block Chaining Message Authentication Code (CBC-MAC). In IEEE 802.11i, CCMP uses a 128-bit key. The block size is 128 bits. The CBC-MAC size is 8 octets, and the nonce size is 48 bits. There are two bytes of IEEE 802.11 overhead. The CBC-MAC, the nonce, and the IEEE 802.11 overhead make the CCMP packet 16 octets larger than an unencrypted IEEE 802.11 packet. Although slightly slower, the larger packet is not a bad exchange for increased security.

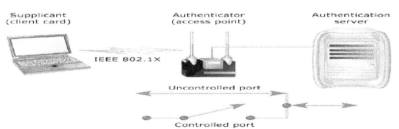 CCMP protects some fields that aren't encrypted. The additional parts of the IEEE 802.11 frame that get protected are known

FIGURE 45 IEEE802.1X USE IN IEEE802.11I SYSTEM

asadditional authentication data (AAD). AAD includes the packets source and destination and protects against attackers replaying packets to different destinations.

IEEE 802.1X

- IEEE 802.1X provides a framework to authenticate and authorize devices connecting to a network. It prohibits access to the network until such devices pass authentication. IEEE 802.1X also provides a framework to transmit key information between authenticator and supplicant.

IEEE 802.1X has three main pieces as shown in Figure 46

BLUETOOTH

Bluetooth is a specification (IEEE 802.15.1) for the use of low-power radio communications to link phones, computers and other network devices over short distances without wires. The name Bluetooth is borrowed from Harald Bluetooth, a king in Denmark more than 1,000 years ago.

Bluetooth technology was designed primarily to support simple wireless networking of personal

FIGURE 46 BLUETOOTH SYSMLE

consumer devices and peripherals, including cell phones, PDAs, and wireless headsets. Wireless signals transmitted with Bluetooth cover short distances, typically up to 30 feet (10 meters). Bluetooth devices generally communicate at less than 1. Bluetooth networks feature a dynamic topology called a *piconet* or *PAN*. Piconets contain a minimum of two and a maximum of eight Bluetooth peer devices. Devices communicate using protocols that are part of the Bluetooth Specification. Definitions for multiple versions of the Bluetooth specification exist including versions 1.1, 1.2 and 2.0.

Although the Bluetooth standard utilizes the same 2.4 Ghz range as 802.11b and 802.11g, Bluetooth technology is not a suitable Wi-Fi replacement. Compared to Wi-Fi, Bluetooth networking is much slower, a bit more limited in range, and supports many fewer devices.

How Bluetooth Works

When you use computers, entertainment systems, or telephones, the various pieces and parts of the systems make up a community of electronic devices. These devices communicate with each other using a variety of wires, cables, radio signals and infrared light beams, and an even greater variety of connectors, plugs and protocols.

There are many different ways that electronic devices can connect to one another. For example:

- Component cables
- Electrical wires
- Ethernet cables
- WiFi
- Infrared signals

The art of connecting things is becoming more and more complex every day. In this article, we will look at a method of connecting devices, called Bluetooth, that can streamline the process. A Bluetooth connection is wireless and automatic, and it has a number of interesting features that can simplify our daily lives.

The Problem

When any two devices need to talk to each other, they have to agree on a number of points before the conversation can begin. The first point of agreement is physical: Will they talk over wires, or through some form of wireless signals? If they use wires, how many are required -- one, two, eight, 25? Once the physical attributes are decided, several more questions arise:

- How much data will be sent at a time? For instance, serial ports send data 1 bit at a time, while parallel ports send several bits at once.

- How will they speak to each other? All of the parties in an electronic discussion need to know what the bits mean and whether the message they receive is the same message that was sent. This means developing a set of commands and responses known as a protocol.

Wireless Security Threats and Risk Mitigation

As discussed previously, the most tangible benefit of wireless is cost reduction. In addition to increasing productivity, WLANs increase work quality. However, a security breach resulting from a single unsecured access point can negate hours spent securing the corporate network and even ruin an organization. You must understand the security risks of WLANs and how to reduce those risks. After completing this section, you will be able to describe WLAN security issues and the features available to increase WLAN security.

Wireless LAN Security Threats

With the lower costs of IEEE 802.11b/g systems, it is inevitable that hackers have many more unsecured WLANs from which to choose. Incidents have been reported of people using numerous open source applications to collect and exploit vulnerabilities in the IEEE 802.11 standard security mechanism, Wired Equivalent Privacy (WEP). Wireless sniffers enable network engineers to passively capture data packets so that they can be examined to correct system problems. These same sniffers can be used by hackers to exploit known security weaknesses.

"War driving" originally meant using a cellular scanning device to find cell phone numbers to exploit. War driving now also means driving around with a laptop and an 802.11b/g client card to find an 802.11b/g system to exploit. Most wireless devices sold today are WLAN-ready. End users often do not change default settings, or they implement only standard WEP security, which is not optimal for securing wireless networks. With basic WEP encryption enabled (or, obviously, with no encryption enabled), collecting data and obtaining sensitive network information, such as user login information, account numbers, and personal records, is possible.

A rogue access point (AP) is an AP placed on a WLAN and used to interfere with normal network operations, for example, with denial of service (DoS) attacks. If a rogue AP is programmed with the correct WEP key, client data could be captured. A rogue AP also could be configured to provide unauthorized users with information such as MAC addresses of clients (both wireless and wired), to capture and spoof data packets, or, at worst, to gain access to servers and files. A simple and common version of a rogue AP is one installed by employees with authorization. Employees install access points intended for home use without the necessary security configuration on the enterprise network, causing a security risk for the network.

Mitigating Security Threats

To secure a WLAN, the following components are required:

- **Authentication**: To ensure that legitimate clients and users access the network via trusted access points

- **Encryption**: To provide privacy and confidentiality

- **Intrusion Detection Systems (IDS) and Intrusion Protection Systems (IPS)**: To protect from security risks and availability

The fundamental solution for wireless security is authentication and encryption to protect the wireless data transmission. These two wireless security solutions can be implemented in degrees; however, both apply to small office/home office (SOHO) and large enterprise wireless networks. Larger enterprise networks need the additional levels of security offered by an IPS monitor. Current IPS systems do not only detect wireless network attacks, but also provide basic protection against unauthorized clients and access points. Many enterprise networks use IPS for protection not primarily against outside threats, but mainly against unintentional unsecured access points installed by employees desiring the mobility and benefits of wireless.

Emerging Wireless Technologies

The demand for wireless data services is growing by leaps and bounds while the amount of available radio spectrum remains relatively constant. The increasing stress created by exploding demand and spectrum scarcity causes us to pay particular attention to technologies that could potentially reap 10x to 1000x increases in spectrum efficiency. Following emerging wireless technologies are included in the research:

1. LTE-Advanced:It is one of major technology for 4G (IMT-Advanced) under standardization by 3GPP release 10. The key technologies in standard specifications are carrier aggregation, HetNet, Relay, SON, and SU-MIMO.

2. Gigabit WLAN: It is 60 GHz unlicensed band wireless systems, which can carry Gbps of data, enable several new applications: high definition video streaming wireless in real time, high speed wireless gaming, and wireless docking and connection to displays. IEEE 802.11ad was formed in January 2009 to make industry standard for 60 GHz wireless systems as an amendment to the existing IEEE 802.11-2007 (modifications to the 802.11 PHY and the 802.11 MAC).

3. Gognitive radio in TVWS: The technologies for the cognitive radios over TV white space are under standardization by IEEE 802.22 and 802.11af.

4. Zigbee for M2M: ZigBee is a low-cost, low-power, wireless mesh networking standard based on the IEEE 802.15.4-2003 for Wireless Personal Area Networks. Zigbee is one of key enabling technologies for M2M (Machine-to-Machine) applications: smart grids. connected home, building automation, mobile helath, security, and automatic control.

5. NFC: Near field communication is a short-range wireless technology for mobile transaction applications. Industry standard for NFC technology is under development by the NFC Forum.

Among the total of 44 IPR holders, Samsung Electronics is the leader followed by Broadcom, Motorola, Qualcomm, Philips, Nokia, LG Electronics, Intel, STMicroelectonics, and Microsoft.

LTE-Advanced is a term used for the version of LTE that addresses IMT-Advanced requirements, as specified in Release 10. The ITU ratified LTE-Advanced as IMT-Advanced in November 2010. LTE-Advanced is both backwards- and forwards-compatible with LTE, meaning LTE devices will operate in newer LTE-Advanced networks, and LTE-Advanced devices will operate in older LTE networks.

In preparation for the next generation of wireless technology, called IMT-Advanced by the International Telecommunication Union (ITU), LTE-Advanced was standardized by 3GPP in Release 10 and Release 11. In November 2010, the ITU ratified LTE-Advanced as IMT-Advanced. LTE-Advanced is a further evolution of LTE, an OFDMA-based technology, specified in Release 8 and 9, which is supported by a tremendous ecosystem of manufacturers and operators worldwide, and has already proven itself to be the global next generation technology.

It is expected that LTE-Advanced will first be commercially available in 2013, with wider deployments by 2015. LTE-Advanced will be both backwards- and forwards-compatible with LTE, meaning LTE devices will operate in newer LTE-Advanced networks, and LTE-Advanced devices will operate in older LTE networks.

3GPP developed the following capabilities for LTE-Advanced with specifications functionally frozen for Release 11 in September 2012:

- Wider bandwidth support for up to 100 MHz via aggregation of 20 MHz blocks (Carrier Aggregation)

- Uplink MIMO (two transmit antennas in the device)

- Higher order downlink MIMO of up to 8 by 8 in Release 10

- Coordinated Multipoint Transmission (CoMP) with two proposed approaches: coordinated scheduling and/or beamforming, and joint processing/transmission in Release 11

- Heterogeneous network (Het-net) support including enhanced Inter-Cell

Item	IMT-Advanced Requirement	LTE-Advanced Projected Capability
Peak Data Rate Downlink		1 Gbps
Peak Data Rate Uplink		500 Mbps
Spectrum Allocation	Up to 40 MHz	Up to 100 MHz
Latency User Plane	10 msec	10 msec
Latency Control Plane	100 msec	50 msec
Peak Spectral Efficiency DL[133]	15 bps/Hz	30 bps/Hz
Peak Spectral Efficiency UL	6.75 bps/Hz	15 bps/Hz
Average Spectral Efficiency DL	2.2 bps/Hz	2.6 bps/Hz
Average Spectral Efficiency UL	1.4 bps/Hz	2.0 bps/Hz
Cell-Edge Spectral Efficiency DL	0.06 bps/Hz	0.09 bps/Hz
Cell-Edge Spectral Efficiency UL	0.03 bps/Hz	0.07 bps/Hz

FIGURE 47 IMT-ADVANCED REQUIREMENTS AND ANTICIPATED LTE-ADVANCED CAPABILITY

Advance will be the ideal technology for these new bands. Even in existing bands, operators are likely to eventually upgrade their LTE networks to LTE-Advanced to obtain spectral efficiency gains and capabilities.

Federal Information Processing Standards

The Federal Information Processing Standard (FIPS) Publication 140-2, is a computer security standard, developed by a U.S. Government and industry working group to validate the quality of cryptographic modules. FIPS publications (including 140-2) can be found at the following. Note that at the time of writing, Publication 140-3 is at Draft status, and may not represent the completed standard. The FIPS standard provides four (4) security *levels*, to ensure adequate coverage of different industries, implementations of cryptographic modules and organizational sizes and requirements. These levels are described below:

- Level 1 - Security Level 1 provides the lowest level of security. Basic security requirements are specified for a cryptographic module (e.g., at least one Approved algorithm or Approved security function shall be used). No specific physical security mechanisms are required in a Security Level 1 cryptographic module beyond the basic requirement for production-grade components. An example of a Security Level 1 cryptographic module is a personal computer (PC) encryption board.

- Level 2 - Security Level 2 enhances the physical security mechanisms of a Security Level 1 cryptographic module by adding the requirement for tamper-evidence, which includes the use of tamper-evident coatings or seals or for pick-resistant locks on removable covers or doors of the module. Tamper-evident coatings or seals are placed on a cryptographic module so that the coating or seal must be broken to attain physical access to the plaintext cryptographic keys and critical security parameters (CSPs) within the module. Tamper-evident seals or pick-resistant locks are placed on covers or doors to protect against unauthorized physical access.

- Level 3 - In addition to the tamper-evident physical security mechanisms required at Security Level 2, Security Level 3 attempts to prevent the intruder from gaining access to CSPs held within the cryptographic module. Physical security mechanisms required at Security Level 3 are intended to have a high probability of detecting and responding to attempts at physical access, use or modification of the cryptographic module. The physical security mechanisms may include the use of strong enclosures and tamper detection/response circuitry that zeroes all plaintext CSPs when the removable covers/doors of the cryptographic module are opened.

- Level 4 - Security Level 4 provides the highest level of security defined in this standard. At this security level, the physical security mechanisms provide a complete envelope of protection around the cryptographic module with the intent of detecting and responding to all unauthorized attempts at physical access. Penetration of the cryptographic module enclosure from any direction has a very high probability of being detected; resulting in the immediate zeroization of all plaintext CSPs. Security Level 4 cryptographic modules are useful for operation in physically unprotected environments.

Exercise

Quizzes:

Q.1) What is difference between Wireless Local Area Network (LAN) and Wireless Metropolitan Area Networks (MAN)?

Answer) Links two or more devices using a wireless distribution method, providing a connection through access points to the wider Internet is a LAN. Connects several wireless LANs is a WAN.

Q.2) What are Wireless Operating Mode?

Answer) The IEEE 802.11 standards specify two operating modes: infrastructure mode and ad hoc mode. Infrastructure mode is used to connect computers with wireless network adapters, also known as wireless clients, to an existing wired network with the help from wireless router or access point. The 2 examples which I specified above operate in this mode.

Q.3) Is Ad hoc mode used to connect wireless clients directly together, without the need for a wireless router or access point? **(state whether true or false)**

Answer) True

Q.4) Either Wireless routers pass information between devices connected to them as well as to the Internet by putting the information in small "packets"? **(state whether true or false)**

Answer) True

Q.5) There is no difference between Smartphones and tablet? (state whether true or false)

Answer) False

Q.6) What is the functions of IEEE 802.1X

Answer)
IEEE 802.1X provides a framework to authenticate and authorize devices connecting to a network. It prohibits access to the network until such devices pass authentication. IEEE 802.1X also provides a framework to transmit key information between authenticator and supplicant.

Assignment

Research about how to expand Wireless Network Cover?

Answer) Information can be found here:
ttp://www.tenda.cn/tendacn/support/show.aspx?articleid=1256

PROJECT

Decentralized wireless networks could have applications in distributed sensing and robotics and maybe even personal communications. Research this concept and draw diagram in context of Ad hoc networks.

Answer) Reference to this can be found here: http://web.mit.edu/newsoffice/2011/exp-ad-hoc-0310.html

Wireless LANs

Wireless LAN Overview

Wireless LANs based on the IEEE 802.11 standards allow wire- free networking in the local area network environment using the unlicensed 2.4 or 5.3 GHz unlicensed radio band. They're used everywhere from homes to Fortune 500 companies to hotspot Internet access. This article will offer a brief summary of the various network topologies in various environments.

Simple home Wireless LANs

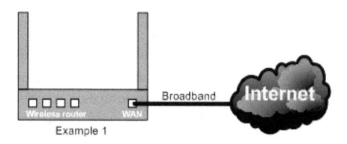

Example 1

Figure 48A SIMPLE WIRELESS LAN

In the most common and cheapest example of a home Wireless LAN, Figure 1 shows a single device acting as the Firewall, Router, Switch, and Wireless Access Point. These Wireless Routers can provide a wide range of functions such as:

- Protects the home network from outside intruders

- Allows the sharing of a single Internet IP address from an ISP (Internet Service Provider)

- Provides Wired Ethernet service for typically 4 computers but can also be expanded with another Ethernet Switch or Hub

- Serves as a Wireless Access Point for multiple wireless computers

These devices come from a variety of manufacturers such as Linksys (Cisco), D-Link, Netgear, SMC, Belkin, and other companies. The basic models typically have a single Wi-Fi radio offering 2.4 GHz 802.11b/g operation while the higher end models will offer dual-band Wi-Fi radios or high-speed MIMO capability. Dual-band Access Points have two radios which provide 2.4 GHz 802.11b/g and 5.3 GHz 802.11a capability while MIMO Access Points use multiple radios to boost performance in the 2.4 GHz range. Dual-band Access Points are essentially two

Access Points in one and can serve two non-interfering frequencies at the same time while the newer MIMO devices boost speed in the 2.4 GHz range along with superior range. Unfortunately, the 2.4 GHz range is often congested and manufacturers have stayed away from dual-band MIMO devices because of cost concerns since they're already the most expensive to begin with. Dual-band devices don't have the highest performance or range, but allow you to operate in the relatively uncongested 5.3 GHz range and allow two devices to operate at full speed simultaneously if they are in different bands.

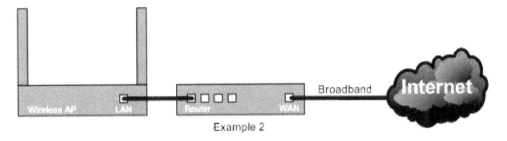

Figure 49 WIRELESS ACCESS POINT

Figure 50 is a less common example of a home network where the Wireless Access Point is a separate device. This topology is more expensive but offers more flexibility. Consolidated router/wireless devices may not offer all the features desired by power users. In this configuration, it's possible for the Access Point to cost more than an equivalent Router and AP in one and that's probably due to the fact that there are fewer sold since most people prefer the combined functionality. Some people require higher end routers and switches that have features such as bandwidth throttling and gigabit Ethernet and having a modular design allows them the flexibility they need.

Wireless Bridging

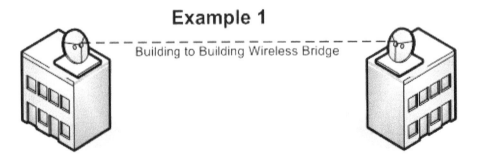

Figure 50 WIRELESS BRIDGING

Wireless Bridges allow buildings to connect wirelessly when wiring is too expensive or a second redundant connection is needed as a backup for a wired connection. 802.11 devices are commonly used for these application as well as optical line-of-sight Wireless bridges. 802.11 radio based solutions are usually much cheaper and don't require a line-of-sight between the antennas to operate, but are significantly slower than optical solutions. 802.11 solutions typically operate in the 5 to 30 mbps range while optical solutions operate in the 100 to 1000 mbps range. Both types of bridges can operate beyond 10 miles although the radio based solution is more likely to reach these distances because it doesn't require line-of-sight. The down side to radio based solutions is the lower speed and the possibility of RF (radio frequency) interference while optical solutions aren't affected by RF. The down side of optical solutions is the higher entry price and the fact that line-of-sight is not always possible between two locations.

Example 2

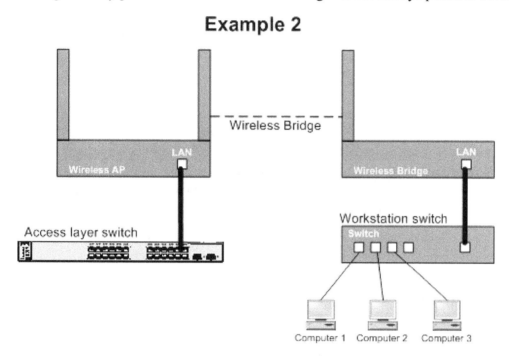

Figure 51 TYPICAL WIRELESS BRIDGE IN USE

Figure 52 Illustrates a typical scenario where a Wireless Bridge is used to wirelessly extend an Ethernet network. There are many types of 802.11 bridges and some of them use proprietary methods of interlinking and may not always offer the best compatibility or security. A preferable solution is to use a simple Wireless Bridge that can connect to any common infrastructure-type Access Point as a regular WPA client to provide a secured wireless connection. Once bridged, an additional Ethernet Switch can be used to expand the port capacity and link multiple Wired Ethernet computers to the LAN over the wireless bridge. This is a cheaper option than outfitting multiple fixed position Desktop PCs with wireless Ethernet cards and having to configure them.

Brief History

The history of wireless networks and of wireless networking goes hand in hand. Without the discovery of technology such as the radio, wireless technology would not exist at all today. The history of wireless networking goes as far back as the 1800's with the advent of radio waves. The advent of more technology grew throughout the years and expanded to what we communicated with today.

In 1888, a Hamburg, Germany born physicist named Heinrich Rudolf Herz produced his first radio wave ever. By 1894 this radio wave production became a way of communication. Telegraph wires were used to receive the radio waves in signal form. Herz opened the way for radio, television, and radar with his discovery of electromagnetic waves. An Italian inventor named Marchese Guglielmo Marconi then expanded the radius of radio wave sending to two miles, becoming the "father of the radio." By 1899, this form of telecommunication could travel pretty far for its time. Marconi could send a signal 9 miles across the Bristol Channel. He eventually expanded the radius to 31 miles across the English Channel to France. By 1901 the communication area became immense. Marconi could send signals across the entire Atlantic Ocean.

World War II became a big stepping stone for the radio wave. The United States was the first party to use radio waves for data transmission during the war. This use of radio waves could have quite possibly won the war for the Americans. The use of radio wave data communication lead to a lot of speculation to whether the radio signals could be expanded into something bigger than it currently was. In 1971, a group of researchers under the lead of Norman Abramson, at the University of Hawaii, created the first "packet-switched" radio communications network entitled "Alohanet." Alohanet was the first wireless local area network, otherwise known as a WLAN. The first WLAN was not much, but it was a large discovery. The Alohanet WLAN was comprised of seven computers that communicated to each other. In 1972, Alohanet connected with the WLAN system Arpanet on the mainland. This length of connect was ground breaking in telecommunications between computers.

The first types of WLAN technology used an interface in which became over crowded for communication. Small appliances and industrial machinery caused interference so the technology had to be updated. The second type of WLAN technology to be released ended up being four times faster than its predecessor at 2Mbps per second. We use the third format of WLAN today, though our current WLAN system runs at the same speed as the second system released.

In 1990, the 802.11 Working Group was established to work towards a WLAN standard for all computers to communicate from. In 1997, IEEE 802.11 was accepted as the standard data communication format for wireless local area networks. The technology continues to grow today. Governments and large corporations are constantly looking out for the latest and fastest standard to work from.

The expansion of wireless networking will likely continue for decades to come.

Frequency and Data Rates

This section describes the basic radio frequency (RF) information necessary to understand RF considerations in various wireless local area network (WLAN) environments. This chapter includes information on the following topics:

- Regulatory domains and frequencies

- Understanding the IEEE 802.11 standards

- RF spectrum implementations including 802.11b/g and 802.11a

- Planning for RF deployment

- Manually fine-tuning WLAN coverage

- Radio Resource Management (RRM)

RF Basics

In the United States, there are three bands allocated for unlicensed industrial, scientific, and medical (ISM) usage. These ISM bands are defined as follows:

- 900 MHz (902 to 928 MHz)

- 2.4 GHz (2.4 to 2.4835 GHz) (IEEE 802.11b/g operates in this frequency range)

- 5 GHz (5.15 to 5.35 and 5.725 to 5.825 GHz) (IEEE 802.11a operates in this frequency range)

Each range has different characteristics. The lower frequencies exhibit better range, but with limited bandwidth and thus lower data rates. The higher frequencies exhibit less range and are subject to greater attenuation from solid objects.

The following sections cover some of the specific RF characteristics used by 802.11 radios for improving communications in the 2.4 and 5 GHz frequency ranges.This section provides a summary of regulatory domains and their operating frequencies.

Regulatory Domains

Devices that operate in unlicensed bands do not require any formal licensing process, but when operating in these bands, the user is obligated to follow the government regulations for that region. The regulatory domains in different parts of the world monitor these bands according to different criteria, and the WLAN devices used in these domains must comply with the specifications of the relevant governing regulatory domain. Although the regulatory requirements do not affect the interoperability of IEEE 802.11b/g and 802.11a-compliant products, the regulatory agencies do set certain criteria in the standard. For example, the emission requirements for WLAN to minimize the amount of interference a radio can generate or receive from another radio in the same proximity. It is the responsibility of the vendor to get the product certified from the relevant regulatory body. Table 3-1 summarizes the current regulatory domains for Wi-Fi products. The main regulatory domains are FCC, ETSI, and the MKK.

Besides following the requirements of the regulatory agencies, many vendors also ensure compatibility with other vendors through the Wi-Fi certification program.

Table 3-1 Regulatory Domains

Regulatory Domain	Geographic Area
Americas or FCC (United States Federal Communication Commission)	North, South, and Central America, Australia and New Zealand, various parts of Asia and Oceania
Europe or ETSI (European Telecommunications Standards Institute)	Europe (both EU and non EU countries), Middle East, Africa, various parts of Asia and Oceania
Japan (MKK)	Japan
China	People's Republic of China (Mainland China)
Israel	Israel
Singapore	Singapore
Taiwan	Republic of China (Taiwan)

The regulations of Singapore and Taiwan for wireless LANs are particular to these countries only for operation in the 5 GHz band. Singapore and Taiwan are therefore only regulatory domains for 5 GHz operation; for operation in 2.4 GHz, they fall into the ETSI and FCC domains, respectively.

OPERATING FREQUENCIES

The 2.4 GHz band regulations have been relatively constant, given the length of time it has been operating. The FCC allows for 11 channels, ETSI allows for up to 13 channels, and Japan allows up to 14 channels, but requires a special license to operate in channel 14. For 802.11a, countries are moving to open the frequency range 5.250-5.350 GHz (UNII-2) and the frequency range 5.470 to 5.780 GHz for additional 802.11a channels. These various frequencies are covered in more detail in the specific 802.11 sections in this chapter.

OPERATING FREQUENCIES AND DATA RATES

Ratified in September 1999, the 802.11b standard operates in the 2.4 GHz spectrum and supports data rates of 1, 2, 5.5, and 11 Mbps. 802.11b enjoys broad user acceptance and vendor support. 802.11b technology has been deployed by thousands of enterprise organizations, which typically find its speed and performance acceptable for their current applications.

The 802.11g standard, which was ratified in June 2003, operates in the same spectrum as 802.11b and is backward compatible with the 802.11b standard. 802.11g supports the additional data rates of 6, 9, 12, 18, 24, 36, 48, and 54 Mbps.

Table 3-2 lists the various 802.11b/g channel frequencies and specifies whether a regulatory agency allows their use in their domain. Note that not all of these frequencies are available for use in all regulatory domains.

Table 3-2 Operating Frequency Range for 802.11b and 802.11g

Channel Identifier	Center Frequency	FCC (America)	ESTI (EMEA)	TELEC (Japan)	MOC (Israel Outdoor)[1]
1	2412	X	X	X	
2	2417	X	X	X	
3	2422	X	X	X	
4	2427	X	X	X	
5	2432	X	X	X	X
6	2437	X	X	X	X

7	2442	X	X	X	X
8	2447	X	X	X	X
9	2452	X	X	X	X
10	2457	X	X	X	X
11	2462	X	X	X	X
12	2467		X	X	X
13	2472		X	X	X
14^2	2484			X	

Operating Frequencies and Data Rates

Operating in the unlicensed portion of the 5 GHz radio band, 802.11a is immune to interference from devices that operate in the 2.4 GHz band, such as microwave ovens, many cordless phones, and Bluetooth (a short-range, low-speed, point-to-point, personal-area-network wireless standard). Because the 802.11a standard operates in a different frequency range, it is not compatible with existing 802.11b or 802.11g-compliant wireless devices, but it does mean that 2.4-GHz and 5-GHz equipment can operate in the same physical environment without interference.

Choosing between these two technologies does not involve a one-for-one trade-off. They are complementary technologies and will continue to coexist in future enterprise environments. Those responsible for implementing these technologies must be able to make an educated choice between deploying 2.4 GHz-only networks, 5 GHz-only networks, or a combination of both. Organizations with existing 802.11b networks cannot simply deploy a new 802.11a network for existing APs and expect to have their 802.11a 54 Mbps coverage in the same areas as their 11Mbps 802.11b coverage. The technical characteristics of both these bands simply do not allow for this kind of coverage interchangeability.

802.11a provides data rates of 6, 9, 12, 18, 24, 36, 48, with a maximum data rate of 54 Mbps, though generally at shorter ranges for a given power and antenna gain, but it has up to 23 nonoverlapping channels (depending on the geographic area) compared to the three nonoverlapping channels of 802.11b/g. This results in increased network capacity, improved scalability, and the ability to create microcellular deployments without interference from adjacent cells.

The 5 GHz band in which 802.11a operates is divided into several different sections. Each of the Unlicensed National Information Infrastructure (UNII) bands presented was originally intended for different uses, but all can currently be used by indoor 802.11a with appropriate power restrictions. Initially, the FCC defined only the UNII-1, UNII-2, and UNII-3 bands, each of which had four channels. The channels were spaced 20 MHz apart with an RF spectrum bandwidth of 20 MHz, thereby providing nonoverlapping channels.

There are differing limitations on these three UNII bands. Restrictions vary between them for transmit power, antenna gain, antenna styles, and usage. The UNII-1 band is designated for indoor operations, and initially had a restriction of permanently attached antennas. The UNII-2 band was designated for indoor or outdoor operations, and permitted external antennas. The UNII-3 band was intended for outdoor bridge products and permitted external antennas, but the UNII-3 band can now be used for indoor or outdoor 802.11a WLANs as well.

The channels in UNII-1 (5.150 to 5.250 GHz) are 36, 40, 44, and 48. The channels in UNII-2 (5.250-5.350 GHz) are 52, 56, 60, 64 and require Dynamic Frequency Selection (DFS) and Transmitter Power Control (TPC). The channels in the new frequency range (5.470-5.725 GHz) are 100, 104, 108, 112, 116, 120, 124, 128, 132, 136, and 140 also require DFS and TPC. The channels in UNII-3 are 149, 153, 157, 161, 165 (5.725-5.825) and do not require DFS and TPC. Not all channels in a given range can be used in all of the regulatory domains. Figure 3-1 shows the various channels in the UNII-1, 2, and 3 bands, along with the additional 11 new channels.

In February of 2004, the FCC released a revision to the regulations covering the 5 GHz 802.11a channel usage. This revision added 11 additional channels, bringing the available channels capacity to 23 channels (see Figure 53).

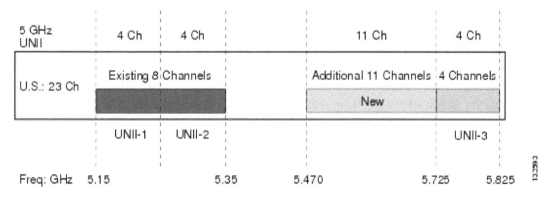

Figure 52 CHANNEL CAPACITIES

The new additional 11 channels are for indoor/outdoor use. To use the 11 new channels, however, radios must comply with two features that are part of the 802.11h specification: TPC and DFS. DFS is required to avoid radar that operates in this frequency range, but it can also be used for other purposes, such as dynamic frequency planning. 802.11h has been supported since Cisco Unified Wireless Network Software Release 3.1. DFS dynamically instructs a transmitter to switch to another channel whenever a particular condition (such as the presence of a radar signal) is met. Before transmitting, the DFS mechanism of a device monitors its available operating spectrum, listening for a radar signal. If a signal is detected, the channel associated with the radar signal is vacated or flagged as unavailable for use by the transmitter. The transmitting device continuously monitors the environment for the presence of radar, both prior to and during operation. Portions of the 5 GHz band are allocated to radar systems, which allow WLANs to avoid interference with incumbent radar users in instances where they are collocated.

TPC allows the AP to negotiate power levels with a WLAN client during that association process. The AP can inform that WLAN client of the range of allowable transmit power to be used with that AP, and may reject clients unable to meet those levels. The WLAN client is able to adjust its transmit power level within the range specified in the TPC negotiations. This ensures that interference from the WLAN is minimized and allows the WLAN client to optimize battery life.

802.11 ARCHITECTURE

The IEEE 802.11 protocol is a network access technology for providing connectivity between wireless stations and wired networking infrastructures. By deploying the IEEE 802.11 protocol and associated technologies, you enable the mobile user to travel to various places — meeting rooms, hallways, lobbies, cafeterias, classrooms, and so forth — and still have access to networked data. Also, beyond the corporate workplace, you enable access to the Internet and even corporate sites can be made available through public wireless "hot spot" networks. Airports, restaurants, rail stations, and common areas throughout cities can be configured to provide this service. This section provides an in-depth view of how IEEE 802.11 works, including the architecture, related protocols, and technologies.

The 802.11 logical architecture contains several main components: station (STA), wireless access point (AP), independent basic service set (IBSS), basic service set (BSS), distribution system (DS), and extended service set (ESS). Some of the components of the 802.11 logical architecture map directly to hardware devices, such as STAs and wireless APs. The wireless STA contains an adapter card, PC Card, or an embedded device to provide wireless connectivity. The wireless AP functions as a bridge between the wireless STAs and the existing network backbone for network access.

An IBSS is a wireless network, consisting of at least two STAs, used where no access to a DS is available. An IBSS is also sometimes referred to as an ad hoc wireless network. A BSS is a wireless network, consisting of a single wireless AP supporting one or multiple wireless clients. A BSS is also sometimes referred to as an infrastructure wireless network. All STAs in a BSS communicate through the AP. The AP provides connectivity to the wired LAN and provides bridging functionality when one STA initiates communication to another STA or a node on the DS. An ESS is a set of two or more wireless APs connected to the same-wired network that defines a single logical network segment bounded by a router (also known as a *subnet*).

The APs of multiple BSSs are interconnected by the DS. This allows for mobility, because STAs can move from one BSS to another BSS. APs can be interconnected with or without wires; however, most of the time they are connected with wires. The DS is the logical component used to interconnect BSSs. The DS provides distribution services to allow for the roaming of STAs between BSSs.

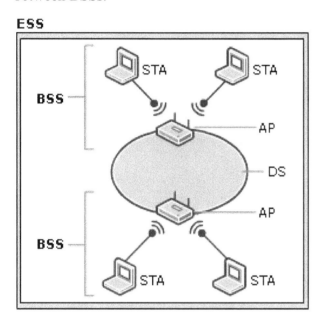
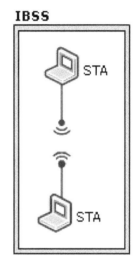

Figure 53 802.11 ARCHITECTURE

802.11 OPERATING MODES

IEEE 802.11 defines the following operating modes:

- Infrastructure mode

- Ad hoc mode

In both operating modes, a Service Set Identifier (SSID), also known as the *wireless network name*, identifies the wireless network. The *SSID* is a name configured on the wireless AP (for infrastructure mode) or an initial wireless client (for ad hoc mode) that identifies the wireless network. The SSID is periodically advertised by the wireless AP or the initial wireless client using a special 802.11 MAC management frame known as a *beacon frame*.

802.11 INFRASTRUCTURE MODE

In *infrastructure mode*, there is at least one wireless AP and one wireless client. The wireless client uses the wireless AP to access the resources of a traditional wired network. The wired network can be an organization intranet or the Internet, depending on the placement of the wireless AP. An extended service set (ESS) is shown in the following figure.

802.11 INFRASTRUCTURE MODE

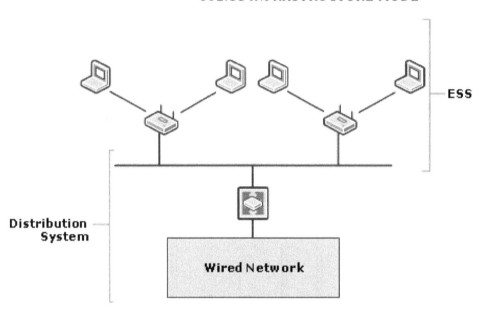

802.11 AD HOC MODE

In *ad hoc mode*, wireless clients communicate directly with each other without the use of a wireless AP, as shown in the following figure.

802.11 WIRELESS CLIENTS IN AD HOC MODE

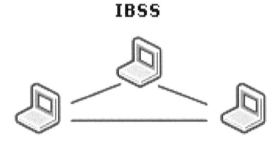

Ad hoc mode is also called *peer-to-peer mode*. Wireless clients in ad hoc mode form an independent basic service set (IBSS). One of the wireless clients, the first wireless client in the IBSS, takes over some of the responsibilities of the wireless AP. These responsibilities include the periodic beaconing process and the authentication of new members. This wireless client does not act as a bridge to relay information between wireless clients. Ad hoc mode is used to connect wireless clients together when there is no wireless AP present. The wireless clients must be explicitly configured to use ad hoc mode. There can be a maximum of nine members in an ad hoc 802.11 wireless network.

Wireless LAN Components

The basic components in a wireless network are:

- The Wired Network

- Access Point or Wireless Router

- Client Device

- Client Bridge

- Repeater

Each component has a specific function, and while some devices can operate in more than one function, they often have specific attributes that best suit them for a given function. Here are the details on each device/function:

The Wired Network

While the wired network isn't a simple "device", it is critical to the wireless network; because without it there is really no function to the wireless portion. The wired network can provide several functions:

- Internet connectivity – Your ISP likely provides you with an Ethernet connection to their router or modem, so your wireless network will need to connect to that. Ethernet is a common network standard used in homes and businesses, it generally uses CAT5, CAT5e, or CAT6 cables for connectivity in the LAN (Local Area

  Network).

- Connection to a server – If you use a media server or file server at home you probably need to connect to it via Ethernet.

- Connection to other network devices – You might have other computers at home or other network devices to connect to.

Access Point or Wireless Router

Both of these devices perform the same *wireless* functions. The point of the AP (Access Point) or Router is to authorize and control the access that Client Devices have to the wireless network, and to connect those client devices to the wired network.mIt controls the speed, security requirements, allowed devices, and many other functions of the wireless network. It's the "center" of your WiFi network.

Client Device

Client devices are really anything that *wirelessly* connects to the AP or wireless router. These can be anything from an Apple or Dell laptop, to your iPhone, even your refrigerator. The other devices below (Client Bridge and repeater) are also client devices, just unique ones.

The client devices have the same wireless systems built into them as an AP or wireless router, they just use them in a different way. There can even be client-device to client-device networks that operate without an AP or router; these are called "ad-hoc" networks. Since they're unique (and rare) we'll talk about ad-hoc networks in some other articles.

Client Bridge

A client bridge is a type of client device that bridges the wireless network with the wired network. It's basically like a reverse AP. The function of the AP is to bridge the wired network onto a wireless network, and the client bridge takes that and re-reverses into another wired segment. This can be useful if you have a device such as a printer or Xbox that doesn't support wireless, but you want to connect it to the network without using CAT5 Ethernet cable. You simply get a client bridge device, connect it to the wireless network, then connect the wired device to the bridge.

Repeater

Repeaters are often a barely-necessary evil. I think of them as a "hack", something that sort-of does the job, but doesn't do it well. Repeaters act sort-of like a client bridge, but instead of bridging the wireless network to a wired network segment, they bridge it to another area of the wireless network. This extends the range of the wireless network to devices that are near the repeater, but it does it at the cost of bandwidth and speed. The repeater uses up twice the bandwidth of a normal client device because it has to capture information then re-send it back out on the same channel that it just received it on.

Range

The range of a residential Wi-Fi network depends on the wireless access point (WAP) or wireless router, its' antenna(s) sensitivity, as well as the exact 802.11 standard being used. Factors that determine a particular WAP or wireless router's range are:

- The specific 802.11 protocol being used (802.11a/b/g/n)

- The overall strength of the device transmitter.

- The nature of obstructions and interference in the surrounding area
  A general rule of thumb in home networking says that 802.11b/g WAPs and routers support a range of up to 150 feet (46 m) indoors and 300 feet (92 m) outdoors. Another rule of thumb holds that the effective range of 802.11a is approximately one-third that of 802.11b/g. 802.11n devices typically have twice the range of 802.11b/g devices.

  All of these rough estimates fall on the high end of the range seen in practice. Obstructions in home such as brick walls and metal frames or siding can greatly reduce the range of a Wi-Fi LAN by 25% or more. Because 802.11a employs a higher signaling frequency than 802.11b/g/n, 802.11a is most susceptible to obstructions. Interference from microwave ovens and other equipment also affects range. 802.11b and 802.11g are both susceptible to these. Of course, it's possible to extend a Wi-Fi LAN to much longer distances by chaining together multiple wireless access points or routers, or simply changing to higher-gain antennas.
  Another benefit of 802.11n technology is much better coverage. Wireless-N devices use "reflections" of the signal (from walls, etc.) to strengthen it and eliminate cold or weak spots in the signal.

Wireless-N Range Extenders

Expand the range of your wireless network! Wireless Range Extenders offer an easy way to

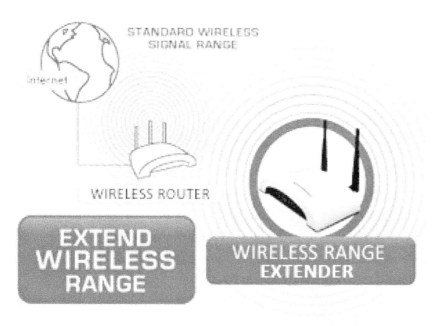

increase the effective coverage of your wireless network.

Unlike adding a traditional access point to your network to expand wireless coverage, wireless range extenders do not need to be connected to the network by a data cable. Just put the wireless range extender within range of your main access point or wireless router, and it "bounces" the signals out to remote wireless devices.

The "relay station" or "wireless repeater" approach saves wiring costs and helps to build wireless infrastructure by driving signals into even those distant, reflective corners and hard-to-reach areas where wireless coverage is spotty or cabling is impractical. The wireless range extender is perfect to help cover large areas in multi-storey homes, warehouse environments, public spaces, wireless "Hot Spots" and outdoor venues - anywhere where you need extra coverage for your wireless network. So, expand your wireless network's effective coverage the easy way, with wireless range extenders.

WIRELESS-N - (802.11B/G/N, 2.4GHZ)

Are you experiencing wireless drop-outs? Poor wireless range? If Wireless G networking doesn't meet your expectations then Wireless N is your answer. Wireless N provides a breakthrough solution for larger homes or offices that have a wide area to cover and want to run multimedia and high-bandwidth applications. With its significant range and speed Wireless N is ideal for streaming video, music and photos, online gaming, Web-surfing and email.

DUAL-BAND WIRELESS-N - (802.11A/B/G/N, 2.4GHZ & 5GHZ)

Ideal for businesses. Known as Dual Band Wireless N, Wireless AN offers all the same benefits as Wireless N but also simultanously offer wireless connectivity in either the widely used 2.4GHz freq. or the interference-free 5GHz freq resulting in the potential bandwidth of up to 600Mbps.

BENEFITS

The emergence and continual growth of wireless LANs are being driven by the need to lower the costs associated with network infrastructures and to support mobile networking applications that offer gains in process efficiency, accuracy, and lower business costs. The following sections explain the mobility and cost savings benefits of wireless LANs.

MOBILITY

Mobility enables users to physically move while using an appliance, such as a handheld PC or data collector. Many jobs require workers to be mobile—these include inventory clerks, healthcare workers, policemen, and emergency care specialists. Of course, wireless networks require a physical tether between the user's workstation and the network's resources, which makes access to these resources impossible while roaming about the building or elsewhere. This freedom of movement results in significant return on investments due to gains in efficiency.

Mobile applications requiring wireless networking include those that depend on real-time access to data usually stored in centralized databases. If your application requires mobile users to be immediately aware of changes made to data, or if information put into the system must immediately be available to others, then you have a definite need for wireless networking. For accurate and efficient price markdowns, for example, many retail stores use wireless networks to interconnect handheld bar-code scanners and printers to databases that have current price information. This enables the printing of the correct price on the items, satisfying both the customer and the business owner.

Another example of the use of wireless networking is in auto racing. Formula-1 and Indy racecars have sophisticated data-acquisition systems that monitor the various on-board systems in the car. When the cars come around the track and pass the respective teams in the pit, this information is downloaded to a central computer, thereby enabling real-time analysis of the performance of the race car.

Not all mobile applications require wireless networking, though. Sometimes the business case doesn't support the need for mobile real-time access to information. If the application's data can be stored on the user's device, and if changes to the data are not significant, then the additional cost of wireless network hardware may not provide enough benefits to justify the additional expense. Keep in mind, though, that other needs for wireless networks may still exist.

Installation in Difficult-to-Wire Areas

The implementation of wireless networks offers many tangible cost savings when performing installations in difficult-to-wire areas. If rivers, freeways, or other obstacles separate buildings that you want to connect, a wireless solution may be much more economical than installing physical cable or leasing communications circuits, such as T1 service or 56Kbps lines. Some organizations spend thousands or even millions of dollars to install physical links with nearby facilities. If you are facing this type of installation, consider wireless networking as an alternative. The deployment of wireless networking in these situations costs thousands of dollars but will result in a definite cost savings in the long run.

The asbestos found in older facilities is another problem that many organizations encounter. The inhalation of asbestos particles is extremely hazardous to your health; therefore, you must take great care when installing network cabling within these areas. When taking necessary precautions, the resulting cost of cable installations in these facilities can be prohibitive.

Some organizations, for example, remove the asbestos, making it safe to install cabling. This process is very expensive because you must protect the building's occupants from breathing the asbestos particles agitated during removal. The cost of removing asbestos covering just a few flights of stairs can be tens of thousands of dollars. Obviously, the advantage of wireless networking in asbestos-contaminated buildings is that you can avoid the asbestos removal process, resulting in tremendous costs savings.

In some cases, it might be impossible to install cabling. Some municipalities, for example, may restrict you from permanently modifying older facilities with historical value. This could limit the drilling of holes in walls during the installation of network cabling and outlets. In this situation, a wireless network might be the only solution. Right-of-way restrictions within cities and counties may also block the digging of trenches in the ground to lay optical fiber for the interconnection of networked sites. Again in this situation, a wireless network might be the best alternative.

Increased Reliability

A problem inherent to wired networks is the downtime due to cable faults. In fact, cable faults are often the primary cause of system downtime. Moisture erodes metallic conductors via water intrusion during storms and accidental spillage or leakage of liquids. With wired networks, users may accidentally break their network connector when trying to disconnect their PC from the network to move it to a different location. Imperfect cable splices can cause signal reflections that result in unexplainable errors. The accidental cutting of cables can bring a network down immediately. Wires and connectors can easily break through misuse and normal use. These problems interfere with the users' ability to utilize network resources, causing havoc for network managers. An advantage of wireless networking, therefore, results from the use of less cable. This reduces the downtime of the network and the costs associated with replacing cables.

Reduced Installation Time

The installation of cabling is often a time-consuming activity. For LANs, installers must pull twisted-pair wires above the ceiling and drop cables through walls to network outlets that they must affix to the wall. These tasks can take days or weeks, depending on the size of the installation. The installation of optical fiber between buildings within the same geographical area consists of digging trenches to lay the fiber or pulling the fiber through an existing conduit. You might need weeks or possibly months to receive right-of-way approvals and dig through ground and asphalt.

The deployment of wireless networks greatly reduces the need for cable installation, making the network available for use much sooner. Thus, many countries lacking a network infrastructure have turned to wireless networking as a method of providing connectivity among computers without the expense and time associated with installing physical media. This is also necessary within the United States to set up temporary offices and "rewire" renovated facilities.

Long-Term Cost Savings

Companies reorganize, resulting in the movement of people, new floor plans, office partitions, and other renovations. These changes often require recabling the network, incurring both labor and material costs. In some cases, the recabling costs of organizational changes are substantial, especially with large enterprise networks. A reorganization rate of 15 percent each year can result in yearly reconfiguration expenses as high as $250,000 for networks that have 6,000 interconnected devices. The advantage of wireless networking is again based on the lack of cable: You can move the network connection by simply relocating an employee's PC.

Security of 802.11 Wireless LANs

As Wireless LANs (WLANs) have been increasingly entrusted to carry mission critical enterprise data and voice communication, the impact of Wireless LAN (WLAN) Denial of Service (DoS) attacks has increased many folds. The recently ratified 802.11w standard that provides Management Frame Protection (MFP) does provide some help in fighting WLAN DoS attacks. But, if you think that 802.11w can put an end to all of your WLAN DoS problems, I beg to differ. Please read on to find out why.

Ever since inception, wireless LANs have been known to be susceptible to Denial of Service (DoS) attacks. Example DoS attacks include radio-level DoS attacks such as RF jamming and MAC-level DoS attacks such as de-authentication flood, disassociation flood, association flood, and virtual (802.11-NAV-field based) jamming. Tools to launch these DoS attacks are freely available on the Internet. There are 2 main reasons as to why WLANs have been vulnerable to DoS attacks. First, the wireless medium is not confined to physical boundaries such as wires and buildings. Hence, attacks can be potentially launched from outside an enterprise (e.g., from parking lots). Second, authentication/encryption of management and control plane frames was never a part of the original 802.11 specification. This makes it is easy for an attacker to transmit spoofed attack packets that appear legitimate.

The IEEE 802.11w standard aims to mitigate certain types of WLAN DoS attacks. 802.11w extends strong cryptographic protection to specific management frames (in a manner that is similar to what 802.11i/RSN defines for data frames). A select set of management frames transmitted after 802.11i/RSN key derivation is protected. MFP is provided for a category of management frames called "Robust Management Frames". De-authentication frames, Disassociation frames, and certain categories of Action Management frames are defined as Robust Management Frames. Action Management Frames are special types of management frames that carry WLAN operation related information – e.g., QoS Management, Spectrum Management or BlockAck session management. Note that management frames transmitted before the derivation of 802.11i/RSN keys are unprotected.

802.11w provides data integrity and replay protection for broadcast/multicast Robust management frames. Additionally, data confidentiality is provided for unicast management frames. A new protocol "Broadcast Integrity Protocol" (BIP) is defined for achieving integrity of broadcast/multicast management frames. BIP makes use of a Message Integrity Code (MIC) that is calculated over the frame body to detect tampering of management frames. A receiver silently drops all tampered frames. The basic premise here is that the MIC computation uses a shared-secret that is available only to authorized WLAN users (and not to an attacker). I will explain this further using a de-authentication attack. An attacker launching a de-authentication attack cannot compute the correct MIC for the spoofed deauth packets. Hence, his or her de-auth packets will be silently rejected by the 802.11w AP/clients in a WLAN. Alternately, he cannot replay any legitimate deauth packets due to replay protection. Thus, 802.11w can protect a WLAN against de-authentication attack.

802.11w definitely helps mitigate certain classes of DoS attacks on WLANs – e.g., de-authentication attack, dis-association attack. However, the following are the limitations of 802.11w in fighting WLAN DoS attacks:

802.11w provides protection for certain specific 802.11 management frames only, specifically, deauthentication frames, disassociation frames, and action management frames. Hence, DoS attacks based on management frames not protected by 802.11w are still possible (e.g., association based attacks, beacon based attacks).

- DoS attacks based on 802.11 data and control frames are outside the scope of 802.11w and continue to be a pain.

- RF jamming based DoS attacks cannot be mitigated via 802.11w.

- Certain logistical issues exist with the 802.11w solution

- 802.11w requires a code change/software upgrade on not just an AP, but also on clients

- 802.11w cannot protect the large number of legacy devices that exist today.

Hence, 802.11w is a good first line of defense in mitigating WLAN DoS attacks and you should adopt it. However, for more robust protection, it should be complemented by a DoS detection and mitigation strategy based on a Wireless Intrusion Prevention System (WIPS). Further, WIPS can help you protect against other wireless security threats that are completely outside of the scope of 802.11w – AP based threats (e.g., Rogue APs), client based threats (e.g., Evil Twins) and threats on WLAN infrastructure (e.g., Skyjacking).

Security Features of 802.11 Wireless LANs per the Standard

Apart from all of the actions in minimizing attacks to WLAN mentioned in the previous section, we will also look at some new standards that intend to improve the security of WLAN. There are two important standards that will be discussed in this paper: 802.1x and 802.11i.

802.1X

One of the standards is 802.1x which was originally designed for wired Ethernet networks. This standard is also part of the 802.11i standard that will be discussed later. The following discussion of 802.1x is divided into three parts, starting with the concept of Point-to-Point Protocol (PPP), followed by Extensible Authentication Protocol (EAP), and continues with the understanding of 802.1x itself.

- **PPP:** The Point-to-Point Protocol (PPP) originally emerged as an encapsulation protocol for transporting IP traffic over point-to-point links. PPP also established a standard for the assignment and management of IP addresses, asynchronous (start/stop) and bit-oriented synchronous encapsulation, network protocol multiplexing, link configuration, link quality testing, error detection, and option negotiation for such capabilities as network-layer address negotiation and data-compression negotiation.

By any measure, PPP is a good protocol. However, as PPP usage grew, people quickly found its limitation in terms of security. Most corporate networks want to do more than simple usernames and passwords for secure access [13]. This leads to the designation of a new authentication protocol, called Extensible Authentication Protocol (EAP).

- **EAP:** The Extensible Authentication Protocol (EAP) is a general authentication protocol defined in IETF (Internet Engineering Task Force) standards. It was originally developed for use with PPP. It is an authentication protocol that provides a generalized framework for several authentication mechanisms. These include Kerberos, public key, smart cards and one-time passwords. With a standardized EAP, interoperability and compatibility across authentication methods become simpler. For example, when user dials a remote access server (RAS) and use EAP as part of the PPP connection, the RAS does not need to know any of the details about the authentication system. Only the user and the authentication server have to be coordinated. By supporting EAP authentication, RAS server does not actively participate in the authentication dialog. Instead, RAS just re-packages EAP packets to hand off to a RADIUS server to make the actual authentication decision.

IEEE 802.1x relates to EAP in a way that it is a standard for carrying EAP over a wired LAN or WLAN. There are four important entities that explain this standard

i. Authenticator

Authenticator is the entity that requires the entity on the other end of the link to be authenticated. An example is wireless access points.

ii. Supplicant

Supplicant is the entity being authenticated by the Authenticator and desiring access to the services of the Authenticator.

iii. Port Access Entity (PAE)

It is the protocol entity associated with a port. It may support the functionality of Authenticator, Supplicant or both.

iv. Authentication Server

Authentication server is an entity that provides authentication service to the Authenticator. It may be co-located with Authenticator, but it is most likely an external server. It is typically a RADIUS (Remote Access Dial In User Service) server

The supplicant and authentication server are the major parts of 802.1x. Figure below shows the general topology of the above mentioned entities:

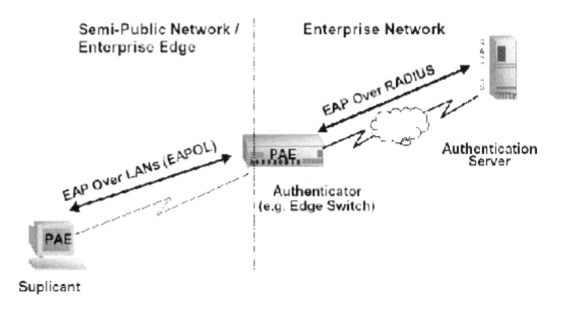

Figure 54 GENERAL TOPOLOGY

EAP messages are encapsulated in Ethernet LAN packets (EAPOL) to allow communications between the supplicant and the authenticator. The following are the most common modes of operation in EAPOL:

1. The authenticator sends an "EAP-Request/Identity" packet to the supplicant as soon as it detects that the link is active.

2. Then, the supplicant sends an "EAP-Response/Identity" packet to the authenticator, which is then passed to the authentication (RADIUS) server.

3. Next, the authentication server sends back a challenge to the authenticator, with a token password system. The authenticator unpacks this from IP, repackages it into EAPOL, and sends it to the supplicant. Different authentication methods will vary this message and the total number of messages. EAP supports client-only authentication and strong mutual authentication. Only strong mutual authentication is considered appropriate for the wireless case.

4. The supplicant responds to the challenge via the authenticator and passes the response onto the authentication server. If the supplicant provides proper identity, the authentication server responds with a success message, which is then passed to the

supplicant. The authenticator now allows access to the LAN, which possibly was restricted based on attributes that came back from the authentication server.

802.11I

In addition to 802.1x standard created by IEEE, one up-and-coming 802.11x specification, which is 802.11i, provides replacement technology for WEP security. 802.11i is still in the development and approval processes. In this paper, the key technical elements that have been defined by the specification will be discussed. While these elements might change, the information provided will provide insight into some of the changes that 802.11i promises to deliver to enhance the security features provided in a WLAN system.

The 802.11i specification consists of three main pieces organized into two layers. On the upper layer is the 802.1x, which has been discussed in the previous section. As used in 802.11i, 802.1x provides a framework for robust user authentication and encryption key distribution. On the lower layer are improved encryption algorithms. The encryption algorithms are in the form of the TKIP (Temporal Key Integrity Protocol) and the CCMP (counter mode with CBC-MAC protocol). It is important to understand how all of these three pieces work to form the security mechanisms of 802.11i standard. Since the concept of 802.1x has been discussed in the previous section, the following section of this paper will only look at TKIP and CCMP. Both of these encryption protocols provide enhanced data integrity over WEP, with TKIP being targeted at legacy equipment, while CCMP is being targeted at future WLAN equipments. However, a true 802.11i system uses either the TKIP or CCMP protocol for all equipments.

TKIP

The temporal key integrity protocol (TKIP) which initially referred to as WEP2, was designed to address all the known attacks and deficiencies in the WEP algorithm. According to 802.11 Planet [6], the TKIP security process begins with a 128-bit temporal-key, which is shared among clients and access points. TKIP combines the temporal key with the client machine's MAC address and then adds a relatively large 16-octet initialization vector to produce the key that will encrypt the data. Similar to WEP, TKIP also uses RC4 to perform the encryption. However, TKIP changes temporal keys every 10,000 packets. This difference provides a dynamic distribution method that significantly enhances the security of the network. TKIP is seen as a method that can quickly overcome the weaknesses in WEP security, especially the reuse of encryption keys. The following are four new algorithms and their function that TKIP adds to WEP:

1. A cryptographic message integrity code, or MIC, called Michael, to defeat forgeries.

2. A new IV sequencing discipline, to remove replay attacks from the attacker's arsenal.

3. A per-packet key mixing function, to de-correlate the public IVs from weak keys.

4. A re-keying mechanism, to provide fresh encryption and integrity keys, undoing the threat of attacks stemming from key reuse.

CCMP

As explained previously, TKIP was designed to address deficiencies in WEP; however, TKIP is not viewed as a long-term solution for WLAN security. In addition to TKIP encryption, the 802.11i draft defines a new encryption method based on the advanced encryption standard (AES). The AES algorithm is a symmetric block cipher that can encrypt and decrypt information. It is capable of using cryptographic keys of 128, 192, and 256 bits to encrypt and decrypt data in blocks of 128 bits. More robust than TKIP, the AES algorithm would replace WEP and RC4. AES based encryption can be used in many different modes or algorithms. The mode that has been chosen for 802.11 is the counter mode with CBCMAC protocol (CCMP). The counter mode delivers data privacy while the CBC-MAC delivers data integrity and authentication. Unlike TKIP, CCMP is mandatory for anyone implementing 802

PROBLEMS WITH THE IEEE 802.11 STANDARD SECURITY

The wireless networking standard, the IEEE 802.11b, has recently become more and more popular due to its convenience and falling prices of the hardware. Users have the ability to transfer large files, access the Web and other high bandwidth activities without having the need to attach network cables to ports that are connected to switches or hubs. They have the freedom to roam around anywhere within the range of the wireless network. This paper will discuss the security features implemented in the 802.11b standard. Following are major problems:

Use of 802.11 without encryption. Unencrypted 802.11 sessions are subject to snooping and hijacking, regardless of how the session is authenticated. As a result, customers desiring confidentiality and session hijacking protection should operate 802.11 networks with encryption enabled.

Weaknesses in WEP. The weaknesses of the WEP encryption scheme are well documented, and cannot be remedied merely by the application of enhanced authentication and key management schemes such as IEEE 802.1X. For example, WEP lacks support for per-packet integrity protection and offers only weak encryption. This enables a wide variety of attacks, including insertion of packets into the data stream. As a result, customers with deployed 802.11 networks using WEP should consider transitioning to alternative ciphers under development by IEEE 802.11 Task Group I, such as TKIP and WRAP.

Lack of authentication for 802.11 management messages. 802.11 management messages include the beacon, probe request/response, association request/response, reassociation request/response, disassociation, and deauthentication. Without authenticating these management messages, denial of service attacks are possible. IEEE 802.1X pre-authentication takes care of most of these vulnerabilities, since it enables authentication and key derivation prior to exchange of management frames. Customers should utilize these enhancements to 802.11 security when available.

1. **Mandatory mutual authentication.** For use with IEEE 802.11, the IEEE 802.11 Tg I specification requires that supplicants and authenticators not send data traffic until mutual authentication is complete. Some pre-standard implementations do not support this. 802.11 Task Group I also mandates use of EAP methods providing mutual authentication, such as EAP SRP or EAP TLS. Most existing implementations do support this today, including Windows XP, which ships with support for EAP TLS.

2. **Use of ciphers providing per-packet authentication as well as encryption.** The IEEE 802.11 Tg I specification defines two new ciphersuites, TKIP and WRAP, both of which include support for per-packet integrity protection and confidentiality. TKIP should be available in the near future, can typically be deployed as an upgrade to existing access points, and includes support for a (weak) message integrity check. However, it is largely based on WEP, and as a result, is only a short term solution. Customers should be planning on migrating to AES-based ciphers such as WRAP in the long term, with keys provided by IEEE 802.1X.

3. **Dictionary attacks on EAP methods.** 802.11 frames, including 802.1X messages, are easily sniffed. For this reason, IEEE 802.11 Task Group I recommends EAP methods resistant to dictionary attack. It's worth heeding this advice, since dictionary attacks enable an attacker to recover the user password, which often can provide access to more than just the 802.11 network. Therefore these attacks are more serious than the previously documented WEP attacks and customers using 802.1X should strongly consider adopting dictionary attack-resistant authentication methods such as EAP TLS, SRP, TTLS and PEAP.

4. **Attacks on the default key.** Some early IEEE 802.1X implementations cannot use the per-session keys derived in IEEE 802.1X to encrypt the data. Instead, these implementations only encrypt data using the multicast/broadcast keys known in the 802.11 lingo as "default keys". Such implementations are vulnerable to many of the WEP attacks, particularly if the default keys are not automatically changed in a frequent and unpredictable way. Since Access Points typically do not have much randomness with which to change default keys securely, administrators may wish to automate this themselves using scripts or SNMPv3. Of course, for this to be secure, the Access Points need to support updating of the default key as well as secure management mechanisms such as SNMPv3 or SSH.

5. **Denial of service attacks based on sending of EAPOL-Logoff frames.** Since the EAPOL logoff frame is not authenticated an attacker can potentially spoof this frame, logging the user off the Access Point. Access Point vendors whose implementations are susceptible to these attacks should fix their implementations. Since the purpose of the

EAPOL-Logoff frame is to signal disconnection, and this is already taken care of by the 802.11 Disassociation messages (which can be authenticated) it is not clear that EAPOL-Logoff frame is really necessary with 802.11. As a result, Access Points should consider filtering these messages and the IEEE 802.11 Tg I specification should clarifying this issue going forward.

6. **Denial of service attacks based on sending of EAPOL-Start frames.** An attacker can attempt to bring down an Access Point by flooding it with EAPOL-Start frames. Access Point vendors whose implementations are susceptible to these attacks should fix their implementations. The key to avoiding problems is not to allocate significant resources on receipt of an EAPOL-Start frame.

7. **Denial of service attacks based on cycling through the EAP Identifier space.** An attacker could attempt to bring down an Access Point by consuming the EAP Identifier space (0-255). Access Point vendors whose implementations are susceptible to these attacks should fix their implementations. Since the EAP Identifier is only required to be unique within a single Port or 802.11 Association, there is no need for an Access Point to lock out further connections once the Identifier space has been exhausted. This issue should be clarified in the revision to the IEEE 802.1X specification.

8. **Denial of service attacks based on sending of premature EAP Success packets.** The IEEE 802.1X specification enables a client to avoid bringing up its interface where the required mutual authentication has not been completed. This enables a well implemented Supplicant to avoid being fooled by a rogue Authenticator sending premature EAP Success packets. Supplicant implementations that are vulnerable to this attack should fix their implementations. This issue should be clarified within the revisions to the EAP and IEEE 802.1X specifications.

Security Requirements and Threats

Wireless local area networks (WLANs), like any other networking technology, needs to be protected from the many security threats out there. Though recent developments have been designed to help ensure privacy for authenticated WLAN users, WLAN clients and enterprise infrastructure, your WLAN can still be vulnerable to a variety of threats that are unique to WLANs. Hackers may try to attack the network, or an employee may create a security breach that leaves the corporate WLAN or a client device vulnerable to attack.

These threats cannot necessarily be mitigated by the traditional firewall technologies or virtual private networks (VPNs), nor can they be totally eliminated through encryption and other authentication methods used in conventional enterprise network security systems. An intrusion detection and prevention system (IDS/IPS) specifically designed for WLANs addresses the risks associated with this networking technology.

A new class of security threats to enterprise networks

It is universally believed that network security is safer on the physical network as opposed to wireless. A WLAN breaks the barrier provided by the building perimeter as the physical security envelope for a wired network because radio signals used by the WLAN cannot be confined within the physical perimeter of a building, and usually cut through walls and windows. This creates a backdoor for unauthorized users to attempt to connect to the enterprise network. Some specific security threats for WLANs are:

- **Rogue APs:** WLAN Access Points (APs) are inexpensive, easy to install, and small enough to be carried by a person. Unauthorized WLAN APs can be connected to an enterprise network unwittingly or with malicious intent—without the knowledge of IT— by simply carrying the device inside the enterprise and connecting it to an Ethernet port on the network. Since rogue APs are typically deployed by employees looking for quick wireless access, they are usually installed without any WLAN security controls (such as Access Control Lists, WPA, WPA2, AES, TKIP, 802. 1X, 802.11 i, etc.). These can be connected to virtually any Ethernet port on the network, bypassing existing WLAN security control points. The radio coverage of rogue APs cannot be confined within the building perimeter of the enterprise (unless you're using the paint), meaning that unauthorized users can connect to the enterprise network through these rogue APs. The invisibility of wireless medium makes this kind of access difficult to prevent.

- **Soft APs:** With client cards and embedded WLAN radios in some PDAs and laptops, a threat called *"soft AP"* is on the rise. A soft AP functions as an AP under software control and can be launched inadvertently or through a virus program, allowing unauthorized users to connect to the enterprise network through soft APs.

- **MAC spoofing:** APs in a WLAN transmit beacons (or probe responses) to advertise their presence in the air. The beacons of an AP contain information about its media access control (MAC) address, which is its identity, and service set identifier (SSID), which is the identity of the network it supports. Wireless clients listen to beacons from different APs in the vicinity. Clients typically connect to an AP that advertises the desired SSID and transmits a strong beacon signal. A number of WLAN AP models available in the market allow their MAC addresses and SSIDs to be user defined. APs as well as many software tools enable setting of MAC addresses and SSIDs of AP devices to virtually any user-defined values. In MAC spoofing, the attacker programs the AP to advertise exactly the same identity information as that of the victim AP. A MAC Spoofing AP can connect to the wired enterprise network as a rogue AP and evade detection by site survey tools. In addition, a MAC spoofing AP can lure authorized wireless clients in the enterprise WLAN into establishing a connection and providing confidential information.

- **Honeypot APs:** Multiple WLANs can co-exist in the same space, enabling users to connect to any available network, whether their own network or another network in the vicinity with overlapping radio coverage. This access to co-existing WLANs can be exploited by hackers who set up an unauthorized wireless network by powering on an AP in the vicinity (e.g. street or parking lot) of your enterprise wireless network. These APs, called *"Honeypot"* APs or *"Evil Twins,"* entice authorized enterprise clients into connecting to them by transmitting a stronger beacon signal and MAC spoofing. An authorized user unwittingly connecting to a Honeypot AP creates security vulnerability by inadvertently providing sensitive information such as its identity, username and password. Authorized wireless clients in the enterprise WLAN can also accidentally connect to non-malicious neighboring APs referred to as *"client mis-associations,"* creating security vulnerability as the wireless clients may inadvertently provide confidential information to such APs and create a *bridg*e between your secure enterprise network and the neighboring APs.

- **Denial of service:** WLANs are being increasingly entrusted with carrying mission-critical applications such as database access, VoIP, e-mail, and Internet access and project data files. These applications can be disrupted by a denial of service (DoS) attack, causing network downtime, user frustration, and loss of productivity. 802.11 WLAN transmissions being a shared medium, they are easily susceptible to DoS attacks. Additionally, *"soft spots"* in the 802.11 MAC protocol can easily be exploited to launch DoS attacks.

- **Ad-hoc networks:** The 802.11 WLAN standard has provisions for establishing peer-to-peer wireless connections between wireless clients, which can then form an ad-hoc network among themselves. However, the ad-hoc networks can create security vulnerabilities. For example, an intruder on the street can form a peer-to-peer ad-hoc wireless connection with an authorized laptop on the enterprise network and can then launch security attacks on the laptop using this wireless connection. For example, if the laptop has a setting to share certain resources (files, directories, etc.) with other authorized laptops in the enterprise, the intruder can get access to these resources.

Loss of Confidentiality

Networks carry all sorts of confidential data, so security is a highly important part of any wireless network structure. Security ensures that the same level of data integrity and confidentiality as a wired network are maintained. Without properly implemented security measures, any wireless network adapter coming within range of another network adapter or access point can join the network. The amount of non secure wireless access points is alarming – a recent study showed how over 90% of Access Points have little or no security enabled. Somebody could conduct a little research of find out that 3 out of 5 of the public access points checked had either no security at all or WEP - which allowed to crack the key within 15 minutes using freely available tools on the Internet.

Loss of Integrity

Loss of integrity is a serious security thread. This is another goal of a wireless network and it makes sure that the data coming and going out of the network is genuine and is not tampered with. This service makes sure that no Page unauthorized user has played a role of man in the middle and has been able to modify the information. The bottom line is that this service just asks the question that, "Whether the data flowing through the network is trust worthy or has it been tampered with?

One of the main weaknesses of Wireless LANs, which appears to be a running theme in the IT world, is incorrect configuration. Many providers supply the products out of the box with an insecure configuration. Although WEP is not secure it does provide a level of security above no encryption and therefore should be used, but still 50 percent of implemented Wireless LANs still fail to configure it. WEP has been implemented incorrectly this results in a number of weaknesses that compromise security of Wireless LAN's. WEP is susceptible to statistical attacks. These become increasingly practical, as more cipher texts that use the same key stream are known. Once one of the plaintexts becomes known, it is trivial to recover all of the others. Overall, WEP fails in a number of ways allowing attackers to decrypt, intercept, inject and encrypt traffic in a Wireless LAN.

Loss of Network Availability

Loss of Network Availability is a problem of denial of network involves some form of DoS and (DDoS) attack, such as jamming. Jamming occurs when a malicious user deliberately emanates a signal from a wireless device in order to overwhelm legitimate wireless signals. Denial of Service (DoS) and Distributed Denial of Service (DDoS) attacks are assaults on a network that flood it with so many additional requests that regular traffic is either slowed or completely interrupted. Unlike single bullet intrusion attacks which cause information damage or leakage, DoS attacks disrupt the availability of network resources and can interrupt network service for a long period of time.

Typical victims for DoS attacks are online businesses, carriers and service providers. DoS attacks target revenue-generating organizations by overtaxing link capacity. This costs them both direct and indirect damages. Direct damages include revenue loss or increased network costs. Indirect damages are related to business reputation and increased operational expenses.

The common form of DoS attacks is DDoS attacks, where hackers take advantage of bot-infected, compromised computers to launch large-scale attacks, as shown in the first graphic.

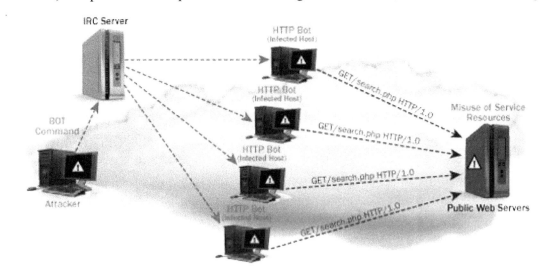

In DDoS attacks, the attacking computer hosts are often personal computers with broadband connections to the Internet that have been compromised by viruses or Trojan programs called Bots. (The compromised computers are usually referred to as "zombies"). Perpetrators of an attack remotely control the zombies and direct the attack, often through a BotNet command and control (C&C) channel such as an Internet Relay Chat (IRC) room. By combining the many existing variants of the same tool/attack and with enough slave hosts, the victims of DDoS attacks are large websites, root servers, large enterprises and ISPs who require massive bandwidth for their services to be disrupted. DDoS tools are extremely easy to develop, with propagation and seeding achieved through a range of resources including IRC, P2P, email worms, malicious websites and social engineering. The results of such DDoS attack are devastating, ranging from service slowdowns to complete service shutdowns for hours – or days.

Other Security Risks

SHIFTING RELATIONSHIPS

Wireless devices have constantly shifting network relationships with other wireless devices. Accidental association takes place when a wireless laptop running the LAN-friendly Windows XP or a misconfigured client automatically associates and connects to a user station in a neighboring network. This enables intruders to connect to innocent user's computers often without their knowledge, compromise sensitive documents on the user station, and expose it to even further exploitation. This danger is compounded if the station is connected to a wired network, which is also now accessible.

Network & Device Vulnerabilities

Insecure wireless LAN devices, such as access points and user stations, can seriously compromise both the wireless network and the wired network. Hackers target insecure devices, using specialized tools to break encryption and authentication.

Threats & Attacks

Wireless networks introduce multiple venues for attack and penetration that are either much more difficult or completely impossible to execute with a standard, wired network. (threats and attacks will be discussed more in details in later chapters)

Exposure of the Wired Network

Most enterprise wireless LANs connect back to a wired network at some point. Hackers can use any insecure wireless station as a launch pad to breach the network. Additionally, misconfigured access points can act as a bridge to the wired network, sending multicast, wired data, and credentials into the air, where they can be intercepted by intruders and hackers on the wireless side of the network. Also, enterprises that use routing protocols, such as HSRP (hot standby routing protocol), can fall prey to hackers doing wireless reconnaissance for topography information about the wired network. These types of protocols reveal information that can enable a hacker to do traffic analysis of the enterprise, such as the devices in use, MAC addresses, IP addresses, and traffic routes.

Passive Attacks

In such a type of attack the information which flows through is not modified but just monitored. Such attacks occur generally when an unauthorized person would intercept the information and then use it for illegal purposes. Passive attacks are of two types, Eavesdropping or traffic analysis and they both are described below:

1. Eavesdropping

In such a type of attack the attacker would passively keep on monitoring the transmissions from clients to access points without changing any message content. Eaves dropping can be defined as accidently or deliberately overhearing a conversation and thus gaining vital information which is not easily available. This is commonly termed as unethical and attackers use it to obtain important information like bank accounts, passwords or even social security numbers. A common example to this may be an attacker running a packet sniffer on a poorly configured wireless router and monitoring the incoming and outgoing traffic.

2. Traffic Analysis

Traffic analysis is an important concern in computer security. In this the attacker, in a more subtle way would intercept and then monitor messages in order to infer information from the patterns in communication. The major concern here is that messages can be intercepted even if they are either encrypted or decrypted. Thus more the number of messages intercepted, stored or even observed, more the information can be deduced from traffic.

Operational Issues

Wireless LANs have operational issues that can compromise the usability of the wireless network, issues that impact availability, performance, security, and cost. To alleviate these issues, wireless LANs require effective operational support mechanisms to run smoothly. Support for wireless LANs cannot depend on traditional wire-based support tools, but instead, must have tools that monitor performance, diagnose faults, and monitor for network use and misuse.

Risk Mitigation

Mitigating Security Threats

To secure a WLAN, the following components are required:

- **Authentication**: To ensure that legitimate clients and users access the network via trusted access points

- **Encryption**: To provide privacy and confidentiality

- **Intrusion Detection Systems (IDS) and Intrusion Protection Systems (IPS)**: To protect from security risks and availability

The fundamental solution for wireless security is authentication and encryption to protect the wireless data transmission. These two wireless security solutions can be implemented in degrees; however, both apply to small office/home office (SOHO) and large enterprise wireless networks. Larger enterprise networks need the additional levels of security offered by an IPS monitor. Current IPS systems do not only detect wireless network attacks, but also provide basic protection against unauthorized clients and access points. Many enterprise networks use IPS for protection not primarily against outside threats, but mainly against unintentional unsecured access points installed by employees desiring the mobility and benefits of wireless.

Enterprises can reduce the amount of risk which haunts their systems by applying countermeasures and make sure that they look after threats and vulnerabilities. Management combined with operational and technical countermeasures can be the best technique used to lessen the risks with wireless LANs. Countermeasures also depend on the amount of monetary resources a company is willing to dedicate to network security. Generally it is a tendency of small companies to compromise on security but when it comes to big financial institutions, or to the matter of fact any company pertaining to customer information; it would have a big budget for network security. The paper Wireless Network Security by Tom et al. describes various counter measures which an organization can follow in order to keep

their wireless LANS secure and free from intrusions. In this paper we will go through some of the measures and discuss their impact in brief.

Management Countermeasures

The main management countermeasure is to have a comprehensive security policy specifying all the precautions that should be taken in order to prevent any unauthorized access. Some of the questions and measures are given below with respect to management that can be addressed to mitigate the risks:

- Is there a requirement of Internet in the organization?

- Prepare a list of people who have access to the companies WLANs service.

- Identify all those people who can access and modify access points and their configurations.

- Limit the number of websites and data exchange every employee can make as per the roles they play in the company.

- Clearly specify all the kind of information which can flow through the access points.

- Develop guidelines for employees on the way to protect organization's resources and information.

- Limit the number of users who can access data sources from outside the company's network and provide guidelines for employees who do so

Each company should prepare a policy as per their requirements and make sure that it is updated when necessary. By keeping such a security policy, organizations would be able to educate their employees the importance of privacy of corporate data and also help them in achieving them.

As the society increases its dependency on computers and networks, we are increasingly surrounded by a variety of threats – computer viruses, leakage of personal information, unauthorized access from outside an organization, and more. Addressing this diversity of threats with effective security countermeasures has become a priority for our customers.

Such security threats are not limited to personal computers, servers, or networks. Even basic printers and multifunction products – need countermeasures against the same faced by more sophisticated IT products. As time has progressed, MFPs have become information terminals.

Security threats in offices

Unauthorized access via networks ↓

Unauthorized access via telephone lines ↓

Unauthorized access via the device's operator panel ↓

Information leaks from storage media ↓

Information leaks due to carelessness ↓

Information leaks via
hard copies ↓

-

Tapping and alteration of
information over the network
↓

-

Security threats can be reduced by considering multifunction copiers as IT equipment and operate them with appropriate diligence. As a forerunner in the field of security countermeasures of multifunction copiers, Ricoh addresses every conceivable security threat:

COUNTERMEASURES AGAINST UNAUTHORIZED ACCESS VIA NETWORKS

While the multifunction products can be found over the network, they do not allow the intruder to access their internal features. User authentication and filtering reduce the risk of information leaks via networks.

- User authentication
- Network port security
- IP address filtering
- Job logs / access logs
- Firmware validation

COUNTERMEASURES AGAINST UNAUTHORIZED ACCESS VIA TELEPHONE LINES

Although telephone lines connected to devices can be a lead-in for external access, Ricoh's multifunction products are designed not to allow access to the internal networks via telephone lines. People of malicious intent cannot access the internal networks of the company via a telephone line for fax.

- Security for fax lines

COUNTERMEASURES AGAINST TAPPING AND ALTERATION OF INFORMATION OVER THE NETWORK

Multifunction products exchange critical information with personal computers and servers over networks. Unprotected, this information is exposed to risks of alteration by people with malicious intent who tap into the network. Ricoh's multifunction products can encrypt network communications to reduce those risks.

- IPsec communications
- Encryption over SSL/TLS
- SNMPv3-encrypted communications
- S/MIME for scan-to-e-mail
- WPA (Wi-Fi protected access) support
- PDF password encryption

COUNTERMEASURES AGAINST UNAUTHORIZED ACCESS VIA THE OPERATOR PANEL

When multifunction products are installed in an office, they are exposed to security risks of unauthorized operations via the operator panel. Many cases of information leaks are reportedly committed by insiders. Using the user authentication features to properly set up access privileges to individual users reduces those risks. It is important to properly manage and run devices without letting users access the information and functions they do not need.

- User authentication
- User authentication by authentication cards
- User access restriction
- User lockout function
- Job logs / access logs

COUNTERMEASURES AGAINST INFORMATION LEAKS VIA STORAGE MEDIA

Multifunction products have a built-in storage device, such as a hard disk drive, for storing address books and accumulated documents. The hard disk drive also contains temporary work images for transmission, reception and printing. If the storage devices are removed, your important information may be read elsewhere. Using the data encryption and overwrite-and-erase functions reduces the risk of information leaks.

- Hard disk drive (HDD) encryption

- DataOverwriteSecurity System (DOSS)

COUNTERMEASURES AGAINST INFORMATION LEAKS VIA HARD COPIES

If a document is left on the tray of a multifunction copier, it can be taken away or viewed by unauthorized persons. It can be a source of information leakage. The risk can be minimized by using the user authentication and locked printing features. Make sure that users make just as many copies as required and that they do not leave hardcopy output unattended on the tray.

- Locked print

- User authentication

COUNTERMEASURES AGAINST INFORMATION LEAKS DUE TO CARELESSNESS

Sometimes one can make copies of confidential information without knowing it, and the information can be spread and taken away. Sometimes one can fax a document to the wrong destination. Carelessness can be a source of information leaks. Ricoh's multifunction copiers feature functions that can help minimize the risk of information leaks due to carelessness of the user.

- Displaying confirmation of transmission

- Re-entering a fax number to confirm destination

- Unauthorized copy control

Request for the User (Request to Use the Security Functions)

Ensuring device security requires security settings suitable for the specific operating environment.
To prevent malicious attackers from causing damage, read the following instructions and properly install and set up the device:

<BEFORE USING THE DEVICE>

1. Install the device in an environment under appropriate physical security control so that the device will not be taken away or destroyed.

2. Select an administrator and a supervisor who are authorized to manage the device. Make sure that the device is used under logical control of the administrator and the supervisor.

3. The administrator should become familiar with the operating instructions before using the security functions.

4. The administrator should instruct users on how to correctly use the security functions to conform to their site security policies.

5. It is recommended that the log be regularly audited. Check for exceptions and abnormal operations.

6. When the device is connected to a network, make sure that the network is protected, for instance, by a firewall.

7. To use the security communications functions to protect data during communications, make sure that all connected devices support the relevant security communications functions, such as encryption.

<UPON TERMINATING THE USE OF THE DEVICE>

Make sure that none of your information assets are left inside the device. To prevent information leakage, erase the information when when returning it, disposing of it, or transferring it to another environment.

Operational Countermeasures

One of the most important security measures is the physical security of access points and wireless networks. It is of utmost importance that only authorized users have physical access to routers and servers of the corporate network. Routers and company servers should be kept in a safe place in the company premises and made sure that people with special privileges only access them. Ideally every company has a server room in which all the servers are kept and the door is locked. Access to such rooms can be made available through specialized technologies like palm scans, photo identification, card badge readers or biometric devices and this in turn minimizes the risk of improper access of unauthorized users. Also spy cameras can be placed at various points so as to monitor illegal activity around the server rooms or access points. The major concern of any system administrator is the place where he/she would keep the access point, so that it covers the entire area and does not create any blind spots. But in the process of achieving that the administrator should keep in mind that keeping access points near doors to avoid blind spots would help intruders in gaining unauthorized access just by staying close to the corporate premises. Also system administrators should use tools to monitor and keep the access points coverage secure.

Technical Countermeasures

Technical Countermeasures involve the use of both software and hardware solutions to help securing the wireless networks. The aim of technical countermeasures is to make sure that all the components of the wireless system are secure and to make all the possible effort to avoid intrusion. Software countermeasures comprise of keeping access points strongly configured, updating security software on periodic basis and making sure that authentication takes place in every connection to the access point. On the other hand hardware measures include the use of smart cards, virtual private networks, key infrastructure and biometrics to protect the wireless network.

Emerging Security Standards and Technologies

There are some emerging security standards and technologies that can minimize the security threats of WLAN such as:

AIRDEFENSE

It is a commercial wireless LAN intrusion protection and management system that discovers network vulnerabilities, detects and protects a WLAN from intruders and attacks, and assists in the management of a WLAN. AirDefense also has the capability to discover vulnerabilities and threats in a WLAN such as rogue APs and ad hoc networks. Apart from securing a WLAN from all the threats, it also provides a robust WLAN management functionality that allows users to understand their network, monitor network performance and enforce network policies.

ISOMAIR WIRELESS SENTRY

This is developed by Isomair Company. This wireless sentry automatically monitors the air space of the enterprise continuously using unique and sophisticated analysis technology to identify insecure access points, security threats and wireless network problems. This is a dedicated appliance employing an Intelligent Conveyor Engine (ICE) to passively monitor wireless networks for threats and inform the security managers when these occur. It is a completely automated system, centrally managed, and will integrate seamlessly with existing security infrastructure. No additional man-time is required to operate the system

WIRELESS SECURITY AUDITOR (WSA)

It is an IBM research prototype of an 802.11 wireless LAN security auditor, running on Linux on an iPAQ PDA (Personal Digital Assistant). WSA helps network administrators to close any vulnerabilities by automatically audits a wireless network for proper security configuration. While there are other 802.11 network analyzers such as Ethereal, Sniffer and Wlandump, WSA aims at protocol experts who want to capture wireless packets for detailed analysis. Moreover, it is intended for the more general audience of network installers and administrators, who want a way to easily and quickly verify the security configuration of their networks, without having to understand any of the details of the 802.11 protocols.

Case Study: Implementing a Wireless LAN in the Work Environment

The Situation

Prior to their implementation of a Meru wireless LAN, Greene County Public Schools (GCPS) had a wireless network system that wasn't "making the grade." Their legacy system consisted of mobile carts within each of the schools which were equipped with low-end Linksys® wireless routers. Because of this system configuration, wireless access was only active within the rooms where the carts were connected.

Difficulty of Use and Technology Adoption. Operating under the old system, teachers found the process of connecting a class to the wireless carts difficult and disruptive. At times, they were unable to connect to the devices correctly. The cumbersome nature of the process led to dampened enthusiasm for the system which adversely affected GCPS' efforts to use the technology for instructional purposes.

System Management As GCPS' legacy wireless network grew over time, it became increasingly more disparate. Consequently, the IT team found themselves lacking an efficient way to implement system management and controls—including preventing the infiltration of unauthorized devices. At the same time, with the number of users steadily growing, finding an effective way to segregate student and public access from the private faculty/staff wireless network was also becoming a priority. With no single point of management, the IT staff was spending increasing amounts of time performing hands-on maintenance and troubleshooting of individual components throughout all the different school buildings. They also had to find a way to abate the growing number of students and faculty using their own personal wireless devices on the school network (laptops, mobile phones and other hand held devices). These critical issues related to system management and security became a drain on IT department resources which translated into an unacceptable level of cost for the school system.

Performance. The legacy wireless network lacked the required throughput capability and, in turn, the predictability needed for running critical school applications. The old network would often exhibit "shaky" performance when used for state required Standards of Learning (SOL) testing. As a result, ensuring Quality of Service (QoS) during SOL testing and other on-line assessments became a high priority concern for the IT staff. With a plan for growth in the number of wireless devices in classrooms, GCPS needed a scalable system that provided all the required capacity without compromise in performance.

Scalability. Like most public school systems, GCPS is subject to the push to devote more space to learning and less to other areas of school operations. With physical space at a premium, the IT department was running out of viable options for housing their expanding LAN equipment. This dilemma made the idea of expanding the wireless network under a centralized system an even more attractive option.

THE MERU SOLUTION

With its list of technology priorities in hand, a short window of opportunity to deploy a new solution, and a fixed budget, GCPS turned to their technology service partner, Advanced Network Systems, to find a wireless system that met all of their requirements. During the summer of 2008, GCPS replaced its legacy system with a Meru solution consisting of an MC3100 controller and 74 AP311 dual radio access points. The solution was deployed at the County's high school, middle school and two elementary schools.

REAPING THE BENEFITS OF MERU

According to Dale Herring, the benefits realized as a result of the Meru solution deployment were numerous. "We've been extremely pleased with Meru. We now have a really powerful system that has all the capabilities that we need," said Herring. He added, "From an IT perspective, the Meru system's centralized configuration and management features have cut down on a lot of time we used to spend maintaining all the different systems we had." Herring noted that another benefit of the Meru system is its high level of flexibility. "Because we now have a consistent wireless solution, device compatibility issues have been eliminated; this allows GCPS' IT team to easily share laptops and other devices between schools when demands shift. Since there are no configuration changes to perform, devices move seamlessly from school to school. Having this kind of flexibility means we spend less of our time on management and a smaller budget needed because we don't have to have as many devices at every school." Herring noted, "One of the big reasons we chose a Meru solution is its compatibility and technology investment protection. No matter what type of device is connected to the network, a/b/g or n, Meru's access points can accommodate all the least common denominator in terms of performance as we go forward."

Expanding on the idea of better system performance Herring added, "Because Standards of Learning testing is considered a mission-critical application for the school district, we need to have guaranteed quality of service when it comes to its implementation. 'Hiccups' in the system are incredibly disruptive and are not an option. With Meru's built in QoS, the on-line SOL testing process has gone very smoothly; the system has reliably supported this and all the other bandwidth-intensive applications we use it for."

According to Dale Herring, "We've had a lot of positive feedback and increased use of the wireless system because connectivity is now a more seamless, transparent process. Disruptions to the teaching process in our classrooms are minimal; plus we were able to easily segregate access for students and the public from the private portion of the network. Everyone in the IT department loves the flexibility and we don't worry the way we used to about adding more devices or new applications. We are all definitely benefiting rom having a pervasive system that provides access wherever and whenever it's needed; both inside and outside of the school buildings."

New Opportunities with a Meru Solution

The 2008/2009 school year brought forth new opportunities for GCPS to improve the learning environment using their state-of-the-art Meru wireless network. Students and school personnel alike are reaping the benefits of being able to successfully run applications over the air including web-based assessments, instructional videos and presentations, along with Internet-based learning and staff training.

Opportunities on the horizon are all about learning and teaching processes. The technology and cost/benefit analysis of implementing an e-reader program is now under consideration. The GCPS' IT department is currently piloting e-reader technology to support the County's reading program in the Middle School. If successful, the program will be expanded to all schools. According to Dale Herring, "We considered the option of e-readers before the Meru installation. But now since we have the technology to effectively support this kind of program, the concept has gained a lot of traction and taken on a new meaning. Students are now able to

 access the most up to date material throughout the facility, not just in certain designated locations." With the number of electronic formats consolidating and significant improvements in device battery life, the use of hand-held devices containing e-books has grown significantly within the educational market. Herring added, "The concept of e-readers appeals to students and school administrators alike. Students already lug around enough laptops and heavy books. On the other side, books are expensive and quickly fall out of date which makes it challenging for schools to stay current."

As part of the teacher development and evaluation process, GCPS administrators are using iPod's to wirelessly connect to a web portal to run their classroom observation software. So far this year, over 1000 informal classroom observations have been conducted and recorded. That data collected is used to insure that best instructional practice is being followed, to provided specific feedback to teachers, and to help administrators stay in touch with what is going on in the classrooms. According to Herring, "Using a secure wireless/web-based system, we've made big strides in recording evaluation info in real time and keeping it secure. We essentially eliminated the need to keep data on a device which could get lost or stolen and need for any further data transfer." Purchased with private enterprise grant funds, the implementation of these mobile devices has had a significant, positive impact on the collection, storage and utilization of this vital information.

Plans for the Future

GCPS has plans to expand the implementation of Meru products in its primary school and school board office in the near future. Further out on the horizon are plans for a VoIP telephony solution which could ultimately also be run over their Meru wireless network.

About Greene County Public Schools

Greene County is located in central Virginia at the foot of the Blue Ridge Mountains, with the Shenandoah National Park and the Skyline Drive forming its western boundary. Although rural in nature, this picturesque County is part of the Charlottesville metropolitan region which includes the University of Virginia. As a result, the County has become a community that has experienced significant growth in its residential population as well as business investment and economic development. The Greene County Public School System has a student enrollment of approximately 2,800 and is comprised of seven schools including one primary, two elementary, one middle, one high school, an alternative education center, and a technical educational center. The school system's popular tag phrase, "Every child, every chance, every day," echoes its formal commitment to build a positive, responsible and effective learning community where students, teachers and staff are encouraged to believe, achieve and succeed.

Exercise

Quizzes:

Q.1) What are the basic functions of Wireless Routers ?

Answer) Wireless Routers can provide a wide range of functions such as:

- Protects the home network from outside intruders

- Allows the sharing of a single Internet IP address from an ISP (Internet Service Provider)

- Provides Wired Ethernet service for typically 4 computers but can also be expanded with another Ethernet Switch or Hub

- Serves as a Wireless Access Point for multiple wireless computers

Q.2) TPC allows the AP to negotiate power levels with a WLAN client during association process. (State true of false)

Answer) True

Q.3) What are the components of 802.11 logical architecture?

Answer) The 802.11 logical architecture contains several main components: station (STA), wireless access point (AP), independent basic service set (IBSS), basic service set (BSS), distribution system (DS), and extended service set (ESS). Some of the components of the 802.11 logical architecture map directly to hardware devices, such as STAs and wireless APs.

Q.4) In 802.11 *infrastructure mod*e, there is at least one wireless AP and one wireless client.

 (State true of false)

Answer) True

Q.5) What are functions of client bridge?

Answer) A client bridge is a type of client device that bridges the wireless network with the wired network. It's basically like a reverse AP. The function of the AP is to bridge the wired network onto a wireless network, and the client bridge takes that and re-reverses into another wired segment. This can be useful if you have a device such as a printer or Xbox that doesn't support wireless, but you want to connect it to the network without using CAT5 Ethernet cable. You simply get a client bridge device, connect it to the wireless network, then connect the wired device to the bridge. Ta-da, instant wired network connectivity over wireless.

Q.6) The security stands 802.1 was originally designed for Wireless LANs? (State true of false)

Answer) False

Q.7) What are Passive Attacks

Answer) In such a type of attack the information which flows through is not modified but just monitored. Such attacks occur generally when an unauthorized person would intercept the information and then use it for illegal purposes. Passive attacks are of two types, Eavesdropping or traffic analysis and they both are described below:

Assignment

Research about Wireless-N Range Extenders and find the example of such devices of any famous company.

Answer) Information can be found here: http://www.pcmag.com/article2/0,2817,2399489,00.asp

PROJECT

With reference to case study 3.4, research another case study of educational environment and elaborate what steps are evolve in its implementations.

Answer) Reference to this can be found here:

http://www.sans.org/reading_room/whitepapers/casestudies/case-study-path-secure-multi-role-wireless-lan-higher-education-environment_1544

Introduction to Information Security

Threats and Attacks

Computer security means to protect information. It deals with the prevention and detection of unauthorized actions by users of a computer. Lately it has been extended to include privacy, confidentiality, and integrity. This definition implies that you have to know the information and the value of that information in order to develop protective measures. You also need to know to which individuals need unique identities and how much information may be divulged to the outside world. A rough classification of protective measures in computer security is as follows:

- Prevention—Take measures that prevent your information from being damaged, altered, or stolen. Preventive measures can range from locking the server room door to setting up high-level security policies.

- Detection—Take measures that allow you to detect when information has been damaged, altered, or stolen, how it has been damaged, altered, or stolen, and who has caused the damage. Various tools are available to help detect intrusions, damage or alterations, and viruses.

- Reaction—Take measures that allow recovery of information, even if information is lost or damaged.

The above measures are all very well, but if you do not understand how information may be compromised, you cannot take measures to protect it. You must examine the components on how information can be compromised:

- *Confidentiality.* The prevention of unauthorized disclosure of information. This can be the result of poor security measures or information leaks by personnel. An example of poor security measures would be to allow anonymous access to sensitive information.

- *Integrity.* The prevention of erroneous modification of information. Authorized users are probably the biggest cause of errors and omissions and the alteration of data. Storing incorrect data within the system can be as bad as losing data. Malicious attackers also can modify, delete, or corrupt information that is vital to the correct operation of business functions.

- *Availability.* The prevention of unauthorized withholding of information or resources. This does not apply just to personnel withholding information. Information should be as freely available as possible to authorized users.

- *Authentication.* The process of verifying that users are who they claim to be when logging onto a system. Generally, the use of user names and passwords accomplishes this. More sophisticated is the use of smart cards and retina scanning. The process of authentication does not grant the user access rights to resources—this is achieved through the authorization process.

- *Authorization.* The process of allowing only authorized users' access to sensitive information. An authorization process uses the appropriate security authority to determine whether a user should have access to resources.

Information security is the provision of controls to ensure the protection of the information assets of an organization in such a way the function of the organization is not impeded. It must meet the requirements of the organization. It should protect against both accidental and malicious threats whether these are natural and man-made in origin.

Security Threats

SECURITY THREATS, ATTACKS, AND VULNERABILITIES

Information is the key asset in most organizations. Companies gain a competitive advantage by knowing how to use that information. The threat comes from others who would like to acquire the information or limit business opportunities by interfering with normal business processes.

The object of security is to protect valuable or sensitive organizational information while making it readily available. Attackers trying to harm a system or disrupt normal business operations exploit vulnerabilities by using various techniques, methods, and tools. System administrators need to understand the various aspects of security to develop measures and policies to protect assets and limit their vulnerabilities.

Attackers generally have motives or goals for example, to disrupt normal business operations or steal information. To achieve these motives or goals, they use various methods, tools, and techniques to exploit vulnerabilities in a computer system or security policy and controls.

Goal + Method + Vulnerabilities = Attack.

SECURITY THREATS

Figure 56 introduces a layout that can be used to break up security threats into different areas.

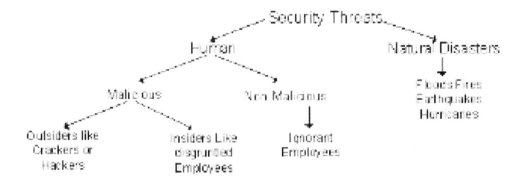

Figure 55 LAYOUT TO BREAK UP SECURITY THREATS

Natural Disasters

Nobody can stop nature from taking its course. Earthquakes, hurricanes, floods, lightning, and fire can cause severe damage to computer systems. Information can be lost, downtime or loss of productivity can occur, and damage to hardware can disrupt other essential services. Few safeguards can be implemented against natural disasters. The best approach is to have disaster recovery plans and contingency plans in place. Other threats such as riots, wars, and terrorist attacks could be included here. Although they are human-caused threats, they are classified as disastrous.

HUMAN THREATS

Malicious threats consist of inside attacks by disgruntled or malicious employees and outside attacks by non-employees just looking to harm and disrupt an organization.

The most dangerous attackers are usually *insiders* (or former insiders), because they know many of the codes and security measures that are already in place. Insiders are likely to have specific goals and objectives, and have legitimate access to the system. Employees are the people most familiar with the organization's computers and applications, and they are most likely to know what actions might cause the most damage. Insiders can plant viruses, Trojan horses, or worms, and they can browse through the file system.

The insider attack can affect all components of computer security. By browsing through a system, confidential information could be revealed. Trojan horses are a threat to both the integrity and confidentiality of information in the system. Insider attacks can affect availability by overloading the system's processing or storage capacity, or by causing the system to crash.

MOTIVES, GOALS, AND OBJECTIVES OF MALICIOUS ATTACKERS

There is a strong overlap between physical security and data privacy and integrity. Indeed, the goal of some attacks is not the physical destruction of the computer system but the penetration and removal or copying of sensitive information. Attackers want to achieve these goals either for personal satisfaction or for a reward.

Here are some methods that attackers use:

- *Deleting and altering information*. Malicious attackers who delete or alter information normally do this to prove a point or take revenge for something that has happened to them. Inside attackers normally do this to spite the organization because they are disgruntled about something. Outside attackers might want to do this to prove that they can get in to the system or for the fun of it.

- *Committing information theft and fraud*. Information technology is increasingly used to commit fraud and theft. Computer systems are exploited in numerous ways, both by automating traditional methods of fraud and by using new methods. Financial systems are not the only ones subject to fraud. Other targets are systems that control access to any resources, such as time and attendance systems, inventory systems, school grading systems, or long-distance telephone systems.

- *Disrupting normal business operations*. Attackers may want to disrupt normal business operations. In any circumstance like this, the attacker has a specific goal to achieve. Attackers use various methods for denial-of-service attacks; the section on methods, tools, and techniques will discuss these.

METHODS, TOOLS, AND TECHNIQUES FOR ATTACKS

Attacks = motive + method + vulnerability.

The method in this formula exploits the organization's vulnerability in order to launch an attack as shown in Figure 2. Malicious attackers can gain access or deny services in numerous ways. Here are some of them:

Viruses. Attackers can develop harmful code known as viruses. Using hacking techniques, they can break into systems and plant viruses. Viruses in general are a threat to any environment. They come in different forms and although not always malicious, they always take up time. Viruses can also be spread via e-mail and disks.

- *Trojan horses*. These are malicious programs or software code hidden inside what looks like a normal program. When a user runs the normal program, the hidden code runs as well. It can then start deleting files and causing other damage to the computer. Trojan horses are normally spread by e-mail attachments. The Melissa virus that caused denial-of-service attacks throughout the world in 1999 was a type of Trojan horse.

- *Worms.* These are programs that run independently and travel from computer to computer across network connections. Worms may have portions of themselves running on many different computers. Worms do not change other programs, although they may carry other code that does.

- *Password cracking.* This is a technique attacker's use to surreptitiously gain system access through another user's account. This is possible because users often select weak passwords. The two major problems with passwords is when they are easy to guess based on knowledge of the user (for example, wife's maiden name) and when they are susceptible to dictionary attacks (that is, using a dictionary as the source of guesses).

- *Denial-of-service attacks.* This attack exploits the need to have a service available. It is a growing trend on the Internet because Web sites in general are open doors ready for abuse. People can easily flood the Web server with communication in order to keep it busy. Therefore, companies connected to the Internet should prepare for (DoS) attacks. They also are difficult to trace and allow other types of attacks to be subdued.

- *E-mail hacking.* Electronic mail is one of the most popular features of the Internet. With access to Internet e-mail, someone can potentially correspond with any one of millions of people worldwide. Some of the threats associated with e-mail are:

- *Impersonation.* The sender address on Internet e-mail cannot be trusted because the sender can create a false return address. Someone could have modified the header in transit, or the sender could have connected directly to the Simple Mail Transfer Protocol (SMTP) port on the target computer to enter the e-mail.

- *Eavesdropping.* E-mail headers and contents are transmitted in the clear text if no encryption is used. As a result, the contents of a message can be read or altered in transit. The header can be modified to hide or change the sender, or to redirect the message.

- *Packet replay.* This refers to the recording and retransmission of message packets in the network. Packet replay is a significant threat for programs that require authentication sequences, because an intruder could replay legitimate authentication sequence messages to gain access to a system. Packet replay is frequently undetectable, but can be prevented by using packet time stamping and packet sequence counting.

- *Packet modification.* This involves one system intercepting and modifying a packet destined for another system. Packet information may not only be modified, it could also be destroyed.

- *Eavesdropping.* This allows a cracker (hacker) to make a complete copy of network activity. As a result, a cracker can obtain sensitive information such as passwords, data, and procedures for performing functions. It is possible for a cracker to eavesdrop by wiretapping, using radio, or using auxiliary ports on terminals. It is also possible to eavesdrop using software that monitors packets sent over the network. In most cases, it is difficult to detect eavesdropping.

- *Social engineering*. This is a common form of cracking. It can be used by outsiders and by people within an organization. Social engineering is a hacker term for tricking people into revealing their password or some form of security information.

- *Intrusion attacks*. In these attacks, a hacker uses various hacking tools to gain access to systems. These can range from password-cracking tools to protocol hacking and manipulation tools. Intrusion detection tools often can help to detect changes and variants that take place within systems and networks.

- *Network spoofing*. In network spoofing, a system presents itself to the network as though it were a different system (computer A impersonates computer B by sending B's address instead of its own). The reason for doing this is that systems tend to operate within a group of other trusted systems. Trust is imparted in a one-to-one fashion; computer A trusts computer B (this does not imply that system B trusts system A). Implied with this trust is that the system administrator of the trusted system is performing the job properly and maintaining an appropriate level of security for the system. Network spoofing occurs in the following manner: if computer A trusts computer B and computer C spoofs (impersonates) computer B, then computer C can gain otherwise-denied access to computer A.

Integrity

Integrity is the next of four core concepts of information security examined in this series. Integrity, in Information Technology terms, means that data remains unchanged while stored or transmitted. Once in place, changes should only be possible to data if the change is authorized. In modern business, enormous amounts of information are created, transmitted, and stored daily. We almost always make the assumption that entries on a web form, e-mails we send, or documents saved will have and retain the data we intended. Nevertheless, how valid is this assumption? Why do we make it?

Accident, mistake, or malice

Accidents happen, so not all integrity failures are due to malice. Integrity failure could be caused by noise or transmission errors, bad sectors or hard disk crashes, or errors in data entry or capture. Tape media are subject to data degradation. Optical media can be scratched. Mistakes can be made by users, customers, or administrators.

We must also beware of malicious changes to data. Such changes may be harder to detect. They may be plausible and otherwise contextually valid. An example might be a "shifted decimal point" in a payment, where $100.00 becomes $10,000. These sorts of attacks on data integrity are often imagined to originate with wily hackers, but could surely come from a disgruntled employee as well. Of course malicious changes also include damage done to programs by viruses, Trojans, or worms.

Verifying and retaining integrity

Computational techniques for verifying data integrity
include: **comparisons**, **checksums**, **message authentication & integrity codes (MAC/MIC)**, and **message digests** such as MD5 or SHA-1 hashes. For example, the Message Digest 5 (MD5) hash is a mathematical algorithm which produces a unique 128 bit number (a hash) created from the data input. If even one bit of data changes, the hash value will change. An example of this in use: most open source programs and packages are distributed along with an MD5 hash. Before installing, the recipient can generate the MD5 hash, and compare it with the (known good) hash provided by the source. If the generated and provided hashes are not the same, the program or package has been changed.

Simpler checksum techniques such as cyclic redundancy checks (CRC) are built-in to hard drives. Modern hard drives also have additional Integrity protection, as they may contain error correction technology, automatically reconstructing data in failing sectors and moving it to new sectors to preserve it.

IMPROVING DATA INTEGRITY

The adoption of best practices needs to be complemented by formalizing accountabilities for the business and IT processes that support and enhance data security.

BUSINESS RESPONSIBILITIES:

A program of data integrity assurance needs to address Detect, Deter (2D); Prevent, Prepare (2P); and Respond, Recover (2R). As data owners, the initiative must come from the business and the role of the IT service provider—in-house or outsourced—should be one of implementation.

GOOD PRACTICES TO ADOPT INCLUDE:

- **Taking ownership of data and accountability for data integrity**—There is no one else in the organization who can do this other than people in the appropriate business unit. This should be obvious when IT services and operations are outsourced, but when these are provided in-house, it is tempting and easy to believe that the data are owned by IT and that IT is responsible for maintaining confidentiality and integrity.

Ownership requires a value assessment in the form of an estimation of the potential cost of lost data integrity, including direct financial losses (as is the case in fraud or major operational disruption), legal costs and reputational damage.

- **Access rights and privileges**—The principles of need to know (NtK) and least privilege (LP) are good practice and, in theory, are not difficult to apply. Social networks and the concept that everyone is an information producer push for greater openness and sharing, and social networks are becoming a force that resists and challenges the implementation of NtK and LP.

  The processes for requesting, changing and removing access rights should be formalized, documented, and regularly reviewed and audited. Privilege creep—when individuals change responsibilities and carry forward historical privileges—constitute a serious business risk that can undermine proper SoD.

IT and End-user Support Responsibilities

Whoever provides information systems and technology operational services (i.e., business unit, in-house IT department, outsourcing service provider) has to demonstrate that appropriate measures are carried out to an appropriate level of maturity and that appropriate performance and risk metrics are collected, monitored and reported.

End-user support teams (either part of IT or independent) are usually responsible for creating accounts and credentials for access to systems and data. These accounts and credentials must be documented fully and implemented only if the relevant authorizations have been formally issued.

CONFIDENTIALITY

Confidentiality is one of four core concepts of Information Security. These services provide the means whereby e-business information is stored and transferred securely (including possibly the identities of participants). They also ensure that private information (such as an individual's medical information) is protected in accordance with legislation such as data protection.

To understand Confidentiality, we must understand the concept of privacy. Further, we must have an understanding of what information *should* be protected, and how to define "authorized" and intended access. At the core, Confidentiality comprises the idea that specific information should not be accessible by those that are not supposed to see it.

All sorts of business and personal information is created, stored, and exchanged. Information could be details of everyday business operations, sales information, marketing, bills and invoices, or many other things. For most of these types of information, there is not an overreaching expectation of extreme privacy or secrecy. It might not be ideal if how much a business spends on electricity became public knowledge, but in reality that bit of information isn't a mission critical secret. Conversely, for any business performing high-volume transactions with customer credit card information as payment, the customers card information is extremely important to protect.

CONFIDENTIAL INFORMATION

So, how do we decide what information should be confidential? We need to consider several factors. First, what's the relative *value* of the information? What is the *risk* if it is exposed? Have you or your business been *entrusted* with the information, with the understanding that it won't be shared with any other party?

KEEPING IT CONFIDENTIAL

<u>Authentication</u> should come first: Is the person or agent who they claim to be? In the physical world we might check a picture ID, or have them present a card and enter a PIN. Computer systems at minimum should ask for a user ID and password.

<u>Authorization</u> comes next: What is this agent's role? Are they a member of a group or department that has access to the information in question? Roles can be things like Accounting, Engineering, Customer, Business Manager, and so forth.

<u>Access Control</u> involves what the agent can or can't do, based on their role. Can they (and should they be able to) read, write, change, add, or delete information?

AVAILABILITY

Availability is essential to information security, because for any such system to satisfy its purpose, the information on it must be available as needed by any authorized personnel. There is a need for the computer systems that store the information, the safety controls that are employed to guard it, and the communication channels that access it to function in the correct manner. Availability systems make certain that they are available all the time, stopping disruptions to information service from the likes of power outages, system upgrades, or hardware failures.

Availability is the third of four concepts examined in this series of articles. In the ubiquitous Internet and wireless access era, information must be available 24/7, or whenever it's needed. All the effort spent securing data from unauthorized access or integrity failures may go to waste.

In the ubiquitous Internet and wireless access era, information must be available 24/7, or whenever it's needed. All the effort spent securing data from unauthorized access or integrity failures may go to waste if it is not accessible when and where it is needed. Business operations rely critically on digital information and electronic information transfer. Perfect backups and massive servers are useless if system and network uptime is minimal. Unreliability brings inefficiency, a recipe for failure. Fortunately, there are numerous solutions available to increase availability. Solutions may be simple or complex, ranging in cost from almost free to as much as you want to spend!

IS IT AVAILABLE?

How do we ensure our information is available? In planning, determine optimized computing and memory capacity, plan for growth, and predict peak usage requirements. High-availability solutions are becoming more affordable and simpler. Load balancing and fail-over solutions should be part of the design, not an add-on or a future consideration. These solutions don't just improve performance; they simplify maintenance, and most importantly in this discussion, ensure availability. Virtual server farms make increasing load capacity simpler, and make restores much faster. If these things don't seem that important to you yet, ask yourself: what is the real cost if employees can't do their jobs; if customers can't be serviced? Aren't planned costs for a better infrastructure better than unplanned costs for a crisis?

DANGERS TO AVAILABILITY

Availability can be compromised in many ways. Denial of Service (DoS) attacks can bring down networks, servers, or applications. A hacker or disgruntled employee could delete important data. If the network is penetrated, control of servers or network hardware can be usurped. In many cases these attacks happen through worms, like "Conficker", without any person's conscious knowledge or intent during the attack. There are many points of failure. Anything, from a server, a database, an application, the LAN, WAN, Wireless net, or Internet connectivity could have an outage. Accidental downtime is possible too, of course. Like Integrity, loss of availability could occur due to error(s) on the part of the support or operations staff.

ACCOUNTABILITY

Accountability is an essential information security concept. The phrase means that every individual who works with an information system should have specific responsibilities for information assurance. The tasks for which a individual is responsible are part of the overall information security plan and are readily measurable by a person who has managerial responsibility for information assurance. One example is the policy statement that all employees must avoid installing outside software on a company-owned information infrastructure. The person in charge of information security should perform periodic checks to be certain that the policy is being followed.

Every information asset should be "owned" by an individual in the organization who is primarily responsible each one.

INFORMATION SECURITY ACCOUNTABILITY IN BUSINESS ENVIRONMENT

In today's business environment, everyone is a manager of information. Clearly articulating the accountability at all levels of the organization will support the appropriate management of information assets. The Deputy Minister is ultimately accountable for the management of information in the custody or under the control of the ministry. This accountability is usually delegated to program managers and individual employees in the ministry. In addition, specific responsibility for providing leadership, expertise, and a focal point for managing information assets is often assigned to a specific function such as an Information Management Director. This section lists a set of possible accountability statements for different levels and functions within the organization.

PROGRAM EXECUTIVES AND MANAGERS

Program Executives and Managers are accountable, within their business area, for:

- Identifying and defining information needed to meet short-term and long-term business objectives;

- Ensuring the accuracy, completeness, and timeliness of information;

- Ensuring practices for the proper collection, creation, storage, access, retention, and disposal of information are in place for employees and contractors and that these practices meet ministry policies and standards;

- Ensuring the proper levels of security and privacy protection are applied to the information based on privacy impact assessments and threat/risk assessments and any relevant information sharing agreements;

- Assessing the information management training needs for staff in the business area; and providing tools, technology and training to support their organization's management of information.

NON-REPUDIATION

Non-repudiation allows an exchange of data between two principals in such a manner that the principals cannot subsequently deny their participation in the exchange. Current non-repudiation schemes, while providing a mandatory proof of origin service, generally provide only discretionary proof of receipt since it is difficult to enforce the return of the proof of receipt by the recipient.

Repudiation is the denial by one of the entities involved in a communication of having participated in all or part of the communication [ISO89]. Non-repudiation is concerned with preventing such a denial. With sender non-repudiation, the originator of a data exchange is provided with a proof of receipt (POR) which proves that the recipient received the data. Receiver non-repudiation provides the recipient with a proof of origin (POO) which proves that the originator sent the data. The proofs of origin and receipt constitute non-repudiation evidence information. Principals can exchange evidence information, either through direct peer-to-peer communication or indirectly via a third-party intermediary

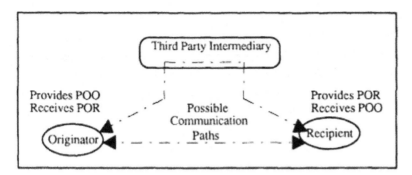

The correct generation of evidence information is crucial to non-repudiation. The proof of origin must associate the identity of the originator with the data exchanged in such a manner that the originator cannot deny this association. Likewise, the identity of the recipient is associated with the proof of receipt. The evidence must be undeniable and unforgettable. These properties are achieved through the use of digital signatures.

A non-repudiation service must provide an arbitration framework for addressing disputes. If a dispute arises, it may be possible for the disputing principals to resolve it themselves by exchanging and examining the evidence information. If this does not suffice, then an agreed arbitrator, which is trusted by both principals, is called upon to reach a settlement. The entities involved in the exchange present evidence to this arbitrator who uses a set of well-defined rules to decide, based on the evidence submitted, whether or not an exchange took place.

The remainder of this section briefly presents the approach of existing non-repudiation schemes. The third-party services required for the operation of our scheme are presented in section 4. In section 5, we give step-by-step details of our non-repudiation protocol. The dispute arbitration process is discussed in section 6 and the decision-making rules are given.

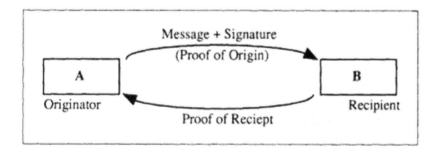

General Approach to the Non-Repudiation Problem

Non-repudiation is sometimes implemented using a simple peer-to-peer protocol whereby the originator sends the message along with his signature, thus providing the recipient with the proof of origin for the message and the recipient, in turn, returns a signed proof of receipt to the originator. Examples of techniques based on this method can be found in [Barb91] and [Herd95]. Generally, the difficulty with such non-repudiation schemes is in enforcing mandatory evidence exchanges. From figure 2 above, it is clear that the recipient will obtain the proof of origin so that the sender non-repudiation is a mandatory service. However, the proof of receipt service is more difficult to implement [KBN88] and is generally discretionary in nature.

RELIABILITY

When security of information systems is considered it is needed to analyze three attributes: confidentiality, availability and integrity. According to reliability theory, one of the key measures is probability of failures or time between failures. When it comes to security systems there is a lack of such metrics. In general security can be seen as a subjective category. So it is very difficult to find adequate metrics or measures of security attributes. But it seems that reliability context and analogies should be helpful. Another problem is if such metrics can be helpful in decision taking during ensuring security process. It seems that measuring security is impossible or at least possible in very limited scope. In authors' opinion every techniques which can be utilized to limit uncertainty during decision taking (in computer security domain) is worth considering.

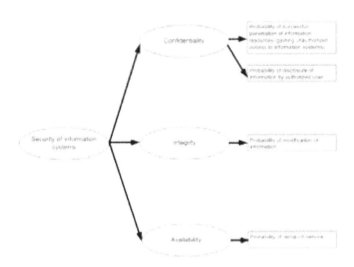

CENTRALIZED OR DECENTRALIZED CONTROLS

DECENTRALIZED management of IT systems. In fact, in smaller organizations where employees are expected to multitask and act with a greater amount of autonomy, it makes sense to allow some decentralization in order to allow flexibility and empower the employees.

However, in large scale operations, most companies have gone to highly centralized management systems, and not just in IT. The reason is increased efficiency and focus. Decentralized management in a large organization can easily result in redundancies and inefficiencies as competing factions within the company attempt to go their own ways. From a customer's standpoint, a company without a standardized IT operation may be less consistent in their quality of service. I think that even with a centralized information system, business units can still have freedom to customize their information system. For example, units separated by region can have their own section of the company webpage to communicate with their specific customer group. Centralization does not have to mean that a business unit has lost its freedom, but rather it can provide a set of tools and guidelines to maximize the potential of the unit's contribution to the company while minimizing the redundancy of work.

Centralized management of IT systems means having a unit within an organization that is dedicated to managing the IT systems for the rest of the organization. One unit is responsible for acquiring, developing, and maintaining hardware and software, as well as developing IT policy for the entire organization. Some advantages of using a centralized system include:

Decreased risk of technological clash by providing oversight to ensure software and hardware are compatible within the organization. With decentralized control, future IT solutions might be limited by compatibility issues between businesses units due to lack of oversight and long term planning. Compatibility is key in ensuring seamless functionality within the organization as well in smoothing out the path for IT system evolution, which is periodically critical in ensuring the long term success of an organization. (What good is a sales employee evaluation if human resources lack the software to read and process it? Or who cares about the new customer management system that doesn't read the old database?)

Lowering redundancies in acquisition and development.

Development and maintenance using established technology and highly reliable operating systems is more likely with centralization. By having one central team of developers, IT staff can share their experiences and avoid the replication of work, instead of one unit wasting months inventing a business solution that another business unit developed last year. Also, use of centralized management system makes information such as HR and supply chain management processes available from one source, reducing the possibility for conflicting sources and redundancies.

UNIFORM POLICY, MANAGEMENT, AND ADMINISTRATION.

Use of centralized management also provides a built in mediation system to research and administer policies for use that are observed throughout the organization. Having recognized experts also enables a company to have one help desk, rather than help desks scattered amongst business units. This allows for a standardization of processes and thus a more comfortable user who does not get varying answers from different help desks. Managers benefit by having a firmer grasp of IT solutions developed in their departments.

Decentralized IT systems give the various departments or units in a business autonomy over their own IT resources unless it is essential to the overall organization policy. (In military speak, this is referred to as "control by negation.") Essentially, each unit (eg marketing, sales, human resources, etc.) is responsible for maintaining and developing their own IT system. Advantages of using a decentralized system includes, but is not limited to:

Inexpensive and easy to set up as compared to a larger, centralized network.
The development of microcomputers accelerated a downsizing trend, prompting a move back to decentralization by many business firms. It is easy and inexpensive to maintain PCs on a network. Therefore, decentralization of the management and control of information systems in the business can be the best solution for many businesses.

Departments are free to develop systems that meet their needs.
In the earliest days, computer networks were often placed in the "basement," with located in only one place. However, advances in technology allows much more flexibility in where networks are located and how they are administered. Increased networking speed and security gives organizations the option to "break" central information technology systems into pieces and spread it around the globe.

Empowerment of employees and increased personal accountability.

Decentralizing an organization's information system gives each IS manager to focus on the local needs of the company's subsidiary and extend it to the global needs. The ability to align local processing with each individual unit's perceived needs lends greater autonomy, and therefore greater scope for motivating user involvement in maintaining and developing the company's IT system.

Security Assessment

Attacks and Attackers

Without security measures and controls in place, your data might be subjected to an attack. Some attacks are passive, meaning information is monitored; others are active, meaning the information is altered with intent to corrupt or destroy the data or the network itself. Your networks and data are vulnerable to any of the following types of attacks if you do not have a security plan in place.

Eavesdropping

In general, the majority of network communications occur in an unsecured or "cleartext" format, which allows an attacker who has gained access to data paths in your network to "listen in" or interpret (read) the traffic. When an attacker is eavesdropping on your communications, it is referred to as sniffing or snooping. The ability of an eavesdropper to monitor the network is generally the biggest security problem that administrators face in an enterprise. Without strong encryption services that are based on cryptography, your data can be read by others as it traverses the network.

Data Modification

After an attacker has read your data, the next logical step is to alter it. An attacker can modify the data in the packet without the knowledge of the sender or receiver. Even if you do not require confidentiality for all communications, you do not want any of your messages to be modified in transit. For example, if you are exchanging purchase requisitions, you do not want the items, amounts, or billing information to be modified.

Identity Spoofing (IP Address Spoofing)

Most networks and operating systems use the IP address of a computer to identify a valid entity. In certain cases, it is possible for an IP address to be falsely assumed— identity spoofing. An attacker might also use special programs to construct IP packets that appear to originate from valid addresses inside the corporate intranet.

After gaining access to the network with a valid IP address, the attacker can modify, reroute, or delete your data. The attacker can also conduct other types of attacks, as described in the following sections.

Password-Based Attacks

A common denominator of most operating system and network security plans is password-based access control. This means your access rights to a computer and network resources are determined by who you are, that is, your user name and your password.

Older applications do not always protect identity information as it is passed through the network for validation. This might allow an eavesdropper to gain access to the network by posing as a valid user.

When an attacker finds a valid user account, the attacker has the same rights as the real user. Therefore, if the user has administrator-level rights, the attacker also can create accounts for subsequent access at a later time.

After gaining access to your network with a valid account, an attacker can do any of the following:

- Obtain lists of valid user and computer names and network information.

- Modify server and network configurations, including access controls and routing tables.

- Modify, reroute, or delete your data.

Denial-of-Service Attack

Unlike a password-based attack, the denial-of-service attack prevents normal use of your computer or network by valid users.

After gaining access to your network, the attacker can do any of the following:

- Randomize the attention of your internal Information Systems staff so that they do not see the intrusion immediately, which allows the attacker to make more attacks during the diversion.

- Send invalid data to applications or network services, which causes abnormal termination or behavior of the applications or services.

- Flood a computer or the entire network with traffic until a shutdown occurs because of the overload.

- Block traffic, which results in a loss of access to network resources by authorized users.

Man-in-the-Middle Attack

As the name indicates, a man-in-the-middle attack occurs when someone between you and the person with whom you are communicating is actively monitoring, capturing, and controlling your communication transparently. For example, the attacker can re-route a data exchange. When computers are communicating at low levels of the network layer, the computers might not be able to determine with whom they are exchanging data.

Man-in-the-middle attacks are like someone assuming your identity in order to read your message. The person on the other end might believe it is you because the attacker might be actively replying *as you* to keep the exchange going and gain more information. This attack is capable of the same damage as an application-layer attack, described later in this section.

Compromised-Key Attack

A key is a secret code or number necessary to interpret secured information. Although obtaining a key is a difficult and resource-intensive process for an attacker, it is possible. After an attacker obtains a key, that key is referred to as a compromised key.

An attacker uses the compromised key to gain access to a secured communication without the sender or receiver being aware of the attack. With the compromised key, the attacker can decrypt or modify data, and try to use the compromised key to compute additional keys, which might allow the attacker access to other secured communications.

Sniffer Attack

A *sniffer* is an application or device that can read, monitor, and capture network data exchanges and read network packets. If the packets are not encrypted, a sniffer provides a full view of the data inside the packet. Even encapsulated (tunneled) packets can be broken open and read unless they are encrypted *and* the attacker does not have access to the key.

Using a sniffer, an attacker can do any of the following:

- Analyze your network and gain information to eventually cause your network to crash or to become corrupted.

- Read your communications.

Application-Layer Attack

An application-layer attack targets application servers by deliberately causing a fault in a server's operating system or applications. This results in the attacker gaining the ability to bypass normal access controls. The attacker takes advantage of this situation, gaining control of your application, system, or network, and can do any of the following:

- Read, add, delete, or modify your data or operating system.

- Introduce a virus program that uses your computers and software applications to copy viruses throughout your network.

- Introduce a sniffer program to analyze your network and gain information that can eventually be used to crash or to corrupt your systems and network.

- Abnormally terminate your data applications or operating systems.

- Disable other security controls to enable future attacks.

Security Management

Information security management is the process by which the value of each of an organization's information assets is assessed and, if appropriate, protected on an ongoing basis. The information an organization holds will be stored, used and transmitted using various media, some of which will be tangible – paper, for example – and some intangible – such as the ideas in employees' minds. Preserving the value of information is mainly a question of protecting the media in which it is contained.

Building an information security management system (as we present it in this unit) is achieved through the systematic assessment of the systems, technologies and media used for information assets, the appraisal of the costs of security breaches, and the development and deployment of countermeasures to threats. Put simply, information security management recognizes the most vulnerable spots in an organization and builds armour plating to protect them.

The diversity of the media used for an organization's information assets is just one of the difficulties to be overcome in building an information security management system. Among other difficulties are the following.

- Effective information security measures often run counter to the mission of an organization. For instance, the safest way to secure a computer and the information on it is to allow no access to it at all!

- The requirement to respect the needs of the users of the organization's information, so that they can continue to do their jobs properly.

We can deduce that no single solution can address all possible security concerns. The only strategy is to engineer a fit-for-purpose solution that achieves a suitable balance between risks and protection against them.

As with all management systems, the engineering of a fit-for-purpose information security management system is achieved through hard work. Part of the hard work is, of course, an understanding of the technologies involved – we provide the necessary details in this unit. Other major tasks are identifying the needs of the different stakeholders and ensuring coverage of every procedure and policy that involves the development, transformation, or dissemination of sensitive information.

Thus, information security management is a development activity analogous to the development of software, and we shall present in this way throughout this unit.

Security Policies

In today's high-tech and interconnected world, every corporation needs a well thought out security policy. Threats exist from both within the walls of each enterprise as well as from external sources such as hackers, competitors, and foreign governments. The goal of corporate security policies is to define the procedures, guidelines, and practices for configuring and managing security in your environment. By enforcing corporate policy, corporations can minimize their risks and show due diligence to their customers and shareholders.

1. Where To Start

2. The first step toward implementing information security is to formulate a security policy. Identify the key assets to secure, and which assets will be extended to whom. The role of the policy is to guide users in knowing what is allowed, and to guide administrators and managers in making choices about system configuration and use. This process will help you establish specific security goals and a plan to tackle them. Before you can manage security you have to have a way to measure its effectiveness. Your corporate security policy provides the acceptable baseline standards against which to measure compliance.

3. There is no need to start from scratch. Rather than analyzing every risk, look at what others are doing. Meet standards of due care by using existing standards and industry "best practices". Pay attention to regulations and requirements from government, industry, and partners.

4. Some small organizations have the tendency to define security policy from the bottom up, starting with the capabilities of the tools at hand. Medium and large enterprises know that sound security policies begin from the top down.

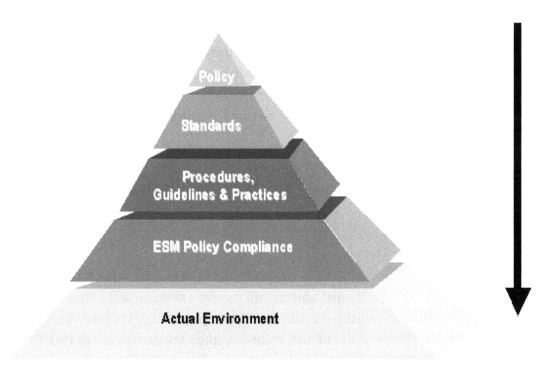

5. As the policy pyramid shows, the best security begins with upper management creating an actual policy or mandate to implement security. The policy should be based on industry standards and regulations such as ISO 17799 and HIPAA. Procedures,

guidelines, and practices form the basis for all security technology. Products such as ESM measure policy compliance with modules and policies for operating systems, databases, and applications. These then interact with the actual computer environment.

6. A thorough security policy doesn't stay static. It is a living document, changing with corporate needs. It evolves to guard against perceived threats and changing system architectures. Tools to implement and measure corporate security policy compliance exist in products like Symantec Enterprise Security Manager and Symantec NetRecon.

7. Organizations must also maintain a "best practice" level of compliance, in order to pass audits measured against standards and regulations.

8. III. Standards And Regulations

9. A host of information security standards and government regulations have been published over the years providing a great foundation for corporate security policy.

10. Standards are often based on user consensus or international adaptation. The ISO/IEC 17799 international standard is based on security requirements established by the British Government form BS 7799 Part I. Its stated purpose is to "give recommendations for information security management for use by those who are responsible for initiating, implementing or maintaining security in their organization". The Center for Internet Security (CIS) is an emerging worldwide standards consortium developing benchmarks to determine if minimum standards of due care are taken. The SANS/FBI Top 20 Internet Security Threats combines top 10 lists from multiple security vendors and experts.

11. Regulations are developed by U.S. and foreign governments to address specific industries such as finance and health care. HIPAA defines security and privacy standards for the health care industry. The Gramm-Leach-Bliley Act is legislation addressing financial services in the United States.

Measuring Security

Information security in an organization needs to be quantified to determine what level of security is implemented in the organization and what aspects still require attention, and to track the progress of the implementation of security measures. When implementing security, it is recommended that it should comply with internationally accepted standards such as ISO 17799 based on BS 7799 to ensure that the minimum controls are in place to provide a secure information system. It is, however, difficult to measure compliance with the standard. There are quite a few software products available, which an organization can use to assist them in implementing information security management. Proteus, CoP-It (the predecessor of Proteus) and COBRA are available products based on the BS 7799 standard. These packages make use of a questionnaire measuring the requirements indicated in the standard. Relevant reports are generated to interpret the results obtained through the audit, ranging from management summaries to indications of compliance and areas of improvement.

The questionnaires used in the products are comprehensive and in-depth, and they contain a great deal of detail on both management and technical concepts.

When implementing information security, it is important to understand that security does not only imply technical controls, but also management processes and business processes. These structures need to be in place to ensure that the detailed processes and technical controls will be implemented correctly and efficiently. Therefore, an organization should first measure its business processes and information security concepts on a high level before starting to implement firewalls everywhere. Having these processes in place will automatically lead to the implementation of the more technical and detailed controls.

Framework for measuring information security

When an organization initiates the process of implementing information security, or after the implementation has been done, there is a certain level of information security in the organization. This information security level will indicate the organization's position and what the organization still needs to do. The following model indicates the different progressive stages or levels through which an organization should go when implementing information security management

Standards

Standards for providing information system security become essential. Standards can define the scope of security functions and features needed, policies for managing information and human assets, criteria for evaluating the effectiveness of security measures, techniques for ongoing assessment of security and for the ongoing monitoring of security breaches, and procedures for dealing with security failures.

Below suggests the elements that, in an integrated fashion, constitute an effective approach to information security management. The focus of this approach is on two distinct aspects of providing information security: process and products. *Process security* looks at information security from the point of view of management policies, procedures, and controls. *Product security* focuses on technical aspects and is concerned with the use of certified products in the IT environment when possible. In Figure 1, the term *technical standards* refers to specifications that refer to aspects such as IT network security, digital signatures, access control, nonrepudiation, key management, and hash functions. Operational, management, and technical *procedures* encompass policies and practices that are defined and enforced by management. Examples include personnel screening policies, guidelines for classifying information, and procedures for assigning user IDs. *Management system audits, certification, and accreditation* deals with management policies and procedures for auditing and certifying information security products.

Codes of practice refer to specific policy standards that define the roles and responsibilities of various employees in maintaining information security. *Assurance* deals with product and system testing and evaluation. *Cultural, ethical, social, and legal issuers* refer to human factors aspects related to information security.

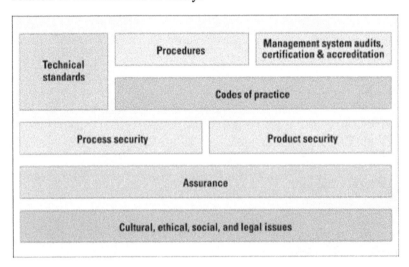

FIGURE 56 INFORMATION SECURITY MANAGEMENT ELEMENTS

Many standards and guideline documents have been developed in recent years to aid management in the area of information security. The two most important are ISO 17799, which deals primarily with process security, and the *Common Criteria,* which deals primarily with product security. This article surveys these two standards, and examines some other important standards and guidelines as well.

ISO 17799

An increasingly popular standard for writing and implementing security policies is ISO 17799 "Code of Practice for Information Security Management." (ISO 17799 will eventually be reissued as ISO 27002 in the new ISO 27000 family of security standards). ISO 17799 is a comprehensive set of controls comprising best practices in information security. It is essentially an internationally recognized generic information security standard. Table 1 summarizes the area covered by this standard and indicates the objectives for each area.

With the increasing interest in security, ISO 17799 certification, provided by various accredited bodies, has been established as a goal for many corporations, government agencies, and other organizations around the world. ISO 17799 offers a convenient framework to help security policy writers' structure their policies in accordance with an international standard.

Much of the content of ISO 17799 deals with security controls, which are defined as practices, procedures, or mechanisms that may protect against a threat, reduce vulnerability, limit the effect of an unwanted incident, detect unwanted incidents, and facilitate recovery. Some controls deal with security management, focusing on management actions to institute and maintain security policies. Other controls are operational; they address the correct implementation and use of security policies and standards, ensuring consistency in security operations and correcting identified operational deficiencies. These controls relate to mechanisms and procedures that are primarily implemented by people rather than systems.

Finally, there are technical controls; they involve the correct use of hardware and software security capabilities in systems. These controls range from simple to complex measures that work together to secure critical and sensitive data, information, and IT systems functions. This concept of controls cuts across all the areas listed in Table 1.

To give some idea of the scope of ISO 17799, we examine several of the security areas discussed in that document. *Auditing* is a key security management function that is addressed in multiple areas within the document. First, ISO 17799 lists key data items that should, when relevant, be included in an audit log:

- User IDs
- Dates, times, and details of key events, for example, log-on and log-off
- Records of successful and rejected system access attempts
- Records of successful and rejected data and other resource access attempts
- Changes to system configuration
- Use of privileges
- Use of system utilities and applications

- Files accessed and the kind of access

- Network addresses and protocols

- Alarms raised by the access control system

- Activation and deactivation of protection systems, such as antivirus systems and intrusion detection systems

It provides a useful set of guidelines for implementation of an auditing capability:

1. Audit requirements should be agreed upon by appropriate management.

2. The checks should be limited to read-only access to software and data.

3. Access other than read-only should be allowed only for isolated copies of system files, which should be erased when the audit is completed or given appropriate protection if there is an obligation to keep such files under audit documentation requirements.

4. Resources for performing the checks should be explicitly identified and made available.

5. Requirements for special or additional processing should be identified and agreed upon.

6. All access should be monitored and logged to produce a reference trail; the use of time stamped reference trails should be considered for critical data or systems.

7. All procedures, requirements, and responsibilities should be documented.

8. The person(s) carrying out the audit should be independent of the activities audited.

Under the area of communications and operations management, ISO 17799 includes *network security management*. One aspect of this management is concerned with network controls for networks owned and operated by the organization. The document provides implementation guidance for these in-house networks. An example of a control follows: Restoration procedures should be regularly checked and tested to ensure that they are effective and that they can be completed within the time allotted in the operational procedures for recovery. Similarly, the document provides guidance for security controls for network services provided by outside vendors. An example of guidance in this area follows: The ability of the network service provider to manage agreed-upon services in a secure way should be determined and regularly monitored, and the right to audit should be agreed upon.

As can be seen, some ISO 17700 specifications are detailed and specific, whereas others are quite general.

Risk and Threat Analysis

As information spreads, dependence on the information system, threats to assets, and vulnerability risks all increase, leaving organizations exposed to information leakage and attacks on the system security. The risk analysis process evaluates the risk of exposure to leakage and attack, and calculates the degree of risk. In other words, the risk analysis process is designed to diagnose the risks of organizations and prevent information leakage and security attacks. The process analyzes and evaluates the assets of organizations, the threats posed to those assets, the vulnerability of the assets, and security countermeasures, thereby contributing to reducing the risk level of organizations. The ultimate objectives of the risk analysis process are to consider the threats to the information system and assess the vulnerability of the information system and its asset value, to analyze and evaluate the asset risk level, to provide countermeasures for removing, accepting or avoiding risk, and, finally, to build a safe environment in which to operate the information system.

We defined a Threat as the coincidence of an Actor, Motivation, and an exploitable Vulnerability. We went on to define Risk as the product of a Threat, Probability, and Business Impact.

Let us start this article with a flow chart illustrating the relationship between some of the concepts in Risk Analysis. We show the corporation in the centre, the threats on the right and the countermeasures on the left. The residual risk exposure, shown at the bottom, is the risk introduced by the threats, but that isn't successfully avoided or mitigated. This residual risk must be accepted by the organization.

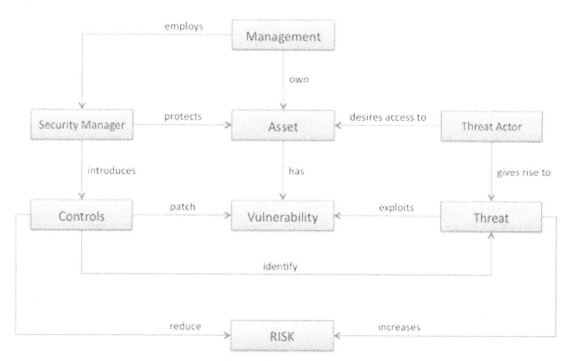

NIST SP800-30 sets out s series of steps that should be carried out during Risk Analysis (also known as Risk Assessment). The steps, shown below, are a hybrid of quantitative and qualitative analysis. Where quantities are known, they should be included, where threats, risks, or assets are subjective, scenarios should be developed. 'High / Med / Low' can be substituted for figures in both likelihood and impact assessments.

The output of a Risk Analysis is the current exposure of the organization and a proposal for the introduction of controls to mitigate some or all of that risk.

When conducting Quantitative Risk Analysis, a loss expectancy is calculated for each asset vulnerability. Each asset must be valued (AV), and the exposure (as a %) of that asset, given the particular vulnerability in question, must also be calculated. For example, confidential business plans worth £1m may cost only £200k to redevelop if they were lost in a fire. The exposure of this asset is therefore 20%. A single loss would cost the business £200,000.

SINGLE LOSS EXPECTANCY (SLE) = ASSET VALUE (AV) X EXPOSURE FACTOR (EF)

The business must then estimate the number of occurrences, annually, of this particular loss. This can be a whole number or a fraction if the event occurs less than once per year. The Annual Rate of Occurrence (ARO) can be predicted based on historical figures. It is essentially the balance of the adversary capability against the countermeasures (controls) put in place by the Security Manager.

Looking back at our flow chart, then, the Asset and Vulnerability are used to calculate the Single Loss Expectancy (SLE) and the Threat, Threat Actor, Controls and Security Manager can be used to estimate the Annual Rate of Occurrence (ARO).

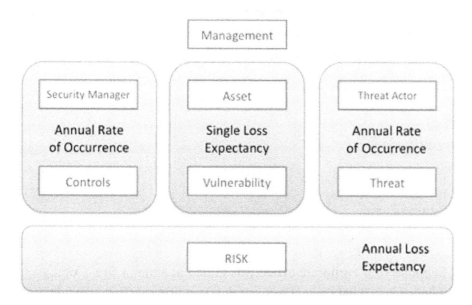

The final calculation – Annual Loss Expectancy (ALE) – is a numeric approximation of risk. It can be used to help the business decide whether the risk should be:

- avoided – through changing business process
- mitigated – through introduction of countermeasures
- accepted – because the cost of avoidance or mitigation outweighs the ALE

ANNUAL LOSS EXPECTANCY (ALE) = SINGLE LOSS EXPECTANCY (SLE) X ANNUAL RATE OF OCCURRENCE (ARO)

Countermeasures or Risk Avoidance measures should only be considered if the cost of adoption is less than the Annual Loss Expectancy for the particular threat. Risk transference (e.g. insurance) could also be considered though, again, if the cost is greater than the ALE, the organization should probably consider 'self-insuring', assuming it is legal to do so.

Identifying and Classifying Assets in Information Security.

The task of identifying assets that need to be protected is a less glamorous aspect of information security. But unless we know these assets, their locations and value, how are we going to decide the amount of time, effort or money that we should spend on securing the assets? In this series on Information Security Management System, we have so far discussed Security policy writing and Security organization structure. Security policy is essential, since it shows the management's commitment to the subject of information security, and establishes an outline giving clear direction in this matter. Security organization creates an administrative infrastructure defining roles and responsibilities of various participants who are entrusted with the responsibility of implementing and monitoring various aspects of information security.

The task of identifying assets that need to be protected is a less glamorous aspect of information security. But unless we know these assets, their locations and value, how are we going to decide the amount of time, effort or money that we should spend on securing the assets?

The major steps required for asset classification and controls are:

A. Identification of the assets

B. Accountability of assets

C. Preparing a schema for information classification

D. Implementing the classification schema

Identification of assets

What are the critical assets? Suppose your corporate office was gutted in a major fire. Coping with this level of disaster will depend on what critical information you previously backed up at a remote location. Another nightmarish scene is that a hacker entered your network and copied your entire customer database. What impact will this have on your business?

Identifying the critical assets is essential for many reasons. You will come to know what is critical and essential for the business. You will be able to take appropriate decisions regarding the level of security that should be provided to protect the assets. You will also be able to decide about the level of redundancy that is necessary by keeping an extra copy of the data or an extra server that you should procure and keep as a hot standby.

Next question that we need to ponder upon is: What exactly is an information asset? Is it the hardware, the software, the programs, or the database?

We can broadly classify assets in the following categories:

Information assets

Every piece of information about your organization falls in this category. This information has been collected, classified, organized and stored in various forms.

Databases: Information about your customers, personnel, production, sales, marketing, finances. This information is critical for your business. It's confidentiality, integrity and availability is of utmost importance.

Data files: Transactional data giving up-to-date information about each event.

Operational and support procedures: These have been developed over the years and provide detailed instructions on how to perform various activities.

Archived information: Old information that may be required to be maintained by law.

Continuity plans, fallback arrangements: These would be developed to overcome any disaster and maintain the continuity of business. Absence of these will lead to ad-hoc decisions in a crisis.

Software assets

These can be divided into two categories:

1. Application software: Application software implements business rules of the organization. Creation of application software is a time consuming task. Integrity of application software is very important. Any flaw in the application software could impact the business adversely.

2. System software: An organization would invest in various packaged software programs like operating systems, DBMS, development tools and utilities, software packages, office productivity suites etc.

Most of the software under this category would be available off the shelf, unless the software is obsolete or non-standard.

Physical assets

These are the visible and tangible equipment and could comprise of:

1. Computer equipment: Mainframe computers, servers, desktops and notebook computers.

2. Communication equipment: Modems, routers, EPABXs and fax machines.
   Storage media: Magnetic tapes, disks, CDs and DATs.

3. Technical equipment: Power supplies, air conditioners.
   Furniture and fixtures

Services

1. Computing services that the organization has outsourced.

2. Communication services like voice communication, data communication, value added services, wide area network etc.

3. Environmental conditioning services like heating, lighting, air conditioning and power.

Accountability of assets

The next step is to establish accountability of assets. This is not difficult for the tangible assets like physical assets. Usually the organization will have a fixed assets register maintained for the purpose of calculating depreciation.

A more difficult task is establishing ownership for the information assets. There will be a number of users for these assets. But the prime responsibility for accuracy will lie with the asset owner. Any addition or modification to the information asset will only be done with the consent of the asset owner. For example, any changes to customer information will be done with the knowledge and consent of the marketing head. Information technology staff will probably make the changes, physically. But ownership clearly lies with the business head who has the prime responsibility for the content in the customer database.

Using these criteria, we have to identify the actual owners of each of the information assets. This is also an important step for one more reason. Only an owner of the asset will be able to decide the business value of the asset. Unless the correct business value of the asset is known, we cannot identify the security requirement of the asset.

The next step is identifying owners of the application software. Application software implements the business rules. As such, the business process owner should be the owner of application software. However, the responsibility of maintaining application software to accurately reflect business rules will be vested with the application developers. As such, the accountability for application software should be with the application development manager.

System software ownership could be with the appropriate persons within the IT team. The owner of these assets will be responsible for maintaining all the system software including protecting the organization against software piracy.

Assets valuation

What is the value of an asset? Like beauty, which is in the eyes of the beholder, an asset's value is best known to the asset owner. It may not be merely the written down value. A more realistic measure is the replacement value. How much is it going to cost if the asset has to be acquired today? Accurate valuation of an information asset is a tricky task. Due care must be taken. A seemingly small item may be immensely difficult to replace today.

True value of the asset will lead us to identify realistic measures needed for protection of the asset.

Preparing a schema for classification

The next task is to create classification levels. The criteria for the classification of assets could be:

1. Confidentiality: Can the information be freely distributed? Alternatively, do we need to restrict it to certain identified individuals?

2. Value: What is the asset value? Is it a high value item, costly to replace or a low value item?

3. Time: Is the information time sensitive? Will its confidentiality status change after some time?

4. Access rights: Who will have access to the asset?

5. Destruction: How long the information will be stored? How can it be destroyed, if necessary?

Each asset needs to be evaluated against the above criteria and classified for easy identification. Let us look at each category for classification.

Confidentiality could be defined in terms of:

- **Confidential**: Where the access is restricted to a specific list of people. These could be company plans, secret manufacturing processes, formulas, etc.

- **Company only**: Where the access is restricted to internal employees only. These could be customer databases, manufacturing procedures, etc.

- **Shared**: Where the resources are shared within groups or with people outside of the organization. This could be operational information and contact information like the internal telephone book to be shared with business partners and agents.

- **Unclassified**: Where the resources are publicly accessible. For example, the company sales brochure and other publicity material.

Classification based on value could be high, medium or low value. A detailed explanation should be prepared giving the reasoning for this classification. A critical component costing a few rupees may be a very high value item as it is not easily available and could stop the production of a high cost item.

Access rights need to be defined for individuals as well as groups. Who is cleared to access confidential information in the organization? And who decides the access rights? Logically, it will be the asset owner who will decide these access rights.

Destruction should be a scheduled and controlled activity. The information that is no longer needed by the company but which could still be useful to competitors, should be destroyed as per a pre-decided schedule and method—depending on the confidentiality classification. For information recorded on hard disk, mere deletion of files does not obliterate information. A more stringent procedure like multiple overwriting may be needed.

Classification schema should lead to an implementable structure. It should be simple to understand and identify.

Implementation of the classification schema

The real test of classification schema is when it is implemented. Information is a fluid resource. It keeps changing its form. The implementation should lead to a uniform way of identifying the information so that a uniform protection could be provided.

Let us take an example. A company's business plan is a confidential document. Let us trace its journey in the corporate world.

The plan will be discussed behind closed doors, known to only a few senior members. In the next step the final plan will be prepared and stored on the MD's computer or that of his secretary. A soft copy of this plan would be sent by email to all executives who need to refer to it. The hard disk of every computer where the plan is stored will also have a backup copy on floppy or other media. Each member will no doubt print it and keep a hard copy folder for reference. An extra copy will also be prepared using the copying machine. If the email is not available, the plan would be sent by fax, post or courier.

So the 'confidential' plan is now distributed across the organization, available on the hard disks of computers belonging to each secretary and each senior executive. You get the general idea. If this can happen to confidential information, imagine how easy it is to get hold of other types of information. The information explosion has given rise to proliferation of information in every nook and corner of the organization.

A practical implementation of classification schema thus becomes very important. The classification label should not give an easy way of identification, which could be misused. It should provide the right amount of protection.

In the example given above, each asset where the confidential information is residing or transiting through will have to be given the same classification level as that of the information itself.

It may be desirable to avoid transmission of confidential documents in soft copy format, for example as an attachment to email. Only a restricted number of hard copies should be circulated. If it is necessary to carry the soft copies, everyone should be instructed to encrypt information for transmission and storage, and to memorize their passwords and keep them secret.

Asset classification is thus the key to various security controls that need to be implemented for asset protection.

Vulnerabilities:

Vulnerability is a weak spot in your network that might be exploited by a security threat. Risks are the potential consequences and impacts of unaddressed vulnerabilities. In other words, failing to do Windows Updates on your Web server is vulnerability. Some of the risks associated with that vulnerability include loss of data, hours or days of site downtime and the staff time needed to rebuild a server after it's been compromised.   Network vulnerabilities are present in every system. Network technology advances so rapidly that it can be very difficult to eradicate vulnerabilities altogether; the best one can hope for, in many cases, is simply to minimize them. Networks are vulnerable to slowdowns due to both internal and external factors. Internally, networks can be affected by overextension and bottlenecks, external threats, DoS/DDoS attacks, and network data interception. The execution of arbitrary commands can lead to system malfunction, slowed performance, and even failure. Indeed, total system failure is the largest threat caused by a compromised system-understanding possible vulnerabilities is critical for administrators.

Internal network vulnerabilities result from overextension of bandwidth (user needs exceeding total resources) and bottlenecks (user needs exceeding resources in specific network sectors). These problems can be addressed by network management systems and utilities such as traceroute, which allow administrators to pinpoint the location of network slowdowns. Traffic can then be rerouted within the network architecture to increase speed and functionality.

External Network Vulnerabilities

DoS and DDoS are external attacks as the result of one attack or a number of coordinated attacks, respectively. Designed to slow down or disable networks altogether, these attacks are among the most serious threats that networks face. Administrators must use tools to monitor network performance in order to catch these threats as soon as possible. Many monitoring systems are configured to send alarms or alerts to administrators when such attacks occur, allowing for network access by intruders to be quickly terminated.

Data interception is another of the most common network vulnerabilities, for both LANs and WLANs. Hackers within range of a WLAN workstation can infiltrate a secure session, and monitor or change the network data for the purpose of accessing sensitive information or altering the operation of the network. User authentication systems are used to keep such interception from occurring. Firewalls can keep unauthorized users from accessing the network in the first place, while base station discovery scans allow for the rooting out of intruders on a given network

ATTACKS:

A *network attack* can be defined as any method, process, or means used to maliciously attempt to compromise network security. There are a number of reasons that an individual(s) would want to attack corporate networks. The individuals performing network attacks are commonly referred to as *network attackers, hackers, or crackers.*

TYPES OF ATTACK:

Classes of attack might include passive monitoring of communications, active network attacks, close-in attacks, exploitation by insiders, and attacks through the service provider. Information systems and networks offer attractive targets and should be resistant to attack from the full range of threat agents, from hackers to nation-states. A system must be able to limit damage and recover rapidly when attacks occur.
There are five types of attack:

PASSIVE ATTACK

A **passive attack** monitors unencrypted traffic and looks for clear-text passwords and sensitive information that can be used in other types of attacks. **Passive attacks** include traffic analysis, monitoring of unprotected communications, decrypting weakly encrypted traffic, and capturing authentication information such as passwords. Passive interception of network operations enables adversaries to see upcoming actions. Passive attacks result in the disclosure of information or data files to an attacker without the consent or knowledge of the user.

ACTIVE ATTACK

In an **active attack,** the attacker tries to bypass or break into secured systems. This can be done through stealth, viruses, worms, or Trojan horses. Active attacks include attempts to circumvent or break protection features, to introduce malicious code, and to steal or modify information. These attacks are mounted against a network backbone, exploit information in transit, electronically penetrate an enclave, or attack an authorized remote user during an attempt to connect to an enclave. Active attacks result in the disclosure or dissemination of data files, DoS, or modification of data.

DISTRIBUTED ATTACK

A **distributed attack** requires that the adversary introduce code, such as a Trojan horse or back-door program, to a "trusted" component or software that will later be distributed to many other companies and users Distribution attacks focus on the malicious modification of hardware or software at the factory or during distribution. These attacks introduce malicious code such as a back door to a product to gain unauthorized access to information or to a system function at a later date.

INSIDER ATTACK

An **insider attack** involves someone from the inside, such as a disgruntled employee, attacking the network Insider attacks can be malicious or no malicious. Malicious insiders intentionally eavesdrop, steal, or damage information; use information in a fraudulent manner; or deny access to other authorized users. No malicious attacks typically result from carelessness, lack of knowledge, or intentional circumvention of security for such reasons as performing a task

CLOSE-IN ATTACK

A **close-in attack** involves someone attempting to get physically close to network components, data, and systems in order to learn more about a network Close-in attacks consist of regular individuals attaining close physical proximity to networks, systems, or facilities for the purpose of modifying, gathering, or denying access to information. Close physical proximity is achieved through surreptitious entry into the network, open access, or both.

One popular form of close in attack is **social engineering** in a social engineering attack, the attacker compromises the network or system through social interaction with a person, through an e-mail message or phone. Various tricks can be used by the individual to revealing information about the security of company. The information that the victim reveals to the hacker would most likely be used in a subsequent attack to gain unauthorized access to a system or network.

PHISHING ATTACK

In phishing attack the hacker creates a fake web site that looks exactly like a popular site such as the SBI bank or paypal. The phishing part of the attack is that the hacker then sends an e-mail message trying to trick the user into clicking a link that leads to the fake site. When the user attempts to log on with their account information, the hacker records the username and password and then tries that information on the real site.

HIJACK ATTACK

Hijack attack In a hijack attack, a hacker takes over a session between you and another individual and disconnects the other individual from the communication. You still believe that you are talking to the original party and may send private information to the hacker by accident.

SPOOF ATTACK

Spoof attack In a spoof attack, the hacker modifies the source address of the packets he or she is sending so that they appear to be coming from someone else. This may be an attempt to bypass your firewall rules.

BUFFER OVERFLOW

Buffer overflow A buffer overflow attack is when the attacker sends more data to an application than is expected. A buffer overflow attack usually results in the attacker gaining administrative access to the system in a command prompt or shell.

Exploit attack

Exploit attack In this type of attack, the attacker knows of a security problem within an operating system or a piece of software and leverages that knowledge by exploiting the vulnerability.

PASSWORD ATTACK

Password attack An attacker tries to crack the passwords stored in a network account database or a password-protected file. There are three major types of password attacks: a dictionary attack, a brute-force attack, and a hybrid attack. A dictionary attack uses a word list file, which is a list of potential passwords. A brute-force attack is when the attacker tries every possible combination of characters.

Network attacks can be classified into the following four types:

1. Internal threats

2. External threats

3. Unstructured threats

4. Structured threats

Threats to the network can be initiated from a number of different sources, hence the reason for network attacks being classified as either external or internal network attacks/threats:

- *External threats:* Individuals carry out external threats or network attacks without assistance from internal employees or contractors. A malicious and experienced individual, a group of experienced individuals, an experienced malicious organization, or inexperienced attackers (script kiddies) carry out these attacks. Such attackers usually have a predefined plan and the technologies (tools) or techniques to carry out the attack. One of the main characteristics of external threats is that they usually involve scanning and gathering information. Users can therefore detect an external attack by scrutinizing existing firewall logs. Users can also install anIntrusion Detection System to quickly identify external threats.

External threats can be further categorized into either structured threats or unstructured threats:

- *Structured external threats:* These threats originate from a malicious individual, a group of malicious individual(s), or a malicious organization. Structured threats are usually initiated from network attackers that have a premeditated thought on the actual damages and losses that they want to cause. Possible motives for structured external threats include greed, politics, terrorism, racism, and criminal payoffs. These attackers are highly skilled on network design, avoiding security measures, Intrusion Detection Systems (IDSs), access procedures, and hacking tools. They have the necessary skills to develop new network attack techniques and the ability to modify existing hacking tools for their exploitations. In certain cases, an internal authorized individual may assist the attacker.

- *Unstructured external threats:* These threats originate from an inexperienced attacker, typically from a script kiddie. Script kiddie refers to an inexperienced attacker who uses cracking tools or scripted tools readily available on the Internet to perform a network attack. Script kiddies are usually inadequately skilled to create the threats on their own. They can be considered bored individuals seeking some form of fame by attempting to crash websites and other public targets on the Internet.

External attacks can also occur either remotely or locally:

- *Remote external attacks:* These attacks are usually aimed at the services that an organization offers to the public. The various forms that remote external attacks can take are:

- Remote attacks aimed at the services available for internal users. This remote attack usually occurs when there is no firewall solution implemented to protect these internal services.

- Remote attacks aimed at locating modems to access the corporate network.

- Denial of service (DoS) attacks to place an exceptional processing load on servers in an attempt to prevent authorized user requests from being serviced.

- War dialing of the corporate private branch exchange (PBX).

- Attempts to brute force password authenticated systems.

- *Local external attacks:* These attacks typically originate from situations where computing facilities are shared and access to the system can be obtained.

- *Internal threats:* Internal attacks originate from dissatisfied or unhappy inside employees or contractors. Internal attackers have some form of access to the system and usually try to hide their attack as a normal process. For instance, internal disgruntled employees have local access to some resources on the internal network already. They could also have some administrative rights on the network. One of the best means to protect against internal attacks is to implement an IntrusionDetection System and to configure it to scan for both external and internal attacks. All forms of attacks should be logged and the logs should be reviewed and followed up.

With respect to network attacks, the core components that should be included when users design network security are:

- Network attack prevention
- Network attack detection
- Network attack isolation
- Network attack recovery

What is Hacking?

The term hacking initially referred to the process of finding solutions to rather technical issues or problems. These days, hacking refers to the process whereby intruders maliciously attempt to compromise the security of corporate networks to destroy, interpret, or steal confidential data or to prevent an organization from operating.

Terminologies that refer to criminal hacking:

- Cracking
- Cybercrime
- Cyberespionage
- Phreaking

To access a network system, the intruder (hacker) performs a number of activities:

- *Footprinting:* This is basically the initial step in hacking a corporate network. Here the intruder attempts to gain as much information on the targeted network by using sources that the public can access. The aim of footprinting is to create a map of the network to determine what operating systems, applications, and address ranges are being utilized and to identify any accessible open ports.

The *methods used to footprint a network* are:

- Access information publicly available on the company website to gain any useful information.
- Try to find any anonymous File Transfer Protocol (FTP) sites and intranet sites that are not secured.

- Gather information on the company's domain name and the IP address block being used.

- Test for hosts in the network's IP address block. Tools such as Ping or Flping are typically used.

- Using tools such as Nslookup, the intruder attempts to perform Domain Name System (DNS) zone transfers.

- A tool such as Nmap is used to find out what the operating systems are that are being used.

- Tools such as Tracert are used to find routers and to collect subnet information.

- *Port scanning:* Port scanning or scanning is when intruders collect information on the network services on a target network. Here, the intruder attempts to find open ports on the target system.
  The *different scanning methods* that network attackers use are:

- Vanilla scan/SYNC scan: TCP SYN packets are sent to each address port in an attempt to connect to all ports. Port numbers 0 – 65,535 are utilized.

- Strobe scan: Here, the attacker attempts to connect to a specific range of ports that are typically open on Windows based hosts or UNIX/Linux based hosts.

- Sweep: A large set of IP addresses are scanned in an attempt to detect a system that has one open port.

- Passive scan: Here, all network traffic entering or leaving the network is captured and traffic is then analyzed to determine what the open ports are on the hosts within the network.

- User Datagram Protocol (UDP) scan: Empty UDP packets are sent to the different ports of a set of addresses to determine how the operating responds. Closed UDP ports respond with the Port Unreachable message when any empty UDP packets are received. Other operating systems respond with the Internet Control Message Protocol (ICMP) error packet.

- FTP bounce: To hide the attacker's location, the scan is initiated from an intermediary File Transfer Protocol (FTP) server.

- FIN scan: TCP FIN packets that specify that the sender wants to close a TCP session are sent to each port for a range of IP addresses.

- *Enumeration:* The unauthorized intruder uses a number of methods to collect information on applications and hosts on the network and on the user accounts utilized on the network. Enumeration is particularly successful in networks that contain unprotected network resources and services:

- Network services that are running but are not being utilized.

- Default user accounts that have no passwords specified.

- Guest accounts those are active.

- *Acquiring access:* Access attacks are performed when an attacker exploits a security weakness so that he/she can obtain access to a system or the network. Trojan horses and password hacking programs are typically used to obtain system access. When access is obtained, the intruder is able to modify or delete data and add, modify, or remove network resources.
  The different types of access attacks are:

- *Unauthorized system access* entails the practice of exploiting the vulnerabilities of operating systems or executing a script or a hacking program to obtain access to a system.

- *Unauthorized privilege escalation* is a frequent type of attack. Privilege escalation occurs when an intruder attempts to obtain a high level of access, like administrative privileges, to gain control of the network system.

- *Unauthorized data manipulation* involves interpreting, altering, and deleting confidential data.

- *Privilege escalation:* When an attacker initially gains access to the network, low level accounts are typically used. Privilege escalation occurs when an attacker escalates his/her privileges to obtain a higher level of access, like administrative privileges, in order to gain control of the network system.
  The *privilege escalation methods* that attackers use are:

- The attacker searches the registry keys for password information.

- The attacker can search documents for information on administrative privileges.

- The attacker can execute a password cracking tool on targeted user accounts.

- The attacker can use a Trojan in an attempt to obtain the credentials of a user account that has administrative privileges.

- *Install backdoors:* A hacker can also implement a mechanism such as some form of access granting code with the intent of using it at some future stage. Attackers typically install back doors so that they can easily access the system later. After a system is compromised, users can remove any installed backdoors by reinstalling the system from a backup that is secure.

- *Removing evidence of activities:* Attackers typically attempt to remove all evidence of their activities.

What are Hackers or Network Attackers?

A hacker or network attacker is someone who maliciously attacks networks, systems, computers, and applications and captures, corrupts, modifies, steals, or deletes confidential company information.

A hacker can refer to a number of different individuals who perform activities aimed at hacking systems and networks and it can also refer to individuals who perform activities that have nothing to do with criminal activity:

- Programmers who hack complex technical problems to come up with solutions.

- Script kiddies who use readily available tools on the Internet to hack into systems.

- Criminal hackers who steal or destroy company data.

- Protesting activists who deny access to specific Web sites as part of their protesting strategy.

Hackers these days are classified according to the hat they wear. This concept is illustrated below:

- ***Black hat hackers*** are malicious or criminal hackers who hack at systems and computers to damage data or who attempt to prevent businesses from rendering their services. Some black hat hackers simply hack security protected systems to gain prestige in the hacking community.

- ***White hat hackers*** are legitimate security experts who are trying to expose security vulnerabilities in operating system platforms. White hat hackers have the improvement of security as their motive. They do not damage or steal company data nor do they seek any fame. These security experts are usually quite knowledgeable about the hacking methods that black hat hackers use.

- ***Grey hat hacker:*** These are individuals who have motives between that of black hat hackers and white hat hackers.

The Common Types of Network Attacks

While there are many different types of network attacks, a few can be regarded as the more commonly performed network attacks. These network attacks are discussed in this section of the Article:

- *Data modification or data manipulation* pertains to a network attack where confidential company data is interpreted, deleted, or modified. Data modification is successful when data is modified without the sender actually being aware that it was tampered with. A few methods of preventing attacks aimed at compromising data integrity are listed here:

- Use digital signatures to ensure that data has not been modified while it is being transmitted or simply stored.

- Implement access control lists (ACLs) to control which users are allowed to access your data.

- Regularly back up important data.

- Include specific code in applications that can validate data input.

- *Eavesdropping:* This type of network attack occurs when an attacker monitors or listens to network traffic in transit then interprets all unprotected data. While users need specialized equipment and access to the telephone company switching facilities to eavesdrop on telephone conversations, all they need to eavesdrop on an Internet Protocol (IP) based network is a sniffer technology to capture the traffic being transmitted. This is basically due to the Transmission Control Protocol/Internet Protocol (TCP/IP) being an open architecture that transmits unencrypted data over the network.
  A few methods of preventing intruders from eavesdropping on the network are:

- Implement Internet Protocol Security (IPSec) to secure and encrypt IP data before it is sent over the network.

- Implement security policies and procedures to prevent attackers from attaching a sniffer on the network.

- Install anti-virus software to protect the corporate network from Trojans. Trojans are typically used to discover and capture sensitive, valuable information such as user credentials.

- *IP address spoofing/IP spoofing/identity spoofing:* IP address spoofing occurs when an attacker assumes the source Internet Protocol (IP) address of IP packets to make it appear as though the packet originated from a valid IP address. The aim of an IP address spoofing attack is to identify computers on a network. Most IP networks utilize the user's IP address to verify identities and routers also typically ignore source IP addresses when routing packets. Routers use the destination IP addresses to forward packets to the intended destination network.
  These factors could enable an attacker to bypass a router and to launch a number of subsequent attacks, including:

- Initiation of a denial of service (DoS) attacks.

- Initiation of man in the middle (MITM) attacks to hijack sessions.

- Redirect traffic.

A few methods of preventing IP address spoofing attacks are:

- Encrypt traffic between routers and external hosts

- Define ingress filters on routers and firewalls to stop inbound traffic where the source address is from a trusted host on the internal network

- *Sniffer attacks:* Sniffing refers to the process that attackers use to capture and analyze network traffic. The packets' contents on a network are analyzed. The tools that attackers use for sniffing are called sniffers or more correctly, protocol analyzers. While protocol analyzers are really network troubleshooting tools, hackers also use them for malicious purposes. Sniffers monitor, capture, and obtain network information such as passwords and valuable customer information. When an individual has physical access to a network, he/she can easily attach a protocol analyzer to the network and then capture traffic. Remote sniffing can also be performed and network attackers typically use them. There are protocol analyzers or sniffers available for most networking technologies including:

- Asynchronous Transfer Mode (ATM)

- Ethernet

- Fiber Channel

- Serial connections

- Small Computer System Inter-face (SCSI)

- Wireless

There are a number of common sniffers that network security administrators and malicious hackers use:

- Dsniff

- Ethereal

- Etherpeek

- Network Associates's Sniffer

- Ngrep

- Sniffit

- Snort

- Tcpdump

- Windump

To protect against sniffers, implement Internet Protocol Security (IPSec) to encrypt network traffic so that any captured information cannot be interpreted.

- *Password attacks:* Password based attacks or password crackers are aimed at guessing the password for a system until the correct password is determined. One of the primary security weaknesses associated with password based access control is that all security is based on the user ID and password being utilized. But who is the individual using the credentials at the keyboard? Some of the older applications do not protect password information. The password information is simply sent in clear or plain text – no form of encryption is utilized! Remember that network attackers can obtain user ID and password information and can then pose as authorized users and attack the corporate network. Attackers can use dictionary attacks or brute force attacks to gain access to resources with the same rights as the authorized user. A big threat would be present if the user has some level of administrative rights to certain portions of the network. An even bigger threat would exist if the same password credentials are used for all systems. The attacker would then have access to a number of systems.
Password based attacks are performed in two ways:

- *Online cracking:* The network attacker sniffs network traffic to seize authentication sessions in an attempt to capture password based information. There are tools that are geared at sniffing out passwords from traffic.

- *Offline cracking:* The network attacker gains access to a system with the intent of gaining access to password information. The attacker then runs some password cracker technology to decipher valid user account information.

A *dictionary attack* occurs when all the words typically used for passwords are attempted to detect a password match. There are some technologies that can generate a number of complex word combinations and variations.
Modern operating systems only store passwords in an encrypted format. To obtain password credentials, users have to have administrative credentials to access the system and information. Operating systems these days also support password policies. Password policies define how passwords are managed and define the characteristics of passwords that are considered acceptable.

Password policy settings can be used to specify and enforce a number of rules for passwords:

1. Define whether passwords are simple or complex

2. Define whether password history is maintained

3. Define the minimum length for passwords

4. Define the minimum password age

5. Define the maximum password age

6. Define whether passwords are stored with reversible encryption or irreversible encryption

Account lockout policies should be implemented if the environment is particularly vulnerable to threats arising from passwords that are being guessed. Implementing an account lockout policy ensures that the user's account is locked after an individual has unsuccessfully tried for several times to provide the correct password. The important factor to remember when defining an account lockout policy is that a policy that permits some degree of user error, but that also prevents hackers from using the user accounts should be implemented.

The following password and account lockout settings are located in the Account Lockout Policy area in Account Policies:

- Account lockout threshold: This setting controls the number of times after which an incorrect password attempt results in the account being locked out of the system.

- Account lockout duration: This setting controls the duration that an account that is locked remains locked. A setting of 0 means that an administrator has to manually unlock the locked account.

- Reset account lockout counter after: This setting determines the time duration that must pass subsequent to an invalid logon attempt occurring prior to the reset account lockout counter being reset.

- *Brute force attack:* Brute force attacks simply attempt to decode a cipher by trying each possible key to find the correct one. This type of network attack systematically uses all possible alpha, numeric, and special character key combinations to find a password that is valid for a user account. Brute force attacks are also typically used to compromise networks that utilize Simple Mail Transfer Protocol (SNMP). Here, the network attacker initiates a brute force attack to find the SNMP community names so that he/she can outline the devices and services running on the network.

A few methods of preventing brute force attacks are listed here:

- Enforce the use of long password strings.

- For SNMP, use long, complex strings for community names.

- Implement an intrusion detection system (IDS). By examining traffic patterns, an IDS is capable of detecting when brute force attacks are underway.

Denial of Service (DoS) attack: A DoS attack is aimed at preventing authorized, legitimate users from accessing services on the network. The DoS attack is not aimed at gathering or collecting data. It is aimed at preventing authorized, legitimate users from using computers or the network normally. The SYN flood from 1996 was the earliest form of a DoS attack that exploited Transmission Control Protocol (TCP) vulnerability. A DoS attack can be initiated by sending invalid data to applications or network services until the server hangs or simply crashes. The most common form of a DoS attack is TCP attacks.

DoS attacks can use either of the following methods to prevent authorized users from using the network services, computers, or applications:

- Flood the network with invalid data until traffic from authorized network users cannot be processed.

- Flood the network with invalid network service requests until the host providing that particular service cannot process requests from authorized network users. The network would eventually become overloaded.

- Disrupt communication between hosts and clients through either of the following methods:

- Modification of system configurations.

- Physical network destruction. Crashing a router, for instance, would prevent users from accessing the system.

There are a number of tools easily accessible and available on the Internet that can initiate DoS attacks:

- Bonk

- LAND

- Smurf

- Teardrop

- WinNuke

A network attacker can increase the enormity of a DoS attack by initiating the attack against a single network from multiple computers or systems. This type of attack is known as a *distributed denial of service (DDoS) attack*. Network administrators can experience great difficulty in fending off DDoS attacks, simply because blocking all the attacking computers can also result in blocking authorized users.

The following measures can be implemented to protect a network against DoS attacks:

- Implement and enforce strong password policies

- Back up system configuration data regularly

- Disable or remove all unnecessary network services

- Implement disk quotas for user and service accounts.

- Configure filtering on the routers and patch operating systems.

The following measures can be implemented to protect a network against DDoS attacks:

- Limit the number of ICMP and SYN packets on router interfaces.

- Filter private IP addresses using router access control lists.

- Apply ingress and egress filtering on all edge routers.

Man in the middle (MITM) attack: A man in the middle (MITM) attack occurs when a hacker eavesdrops on a secure communication session and monitors, captures, and controls the data being sent between the two parties communicating. The attacker attempts to obtain information so that he/she can impersonate the receiver and sender communicating.

For an MITM attack to be successful, the following sequence of events has to occur:

- The hacker must be able to obtain access to the communication session to capture traffic when the receiver and sender establish the secure communication session.

- The hacker must be able to capture the messages being sent between the parties and then send messages so that the session remains active.

There are some public key cryptography systems such as the Diffie-Hellman (DH) key exchange that are rather susceptible to man in the middle attacks. This is due to the Diffie-Hellman (DH) key exchange using no authentication.

What are Viruses?

A virus is a malicious code that affects and infects system files. Numerous instances of the files are then recreated. Viruses usually lead to some sort of data loss and/or system failure.

There are numerous methods by which a virus can get into a system:

1. Through infected floppy disks

2. Through an e-mail attachment infected with the virus

3. Through downloading software infected with the virus

A few *common types of viruses* are:

1. *Boot sector viruses:* These are viruses that infect a hard drive's master boot record. The virus is then loaded into memory whenever the system starts or is rebooted.

2. *File viruses or program viruses or parasitic viruses:* These are viruses that are attached to executable programs. Whenever the particular program is executed, the viruses are loaded into memory.

3. *Multipartite viruses:* These are viruses that are a combination of a boot sector virus and a file virus.

4. *Macro viruses:* These are viruses that are written in macro languages that applications use, of which Microsoft Word is one. Macro viruses usually infect systems through e-mail.

5. *Polymorphic viruses:* These viruses can be considered the more difficult viruses to defend against because they can modify their code. Virus protection software often find polymorphic viruses harder to detect and remove.

If a virus infects a system, use the recommendations listed here:

- Scan each system to gauge how infected the infrastructure is.

- To prevent the virus from spreading any further, immediately disconnect all infected systems.

- All infected systems should be installed from a clean backup copy, that is, a back up taken when the system was clean from virus infections.

- Inform the anti-virus vendor so that the vendor's virus signature database is updated accordingly.

A few *methods of protecting network infrastructure against viruses* are:

1. Install virus protection software on systems

2. Regularly update all installed virus protection software

3. Regularly back up systems after they have been scanned for viruses and are considered clean from virus infection.

4. Users should be educated to not open any e-mail attachments that were sent from individuals they do not recognize.

What are Worms?

As mentioned previously, a virus is a malicious code that infects files on the system. A worm on the other hand is an autonomous code that spreads over a network, targeting hard drive space and processor cycles. Worms not only infect files on one system, but spread to other systems on the network. The purpose of a worm is to deplete available system resources. Hence the reason for a worm repeatedly making copies of itself. Worms basically make copies of themselves or replicate until available memory is used, bandwidth is unavailable, and legitimate network users are no longer able to access network resources or services.

There are a few worms that are sophisticated enough to corrupt files, render systems un-operational, and even steal data. These worms usually have one or numerous viral codes.

A few previously encountered worms are:

- Te *ADMw0rm worm* took advantage of a buffer overflow in Berkeley Internet Name Domain (BIND).

- The *Code Red worm* utilized a buffer overflow vulnerability in Microsoft Internet Information Services (IIS) version 4 and IIS version 5.

- The *LifeChanges worm* exploited a Microsoft Windows weakness, which allowed scrap shell files to be utilized for running arbitrary code.

- The *LoveLetter worm* used a Visual Basic Script to replicate or mass mail itself to all individuals in the Windows address book.

- The *Melissa worm* utilized a Microsoft Outlook and Outlook Express vulnerability to mass mail itself to all individuals in the Windows address book.

- The *Morris worm* exploited a Sendmail debug mode vulnerability.

- The *Nimda worm* managed to run e-mail attachments in Hypertext Markup Language (HTML) messages through the exploitation of HTML IFRAME tag.

- The *Slapper worm* exploited an Apache Web server platform buffer overflow vulnerability.

- The *Slammer worm* exploited a buffer overflow vulnerability on unpatched machines running Microsoft SQL Server.

What are Trojan Horses?

A Trojan horse or Trojan is a file or e-mail attachment disguised as a friendly, legitimate file. When executed though, the file corrupts data and can even install a backdoor that hackers can utilize to access the network.

A Trojan horse differs from a virus or worm in the following ways:

1. Trojan horses disguise themselves as friendly programs. Viruses and worms are much more obvious in their actions.

2. Trojan horses do not replicate like worms and viruses do.

A few *different types of Trojan horses* are listed here:

- *Keystroke loggers* monitor the keystrokes that a user types and then e-mails the information to the network attacker.

- *Password stealers* are disguised as legitimate login screens that wait for users to provide their passwords so that hackers can steal them. Password stealers are aimed at discovering and stealing system passwords for hackers.

- *Hackers use Remote administration tools (RATs)* to gain control over the network from some remote location.

- *Zombies* are typically used to initiate distributed denial of service (DDoS) attacks on the hosts within a network.

Predicting Network Threats

To protect network infrastructure, users need to be able to predict the types of network threats to which it is vulnerable. This should include an analysis of the risks that each identified network threat imposes on the network infrastructure.

Security experts use a model known as STRIDE to classify network threats:

- **S***poofing identity:* These are attacks that are aimed at obtaining user account information. Spoofing identity attacks typically affect data confidentiality.

- **T***ampering with data:* These are attacks that are aimed at modifying company information. Data tampering usually ends up affecting the integrity of data. A man-in-the-middle attack is a form of data tampering.

- **R***epudiation:* Repudiation takes place when a user performs some form of malicious action on a resource and then later denies carrying out that particular activity. Network administrators usually have no evidence to back up their suspicions.

- **I***nformation disclosure:* Here, private and confidential information is made available to individuals who should not have access to the particular information. Information disclosure usually impacts data confidentiality and network resource confidentiality.

- **D***enial of service:* These attacks affect the availability of company data and network resources and services. DoS attacks are aimed at preventing legitimate users from accessing network resources and data.

- *Elevation of privilege:* Elevation of privilege occurs when an attacker escalates his/her privileges to obtain a high level of access like administrative privileges, in an attempt to gain control of the network system.

Identifying Threats to DHCP Implementations

A few threats specific to DHCP implementations are:

- Because the IP address number in a DHCP scope is limited, an unauthorized user could initiate a denial of service (DoS) attack by requesting or obtaining a large numbers of IP addresses.

- A network attacker could use a rogue DHCP server to offer incorrect IP addresses to DHCP clients.

- A denial of service (DoS) attack can be launched through an unauthorized user performing a large number of DNS dynamic updates via the DHCP server.

- Assigning DNS IP addresses and WINS IP addresses through the DHCP server increases the possibility of hackers using this information to attack DNS and WINS servers.

To protect a DHCP environment from network attacks, use the following strategies:

1. Implement firewalls

2. Close all open unused ports

3. If necessary, use VPN tunnels

4. Use MAC address filters

Identifying Threats to DNS Implementations

A few threats specific to DNS implementations:

- Denial of service (DoS) attacks occur when DNS servers are flooded with recursive queries in an attempt to prevent the DNS server from servicing legitimate client requests for name resolution. A successful DoS attack can result in the unavailability of DNS services and eventual network shut down.

- In DNS, footprinting occurs when an intruder intercepts DNS zone information. When the intruder has this information, he/she is able to discover DNS domain names, computer names, and IP addresses being used on the network. The intruder then uses this information to decide which computers he/she wants to attack.

- IP Spoofing: After an intruder has obtained a valid IP address from a footprinting attack, he/she can use the IP address to send malicious packets to the network or access network services. The intruder can also use the valid IP address to modify data.

- In DNS, a redirection attack occurs when an intruder is able to make the DNS server forward or redirect name resolution requests to the incorrect servers. In this case, the incorrect servers are under the intruder's control. A redirection attack is achieved when an intruder corrupts the DNS cache in a DNS server that accepts unsecured dynamic updates.

To protect an external DNS implementation from network attacks, use the following list of recommendations:

DNS servers should be placed in a DMZ or in a perimeter network.

1. Access rules and packet filtering should be configured firewalls to control both source and destination addresses and ports.

2. Host DNS servers on different subnets and ensure that the DNS servers have different configured routers.

3. Install the latest service packs on DNS servers

4. All unnecessary services should be removed.

5. Secure zone transfer data by using VPN tunnels or IPSec.

6. Ensure that zone transfer is only allowed to specific IP addresses.

7. For Internet facing DNS servers, disable recursion, disable dynamic updates, and enable protection against cache pollution.

8. Use a stealth primary server to update secondary DNS servers that are registered with ICANN.

Identifying Threats to Internet Information Server (IIS) Servers (Web servers)

The security vulnerabilities of the earlier Internet Information Server (IIS) versions including IIS version 5 were continuously patched up by service packs and hot fixes available from Microsoft. Previously when IIS was installed, all services were enabled and started, all service accounts had high system rights, and permissions were assigned to the lowest levels. This basically meant that the IIS implementation was vulnerable to all sorts of attacks from hackers. Microsoft introduced the Security Lockdown Wizard in an attempt to address the security loopholes and vulnerabilities that existed in the previous versions of IIS. The Security Lockdown Wizard in IIS 6 has been included in the Web Service Extensions (WSE).

IIS is installed in lock down mode with IIS 6. The only feature immediately available is static content. Users actually need to utilize the WSE feature in the IIS Manager console tree to manually enable IIS to run applications and its features. By default, all applications and extensions are prohibited from running.

To protect IIS servers from network attacks, use the following recommendations:

- To prevent hackers from using default account names, all default account names including the Administrator account and Guest account should be changed. Utilize names that are difficult to guess.

- To prevent a hacker from compromising Active Directory, should the Web server be compromised, the Web server should be a standalone server or a member of a forest other than the forest that the private network uses.

- All the latest released security updates, service packs, and hot fixes should be applied to the Web server.

- All sample applications should be removed from a Web server. A few sample application files are installed by default with IIS 5.0.

- All unnecessary services should be removed or disabled. This would ensure that network attackers cannot exploit these services to compromise the Web server.

- Disable parent path utilization. Hackers typically attempt to access unauthorized disk subsystem areas through parent paths.

- Apply security to each content type. Content should be categorized into separate folders based on content type. Apply discretionary access control lists for each content type identified.

- To protect commonly attacked ports, use IPSec.

- To protect the Web server's secure areas, use the Secure Socket Layer (SSL) protocol.

- To detect hacking activity, implement an intrusion detection system (IDS).

- A few recommendations for writing secure code for ASP or ASP.NET applications are summarized here:

- ASP pages should not contain any hard coded administrator account names and administrator account passwords.

- Sensitive and confidential information and data should not be stored in hidden input fields on Web pages and in cookies.

- Verify and validate form input prior to it being processed.

- Do not use information from HTTP request headers to code decision branches for applications.

- Be wary of buffer overflows

- Use Secure Sockets Layer (SSL) to encrypt session cookies.

Identifying Threats to Wireless Networks

A few threats specific to DNS implementations:

- Eavesdropping attacks: The hacker attempts to capture traffic when it is being transmitted from the wireless computer to the wireless access point (WAP).

- Masquerading: Here, the hacker masquerades as an authorized wireless user to access network resources or services.

- Denial of service (DoS) attacks: The network attacker attempts to prevent authorized wireless users from accessing network resources by using a transmitter to block wireless frequencies.

- Man-in-the-middle attacks: If an attacker successfully launches a man-in-the-middle attack, the attacker could be able to replay and modify wireless communications.

- Attacks at wireless clients: The attacker starts a network attack at the actual wireless computer that is connected to an untrusted wireless network.

To protect wireless networks from network attacks, use the following strategies:

- Administrators should require all wireless communications to be authenticated and encrypted. The common technologies used to protect wireless networks from security threats are Wired Equivalent Privacy (WEP), Wi-Fi Protected Access (WPA), and IEEE 802.1X authentication.

- Regularly apply all firmware updates to wireless devices.

- Place the wireless network in a wireless demilitarized zone (WDMZ). A router or firewall should isolate the private corporate network from the WDMZ. DHCP should not be used in the wireless demilitarized zone.

- To ensure a high level of wireless security, wireless devices should support 802.1X authentication using Extensible Authentication Protocol (EAP) authentication and Temporal Key Integrity Protocol (TKIP). Use IPSec to secure communication between the AP and the RADIUS server.

- The default administrative password that manages the AP should be a complex, strong password.

- The SSID should not contain the name of the company, the address of the company, and any other identification information.

- Do not utilize shared key encryption because it can lead to the compromise of the WEP keys.

- To protect the network from site survey mechanisms, disable SSID broadcasts.

Determining Security Requirements for Different Data Types

When determining security requirements for different data types, it is often helpful to categorize data as follows:

- *Public data:* This category includes all data that is already publicly available on the company's website or news bulletins. Because the data is already publicly available, no risk is typically associated with the data being stolen. Users do, however, need to maintain and ensure the integrity of public data.

- *Private data:* Data that falls within this category is usually well known within an organization's environment but is not well known to the public. A typical example of data that falls within this category is data on the corporate intranet.

- *Confidential data:* Data that falls within this category is data such as private customer information that should be protected from unauthorized access. The organization would almost always suffer some sort of loss if confidential data is intercepted.

- *Secret data:* This is data that can be considered more confidential and sensitive in nature than confidential data. Secret data consists of trade secrets, new product and business strategy information, and patent information. Secret data should have the highest levels of security.

Creating an Incidence Response Plan

The terminology, "incident response" refers to planned actions in response to a network attack or any similar event that affects systems, networks, and company data. An Incident Response plan is aimed at outlining the response procedures that should take place when a network is being attacked or security is being compromised.

The Incident Response plan should assist an organization with dealing with the incident in an orderly manner. Reacting to network attacks by following a planned approach that a security policy defines is the better approach.

These security policies should clearly define the following:

1. The response to follow each incident type.

2. The individual(s) who are responsible for dealing with these incidents.

3. The escalation procedures that should be followed.

An Incident Response plan can be divided into the following four steps:

1. *Response:* Determine how network attacks and security breaches will be dealt with.

2. *Investigation:* Determine how the attack occurred, why the specific attack occurred, and the extent of the attack.

3. *Restoration:* All infected systems should be taken offline and then restored from a clean backup.

4. *Reporting:* The network attack or security breach should be reported to the appropriate authorities.

Before attempting to determine the existing state of a machine that is being attacked, it is recommended that users first record the information listed here:

- The name of the machine

- The IP address of the machine

- The installed operating system, operating system version, and installed service packs.

- All running processes and services

- List all parties that are dependent on the server. These individuals need to be informed of the current situation.

Obtain the following valuable information:

- Application event log information

- System event log information

- Security event log information

- All other machine specific event logs such as DNS logs, DHCP logs, or File Replication logs.

Record all information that indicates malicious activities. This should include:

- All files that have been modified, corrupted, or deleted.

- All unauthorized processes running.

Analyze network security systems.

Security systems for networks are different for all kinds of situations. A home or small office may only require basic security while large businesses may require high-maintenance and advanced software and hardware to prevent malicious attacks from hacking and spamming.

Homes & Small Businesses

- A basic **firewall** or a **unified threat management** system.

- For Windows users, basic **Antivirus software**. An anti-spyware program would also be a good idea. There are many other types of antivirus or anti-spyware programs available.

- When using a wireless connection, use a robust password. Also try to use the strongest security supported by your wireless devices, such as WPA2 with AES. TKIP may be more widely supported by your devices and should only be considered in cases where they are NOT compliant with AES.

- If using Wireless: Change the default SSID network name, also disable SSID Broadcast; as this function is unnecessary for home use. (Security experts consider this to be easily bypassed with modern technology and some knowledge of how wireless traffic is detected by software).

- Enable MAC Address filtering to keep track of all home network MAC devices connecting to your router. (This is not a security feature per se; However it can be used to limit and strictly monitor your DHCP address pool for unwanted intruders if not just by exclusion, but by AP association.)

- Assign STATIC IP addresses to network devices. (This is not a security feature per se; however it may be used, in conjunction with other features, to make your AP less desirable to would-be intruders.)

- Disable ICMP ping on router.

- Review router or firewall logs to help identify abnormal network connections or traffic to the Internet.

- Use passwords for all accounts.

- For Windows users, Have multiple accounts per family member and use non-administrative accounts for day-to-day activities.

- Raise awareness about information security to children.

Medium and Large businesses

- A fairly strong **firewall**, **proxy** or **Unified Threat Management** System

- Strong **Antivirus software** and Internet Security Software.

- For **authentication**, use strong passwords and change them on a bi-weekly/monthly basis.

- When using a wireless connection, use a robust password.

- Raise awareness about **physical security** to employees.

- Use an optional **network analyzer** or network monitor.

- An enlightened administrator or manager.

- Use a VPN, or Virtual Private Network, to communicate between a main office and satellite offices using the Internet as a connectivity medium. A VPN offers a solution to the expense of leasing a data line while providing a secure network for the offices to communicate. A VPN provides the business with a way to communicate between two in a way mimics a private leased line. Although the Internet is used, it is private because the link is encrypted and convenient to use. A medium sized business needing a secure way to connect several offices will find this a good choice.

- Clear employee guidelines should be implemented for using the Internet, including access to non-work related websites, sending and receiving information.

- Individual accounts to log on and access company intranet and Internet with monitoring for accountability.

- Have a back-up policy to recover data in the event of a hardware failure or a security breach that changes, damages or deletes data.

- Disable Messenger.

- Assign several employees to monitor a group like CERT that studies Internet security vulnerabilities and develops training to help improve security.

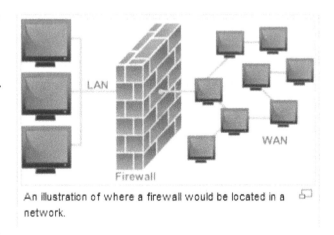

An illustration of where a firewall would be located in a network.

Let us learn some basic concepts of network security systems:

273

Firewall

A firewall can be either software-based or hardware-based and is used to help keep a network secure. Its primary objective is to control the incoming and outgoing network traffic by analyzing the data packets and determining whether it should be allowed through or not, based on a predetermined rule set. A network's firewall builds a bridge between an internal network that is assumed to be secure and trusted, and another network, usually an external (inter)network,

such as the Internet, that is not assumed to be secure and trusted.

FIGURE 57 EXAMPLE OF A FIREWALL

Many personal computer operating systems include software-based firewalls to protect against threats from the public Internet. Many routers that pass data between networks contain firewall components and, conversely, many firewalls can perform basic routing functions.

Proxy server

In computer networks, a proxy server is a server (a computer system or an application) that acts

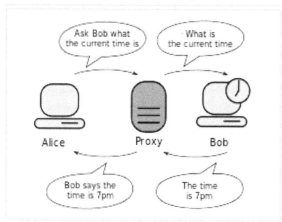

as an intermediary for requests from clients seeking resources from other servers. A client connects to the proxy server, requesting some service, such as a file, connection, web page, or other resource available from a different server and the proxy server evaluates the request as a way to simplify and control its complexity. Today, most proxies are web proxies, facilitating access to content on the World Wide Web.

FIGURE 58 EXAMPLE OF A PROXY SERVER

Antivirus software

An anti-virus or AntiVirus (AV) is software used to prevent, detect and eventually remove malicious programs or malware, such as: viruses, adware, backdoors, malicious BHOs, dialers, fraudtools, hijackers, key loggers, malicious LSPs, rootkits, spyware, Trojan horses and worms.

Virtual Private Networks

Given the ubiquity of the Internet, and the considerable expense in private leased lines, many organizations have been building VPNs (Virtual Private Networks). Traditionally, for an organization to provide connectivity between a main office and a satellite one, an expensive data line had to be leased in order to provide direct connectivity between the two offices. Now, a solution that is often more economical is to provide both offices connectivity to the Internet. Then, using the Internet as the medium, the two offices can communicate.

Summary

Security is a very difficult topic. Everyone has a different idea of what ``security" is, and what levels of risk are acceptable. The key for building a secure network is to define what security means to your organization. Once that has been defined, everything that goes on with the network can be evaluated with respect to that policy. Projects and systems can then be broken down into their components, and it becomes much simpler to decide whether what is proposed will conflict with your security policies and practices.

QUIZ

1. Name at least two network security systems:

   • Proxy

   • Firewall

   • Antivirus software

   • Virtual Private Networks

2. With your own words, define what a Proxy work for:

   This is the process of having one host act in behalf of another

3. Try to define how a Firewall works on a security network:

Its primary objective is to control the incoming and outgoing network traffic by analyzing the data packets and determining whether it should be allowed through or not.

Evaluate the correctness and effectiveness of implementing the network system.

One of the major issues in networks is the performance management for network system usability. To improve network system quality of service, system administrators should evaluate how their systems are working, and should operate their systems to perform users' requests and optimize performance. To manage network system performance, it is important for administrators to be aware of system usability factors such as access delay, processing time, data transfer throughput, and so on.

Several ways to measure network performance have been developed so far. However, performance management is still difficult because of the lack of effective tools to evaluate network system usability.

The goal of our work is to develop a new performance evaluation tool for network system usability. In our approach, we measure system usability and performance through mechanisms installed in the clients. The purpose of our system is to make clear the behavior of the client applications, and allows us to measure system performance for client usability.

In this lesson, we discuss the fundamental principles for client observation and its performance indices, and the design and implementation of the performance evaluation system through observation. In addition, we confirm the effectiveness of our system through experiments.

Necessary functions for evaluation tools

To evaluate network system performance from the point of view of usability, the system administrators must know how their services are working and must improve them to satisfy user requests. Network system performance with regard to usability is determined by how the client provides performance to the user, that is, the system administrator should be aware of client system performance factors such as:

- How long the client takes to access the server.

- How long the client takes to process the transaction.

- How much data is throughput in the client?

Let us consider a common framework to evaluate the performance of the end-point application. The evaluation tool should have the following functions:

- The tool is able to measure the throughput and response speed at the end-point applications, which has an impact on the user. The performance evaluation tool aims to improve the performance of the end-point application. The total system performance doesn't always interrelate with the performance of the network path. Therefore, the network system performance should be evaluated in the client applications.

- The tool should handle various kinds of datalinks. The Internet has been used on various datalinks such as Ethernet, ATM, FDDI, Token Ring, X.25, Integrated Services Digital Network (ISDN), and so on. Transmission Control Protocol/Internet Protocol (TCP/IP) technology is a set of protocols of the upper layer of these datalinks. Therefore, the measurement method should be independent of the datalinks.

- The measurement tool should be independent of applications. There are various applications and application protocols utilized in the Internet. The performance measurement should be a standard framework, and it should not be dependent on a single application and a single application protocol.

- The measurement tool should be able to be applied to existing applications without any modification. It is costly to modify application software to operate the measurement tool. Also, there are number of applications that would be difficult to modify for use with the measurement tool.

- The measurement tool should be able to be applied to running systems. Using computer simulation, it is difficult to calculate all performance factors, and the benchmark is only valid under specified conditions. It is more effective to evaluate running systems by measuring the performance in the actual situation.

- The measurement tool should be able to be applied not only to the network links, but also to the server and client systems. The total performance of the network systems is affected by the servers, the clients, and the network links.

Existing performance measurement tools

Several tools have been developed to evaluate network performance.

- Statistical analysis of servers logs. Statistical analysis from server access logs allows us to determine the operation status of the servers, such as the number of accesses, number of data transfers, and processing time. However, the results of the analysis of server logs determine only the performance of the servers themselves. The performance of the clients and the network links is not included in the results.

- Measurement of network usage and Round Trip Time (RTT). Simple Network Management Protocol (SNMP) is widely used to measure network usage. System administrators can use simple tools such as ping and trace route to measure system usage. However, TCP performance degrades as network usage increases, and it is also affected by the characteristics of the network links. The performance of end-point application is affected by not only the network usage but also by the characteristics, end-to-end throughput, and capacity of the servers and clients.

- Benchmark. We can find some benchmark tools such as SPECweb, WebStone, ttcp, DBS, and so on. These tools provide many indices of exact application performance. However, it is difficult to set up suitable benchmark conditions to reproduce those of servers under actual operating conditions.

- Packet dumping. The analysis of packet dumping provides many indices on the datalink level. Furthermore, some tools such as RMONv2 and ENMA can calculate the indices in the TCP layer. However, packet dumping can only apply to specific datalinks and the traffic shared network. Even in the Ethernet environment, the packets could not be observed in the switched network.

Accordingly, we need a new performance evaluation tool for network systems that can be applied to actual systems operation under various configurations.

Fundamental principles of client observation

The goal of our performance evaluation method is to provide a suitable, common framework to measure network system performance usability. We do this by measuring the actual network system performance from the users point of view.

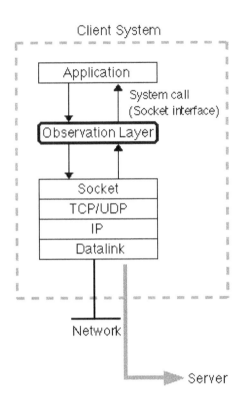

Figure 59 Fundemental concept of performance measurement

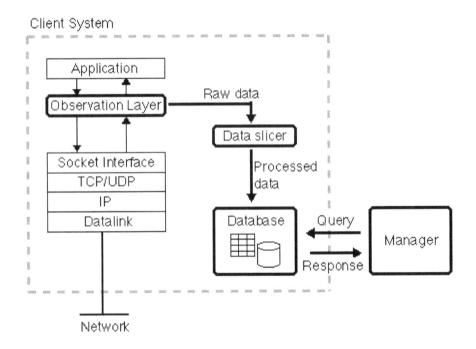

Figure 60 System modeling

Observation layer

The observation layer monitors the system calls between the applications and the OS.

The observation layer has proxy system call functions. The proxy system call functions stands for the application instead of the actual system call functions in the OS. When the application calls the system calls, the proxy system call procedures in the observation layer are invoked. Then the observation layer records time of each state (T1-T7), counts the amount of data transferred in each TCP connection, and simultaneously, invokes the actual system call in the OS.

Data slicer

The data slicer processes the measured raw data in the observation layer with the conditions such as IP address and the port number, and performs the basic analysis.

Database

The data slicer writes the processed data to the database. This database is used for further analysis by the manager.

The database consists of a matrix into which are put the server address, port number, time elapsing in each state, data size, and transfer rate in order time stamp. The structure of the database is quite simple because a data entry for each TCP connection forms a single row of data. Therefore, it reduces the amount of overhead for measurement in the clients.

Furthermore, the database contains an improved multidimensional matrix to comply with future analyses.

Manager

The manager collects the measurement data from the target of the remote clients. It analyzes the data and provides a graphical interpretation of the results. Currently, the manager is implemented as the interface to GNU Plot to view the analysis results.

OVERHEAD FOR THE MEASUREMENT

Our system records the time and counts the data when the application transfers data to/from the network. This procedure affects the performance of the system itself. To evaluate the capability of our system, we compared the throughput with the observation layer and one without it.

Table 18 Configuration of Experiment

Server	Sun Ultra 60 (two UltraSPARC-II 360MHz processors) (Solaris 2.6)

Client	Sun Ultra 10 (UltraSPARC-IIi 333MHz processor) (Solaris2.6)
Server program	Apache 1.3.4
Client program	ApacheBench
Data size	51200 bytes

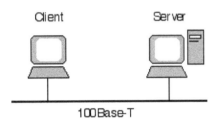

Figure 61 Example of a 100 Base-T

Configuration of experiment

The target system is configured on an Apache HTTP server [11], a Sun Ultra 60 workstation, and an ApacheBench client program on a Sun Ultra 10 workstation. These devices are connected on 100Base-T Ethernet as shown in table.1 and earlier figure.

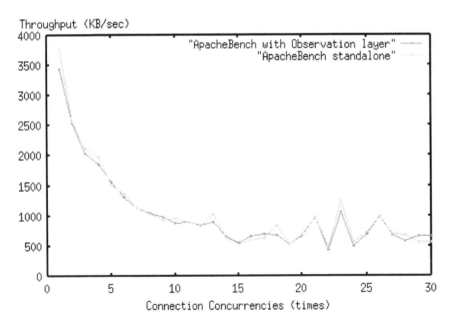

Figure above shows the average throughput (KB/sec) per connection when the data were transferred concurrently. The result shows that the overhead gets to 5 percent or less on average. The overhead could be considered to ignore in the 100Mbps network.

FIGURE 62 AVERAGE THROUGHPUT KB/SEC

Server access log versus our system

The statistical analysis of the server access log was used to evaluate performance thus far. We compared the differences between the analysis results of the server access log and the measurement of our system.

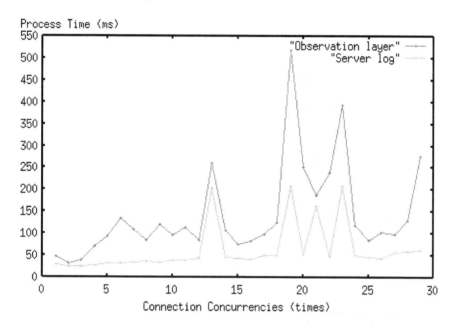

The configurations of the target system are also in above Figure that shows the process time elapsed (milliseconds) from the server log and the Transaction Time (Tt) (ms) in our system.

The result of the server log is less than one of our system, and the maximum difference reaches 40 percent.

The Tt in our system is the entire time elapsed in the transaction, including the time for the connection setup, data transfer, and connection close procedures in the Socket layer. Comparatively, the server log is recorded only the server side application activity. Therefore, the server log cannot measure the performance regarding connection setup/closing. Moreover, the server log is the performance record in the application level. Once the data are put into the buffer in the OS, before the actual transmission, it appears that the data transfers are done early in the server programs.

Summary

In this paper, we described why a new method for network system performance evaluation is needed. Our proposal is to observe the behavior of the client application and exactly measure its performance. Our system can effectively evaluate the network system performance because the client application stands on the end-user side directly.

QUIZ

1. Mention three performance measurement tools:

- Statistical analysis of servers logs.

- Measurement of network usage and Round Trip Time (RTT).

- Benchmark. (SPECweb , WebStone, ttcp, DBS, and so on)

2. Which are the necessary functions for evaluation?

- How long the client takes to access the server.

- How long the client takes to process the transaction.

- How much data is throughput in the client?

3. In system model for fundamental principle of client observation we can mention the following components:

- Observation layer.

- Database.

- Manager.

- Overhead for the measurement.

Designing a network system.

Basics of network architecture.

LAN

Local Area Network.

Standards

The IEEE efforts were called Project 802.

There are three dominant standards: Ethernet (802.3), token ring (802.5), and wireless (802.11).

Ethernet

Ethernet is the most popular LAN architecture today.

It is easy to install and inexpensive.

Data transmission is broken into packets.

The standard method of labeling different versions is Maximum Speed-Transmission Mode-Segment Length or Media Type.

10Base2

It is a bus topology that uses contention (CSMA/CD) and thin coax.

Segments are connected together through a repeater.

It can connect up to five 200-meter segments using four repeaters (5-4-3 rule).

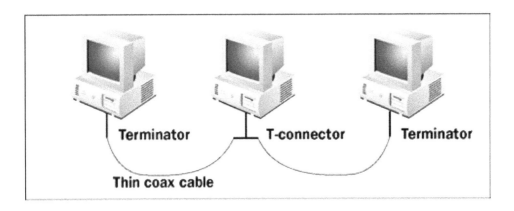

10Base-T

It runs 10 Mbps and uses CSMA/CD.

It is a star-wired bus topology.

It is still used today due to its reliability and ease of use.

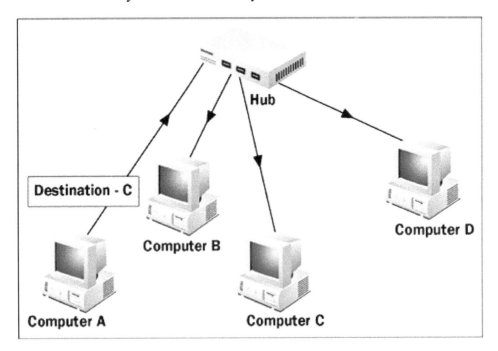

100Base-T

It uses CMSA/CD as a star-wired bus.

There are three subcategories of 100Base-T networks with different cable requirements.

The most common is 100Base-TX (Category 5 or higher UTP).

Switched Ethernet

A switch knows which segment belongs to which device.

It uses a table stored in memory to send a packet.

It increases bandwidth by decreasing traffic and collisions.

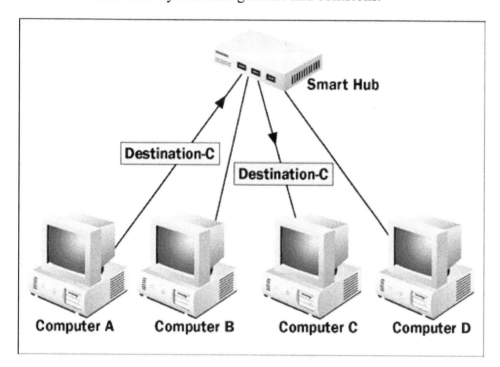

Gigabit Ethernet

1000Base-T is a star topology that uses Category 5 or higher cabling.

It increases speed by sending more bits and using 4 pairs of wires simultaneously.

10G Ethernet

It can be used in both LANs and WANs.

It requires fiber optic cable.

Networks do not encounter collisions.

Token Ring

It has the ability to diagnose and avoid network problems.

It does not slow down when more devices are added to the network.

The packet size can be larger than on an Ethernet network.

IEEE Project 802.5.

16-Mbps speed.

It uses twisted pair cable in a hybrid starring topology.

The packets go to a central hub called the Multistation Access Unit (MAU).

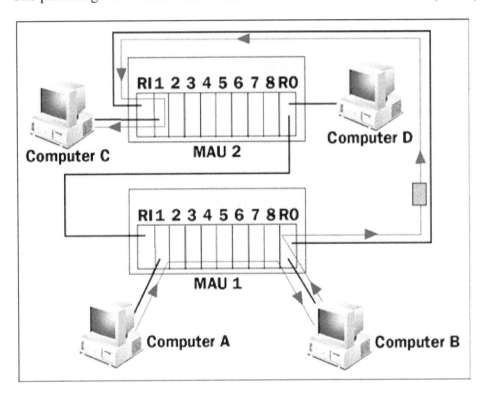

WLAN

Wireless local area network.

It is used when mobility is needed, but it still must remain connected to the network.

802.11b or Wi-Fi (11 Mbps).

802.11a or Wi-Fi5 (108 Mbps).

802.11g (54 Mbps).

Only wireless network interface cards and access points are needed.

An access point acts as a link between wireless and wired networks.

802.11b uses Carrier Sense Multiple Access with Collision Avoidance (CSMA/CA).

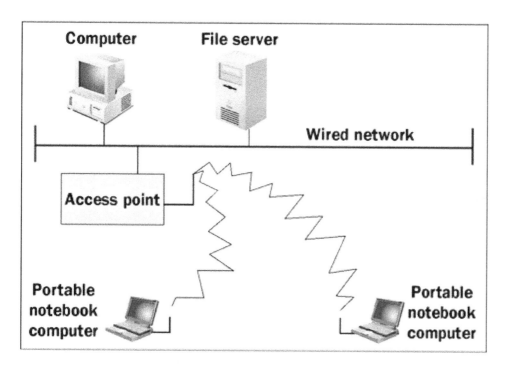

Network Design

Basic rules should be followed for a good network design.

The switches in an Ethernet network must be configured in a hierarchy.

Smaller network segments are better than larger network segments.

Summary

In the early 1980s, the Institute of Electrical and Electronic Engineers (IEEE) began work on developing computer network architecture standards. Known as Project 802, this work established the foundation for three network architecture standards that make up over 95 percent of the LANs in use today. These three dominant standards are Ethernet (802.3), token ring (802.5), and wireless (802.11).

QUIZ

1. For wireless networks is known to use either of the following standard communications numbers?

- 802.11b or Wi-Fi (11 Mbps).

- 802.11a or Wi-Fi5 (108 Mbps).

- 802.11g (54 Mbps).

2. The mnemonic WLAN stands for?

Wireless local area network

3. What the mnemonic IEEE stands for?

Institute of Electrical and Electronic Engineers.

4. What the mnemonic LAN stands for?

Local Area Network.

5. The Institute of Electrical and Electronic Engineers (IEEE) is known also as?

Project 802.

Basic network classifications and topologies.

The pattern or layout of interconnections of different elements or nodes of a computer network is a network topology that might be logical or physical. As opposed to physical design, the transfer of data in a network is referred in Logical Topology (the basic network) where the Physical Topology (the core network) accounts the physical structure of a network that carries devices, cable installations and locations. LAN (local area network) is an example of network that keeps both logical and physical topologies.

There are seven basic types of network topologies in the study of network topology: Point-to-point topology, bus (point-to-multipoint) topology, ring topology, star topology, hybrid topology, mesh topology and tree topology. The interconnections between computers whether logical or physical are the foundation of this classification.

Logical topology is the way a computer in a given network transmits information, not the way it looks or connected, along with the varying speeds of cables used from one network to another. On the other hand the physical topology is affected by a number of factors: troubleshooting technique, installation cost, office layout and cables' types. The physical topology is figured out on the basis of a network's capability to access media and devices, the fault tolerance desired and the cost of telecommunications circuits.

The classification of networks by the virtue of their physical span is as follows: Local Area Networks (LAN), Wide Area Internetworks (WAN) and Metropolitan Area Networks or campus or building internetworks.

Point-to-Point Network Topology

It is the basic model of typical telephony. The simplest topology is a permanent connection between two points. The value of a demanding point-to-point network is proportionate to the number of subscribers' potential pairs. It is possible to establish a permanent circuit within many switched telecommunication systems: the telephone present in a lobby would always connect to the same port, no matter what number is being dialed. A switch connection would save the cost between two points where the resources could be released when no longer required.

Bus Network Topology

LANs that make use of bus topology connects each node to a single cable. Some connector connects each computer or server to the bus cable. For avoiding the bouncing of signal a terminator is used at each end of the bus cable. The source transmits a signal that travels in both directions and passes all machines unless it finds the system with IP address, the intended recipient. The data is ignored in case the address is unmatched. The installation of one cable makes bus topology an inexpensive solution as compared to other topologies; however the maintenance cost is high. If the cable is broken all systems would collapse. Ethernet bus topologies are relatively easy to install and don't require much cabling compared to the alternatives. 10Base-2 ("ThinNet") and 10Base-5 ("ThickNet") both were popular Ethernet cabling options many years ago for bus topologies. However, bus networks work best with a limited number of devices. If more than a few dozen computers are added to a network bus, performance problems will likely result. In addition, if the backbone cable fails, the entire network effectively becomes unusable.

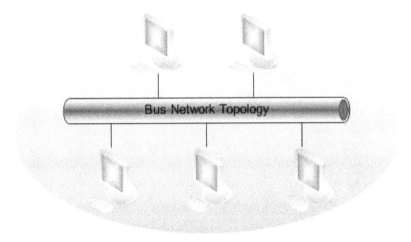

ADVANTAGES OF A LINEAR BUS TOPOLOGY

- Easy to connect a computer or peripheral to a linear bus.

- Requires less cable length than a star topology.

DISADVANTAGES OF A LINEAR BUS TOPOLOGY

- Entire network shuts down if there is a break in the main cable.

- Terminators are required at both ends of the backbone cable.

- Difficult to identify the problem if the entire network shuts down.

- Not meant to be used as a stand-alone solution in a large building.

Tree Topology

Tree Topology Tree topologies integrate multiple star topologies together onto a bus. In its simplest form, only hub devices connect directly to the tree bus, and each hub functions as the "root" of a tree of devices. This bus/star hybrid approach supports future expandability of the network much better than a bus (limited in the number of devices due to the broadcast traffic it generates) or a star (limited by the number of hub connection points) alone.

See the illustration of Tree Network Topology.

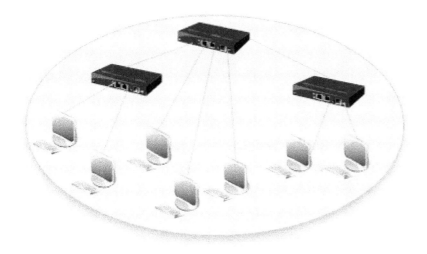

ADVANTAGES OF A TREE TOPOLOGY

- Point-to-point wiring for individual segments.

- Supported by several hardware and software venders.

DISADVANTAGES OF A TREE TOPOLOGY

- Overall length of each segment is limited by the type of cabling used.

- If the backbone line breaks, the entire segment goes down.

- More difficult to configure and wire than other topologies.

Star Network Topology

The topology when each network host is connected to a central hub in LAN is called Star. Each node is connected to the hub with a point-to-point connection. All traffic passes through the hub that serves as a repeater or signal booster. The easiest Star topology to install is hailed for its simplicity to add more nodes but criticized for making hub the single point of failure. The network

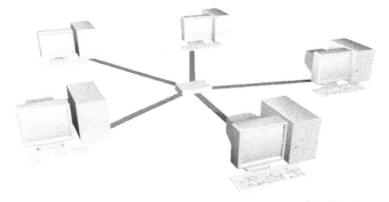

FIGURE 63 STAR TOPOLOGY

could be BMA (broadcast multi-access) or NBMA (non-broadcast multi-access) depending on whether the signal is automatically propagated at the hub to all spokes or individually spokes with those who are addressed.

ADVANTAGES OF A STAR TOPOLOGY

- Easy to install and wire.

- No disruptions to the network then connecting or removing devices.

- Easy to detect faults and to remove parts.

DISADVANTAGES OF A STAR TOPOLOGY

- Requires more cable length than a linear topology.

- If the hub or concentrator fails, nodes attached are disabled.

- More expensive than linear bus topologies because of the cost of the concentrators.

The protocols used with star configurations are usually Ethernet or LocalTalk. Token Ring uses a similar topology, called the star-wired ring

Ring Network Topology

Ring topology is one of the old ways of building computer network design and it is pretty much obsolete. FDDI, SONET or Token Ring technologies are used to build ring technology. It is not widely popular in terms of usability but incase if you find it any where it will mostly be in schools or office buildings.

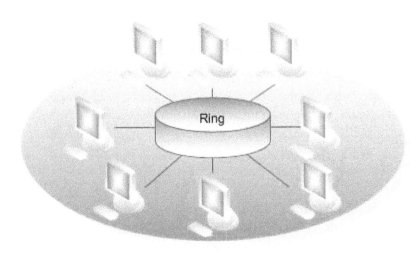

Such physical setting sets up nodes in a circular manner where the data could travel in one direction where each device on the right serves as a repeater to strengthen the signal as it moves ahead.

Mesh Network Topology

The exponent of the number of subscribers is proportionate to the value of the fully meshed networks.

FIGURE 64 RING NETWORK TOPOLOGY

Fully Connected: For practical networks such topology is too complex and costly but highly recommended for small number of interconnected nodes.

Partially Connected: This set up involves the connection of some nodes to more than one node in the network via point-to-point link. In such connection it is possible to take advantage of the redundancy without any complexity or expense of establishing a connection between each node.

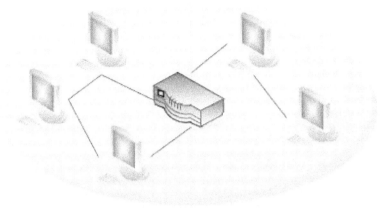

Figure 65 Mesh topology

Tree Network Topology

The top level of the hierarchy, the central root node is connected to some nodes that are a level low in the hierarchy by a point-to-point link where the second level nodes that are already connected to central root would be connected to the nodes in the third level by a point-to-point link. The central root would be the only node having no higher node in the hierarchy. The tree hierarchy is symmetrical. The BRANCHING FACTOR is the fixed number of nodes connected to the next level in the hierarchy. Such network must have at least three levels. Physical Linear Tree Topology would be of a network whose Branching Factor is one.

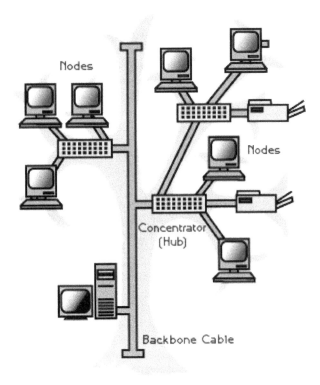

Figure 66 tree network topology

Hybrid Topology

A combination of any two or more network topologies. Note 1: Instances can occur where two basic network topologies, when connected together, can still retain the basic network character, and therefore not be a hybrid network. For example, a tree network connected to a tree network is still a tree network. Therefore, a hybrid network accrues only when two basic networks are connected and the resulting network topology fails to meet one of the basic topology definitions. For example, two star networks connected together exhibit hybrid network topologies. Note 2: A hybrid topology always accrues when two different basic network topologies are connected.

5-4-3 Rule

A consideration in setting up a tree topology using Ethernet protocol is the 5-4-3 rule. One aspect of the Ethernet protocol requires that a signal sent out on the network cable reach every part of the network within a specified length of time. Each concentrator or repeater that a signal goes through adds a small amount of time. This leads to the rule that between any two nodes on the network there can only be a maximum of 5 segments, connected through 4 repeaters/concentrators. In addition, only 3 of the segments may be populated (trunk) segments if they are made of coaxial cable. A populated segment is one which has one or more nodes attached to it . In Figure 4, the 5-4-3 rule is adhered to. The furthest two nodes on the network have 4 segments and 3 repeaters/concentrators between them.

This rule does not apply to other network protocols or Ethernet networks where all fiber optic cabling or a combination of a fiber backbone with UTP cabling is used. If there is a combination of fiber optic backbone and UTP cabling, the rule is simply translated to 7-6-5 rule.

Considerations When Choosing a Topology

- Money. A linear bus network may be the least expensive way to install a network; you do not have to purchase concentrators.

- Length of cable needed. The linear bus network uses shorter lengths of cable.

- Future growth. With a star topology, expanding a network is easily done by adding another concentrator.

- Cable type. The most common cable in schools is unshielded twisted pair, which is most often used with star topologies.

Other definition of Network Topology

A network consists of multiple computers connected using some type of interface, each having one or more interface devices such as a Network Interface Card (NIC) and/or a serial device for PPP networking. Each computer is supported by network software that provides the server or client functionality. The hardware used to transmit data across the network is called the media. It may include copper cable, fiber optic, or wireless transmission. The standard cabling used for the purposes of this document is 10Base-T category 5 Ethernet cable. This is twisted copper cabling which appears at the surface to look similar to TV coaxial cable. It is terminated on each end by a connector that looks much like a phone connector. Its maximum segment length is 100 meters.

In a server-based network, there are computers set up to be primary providers of services such as file service or mail service. The computers providing the service are are called servers and the computers that request and use the service are called client computers.

In a peer-to-peer network, various computers on the network can act both as clients and servers. For instance, many Microsoft Windows based computers will allow file and print sharing. These computers can act both as a client and a server and are also referred to as peers. Many networks are combination peer-to-peer and server based networks. The network operating system uses a network data protocol to communicate on the network to other computers. The network operating system supports the applications on that computer. A Network Operating System (NOS) includes Windows NT, Novell Netware, Linux, Unix and others.

Summary

Knowledge of networking topologies is of core importance of computer networking design. Computer networks can only be developed using the knowledge about these topologies and decide to which topology design is best suited according to the requirement.

QUIZ

1. Define briefly how is conformed a Point-to-Point Network Topology.

It is the basic model of typical telephony.

2. Define briefly how is conformed a Bus Network Topology.

LANs that make use of bus topology connects each node to a single cable.

3. Define briefly how is conformed a Star Network Topology.

The topology when each network host is connected to a central hub in LAN is called Star.

4. Define briefly how is conformed a Ring Network Topology.

Such physical setting sets up nodes in a circular manner where the data could travel in one direction.

5. Define briefly how is conformed a Mesh Network Topology.

The exponent of the number of subscribers is proportionate to the value of the fully meshed networks.

6. Define briefly how is conformed a Tree Network Topology.

Physical Tree Topology would be of a network whose Branching Factor is one.

LAN physical media.

A **local area network (LAN)** is a network used for connecting a business or organization's computers to one another. With a LAN, a concept that goes back to 1970, a company's employees can:

- Exchange information

- Communicate

- Access various services

A local area network usually links computers (or resources such as printers) using a wired transmission medium (most frequently twisted pairs or coaxial cables) over a circumference of about a hundred meters. For larger spaces, the network is considered to be part of a network called a MAN (metropolitan area network), in which the transmission medium is better suited to sending signals over great distances.

Hardware components of a local area network

A local area network is made of computers linked by a set of software and hardware elements. The hardware elements used for connecting computers to one another are:

- The network card: This is a card connected to the computer's motherboard, which interfaces with the physical medium, meaning the physical lines over which the information travels.

- The transceiver: This is used to transform the signals travelling over the physical support into logical signals that the network card can manipulate both when sending and receiving data.

- The socket: This is the element used to mechanically connect the network card with the physical medium.

- The physical connection medium: This is the support (generally wired, meaning that it's in the form of a cable) used to link the computers together. The main physical support media used in local area networks are:

- Coaxial cable: **Coaxial cable**, or coax, is intended for use as transmission line for radio frequency (RF) signals. A few common applications of coaxial cable would be to connect radio transmitters or receivers with their antennas, network connectivity, and the more familiar distribution of cable television to your home. When compared with other modes of transmission, coax cable shows advantage in that the electromagnetic field that carries the signal does not stray from the space between the

FIGURE 67 COAXIAL CABLE

inner and outer conductors. This allows coaxial cable to be safely installed next to metallic objects that would otherwise result in electromagnetic interference and losses of power. We carry coaxial bulk cable in RG-58/U, RG-59/U, RG-6/U, RG-6/UQ, and RG-8/U. In our "How-To" section you will find step-by-step instructions on how to terminate coax cables.

What are twisted pairs?

Figure 68 twister pair coaxial cable

Twisted pair:

- Two wires twisted together form a *twisted pair*.

- Usually, there are several twisted-pairs in a twisted pair cable.

- In higher performance cables each twisted pair will be shielded.

WHY DO THEY PUT TWISTED PAIRS IN CABLES?

It is an extremely effective way to send high-speed signals down a cable because:

- Most electrical noise entering into and/or radiating from the cable can be eliminated.

- Cross-talk (signals leaking between wires in a cable) is minimized.

WHY DO SIGNALS LEAK BETWEEN WIRES?

In addition to energy flowing down a wire, it can flow between wires due to the electrostatic and magnetic effects that occur when voltages or currents in the wire change. In understanding electrostatic effects, consider that "insulation between two conductors" is the definition of a capacitor. More surface area (longer cables) means more inter-wire capacitance. Adjacent wires in the same cable behave as though capacitors are connecting them together, thus higher frequency signals can leak, or "cross talk", from wire to wire through this capacitance.

HOW DOES TWISTED PAIR CABLING MININIZE THE EFFECTS OF CAPACITANCE?

A. Cross-talk (leaking signals)

Signals are sent down twisted-pair wires such that when one wire in the pair becomes positive the other wire becomes negative by the same amount. Any other wires close to this pair will be affected by cross-talk equal to the sum of the two signals, so if this sum is zero (or nearly zero) then the affects of cross-talk are eliminated.

Notice in period 1 in the illustration below the signal sent through the orange wire shows up on the black wire. In period 2 the signal sent through the white wire shows up on the black wire. In period 3 the signal sent through the orange wire and it's opposite polarity signal on the white wire cancel each other out, leaving no effect on the black wire.

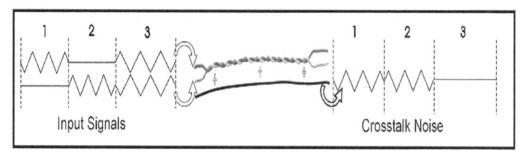

B. Immunity to Electrical Noise

The receiving electronics is intended to detect only the difference in polarity between the two wires in the twisted pair. Since electrical noise affects both wires of a twisted pair equally the receiving electronics gets a true signal by rejecting signals on the twisted pair that move toward the same polarity.

Question:

If I am using a good, certified, twisted pair cable and I test for opens, shorts and even perform high voltage insulation tests, is this enough to assure the quality of my assemblies?

Answer:

Continuity, resistance, and insulation tests can tell you if the connections are correct but they can NOT tell you anything about the noise canceling effects provided by twisted pairing. A common and serious error in a twisted pair cable is a "*split pair*".

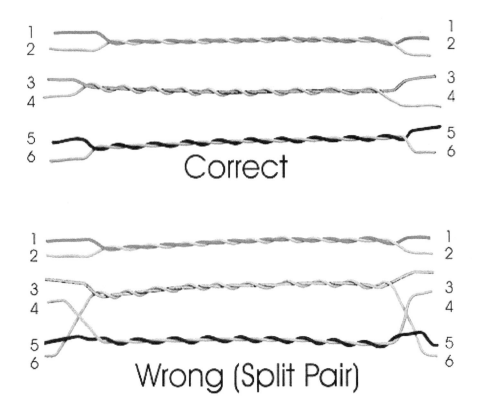

This error occurs when one wire from each of two different pairs gets swapped on both ends of the cable. In our example above, you can see that the white wire of the blue & white twisted pair (pin 4) and the white wire of the black & white twisted pair (pin 6) have been swapped on both ends. The result is a cable that will pass a standard continuity test, but will have serious cross-talk problems. Split pair errors can easily happen in twisted pair cables where one wire of each pair is the same color. Some twisted pair cables have wires of all the same color, making this type of error even easier to produce and harder to find. Even when all the colors are different, it is not that hard to make a mis-wire on one end that is caught during a continuity test and then "fix it" at the other end so that the continuity test passes but a split pair error now exists.

WHAT TESTERS DETECT SPLIT PAIRS?

Some of our testers can detect split pairs by checking that specific wires behave electrically like they are twisted together thus canceling the capacitance coupling effects. **Twisted pair testing is available on the following Cirris testers:** Signature 500, Signature 1000H+, 1100H+, Touch 1 and easy-wire CH.

However, there is more to twisted pair testing than just using the right tester!

TIPS TO SUCCESSFULLY DETECT SPLIT PAIRS

Even with a tester capable of testing for split pairs, there are other challenges when testing twisted pair cables. Test fixturing, twisted pair cable quality and cable length all play an important role in testing for split pairs. Keep in mind the following issues when testing your twisted pair assemblies.

- Do not let the test fixturing degrade your test. Keep your interface wire lengths as short as possible (testing directly on Cirris adapter cards plugged into the tester is preferable) If the interface cable length is more than an inch or two, it must be constructed with the same twisted pairing as the cable to be tested. Also the total length of interface cables (both sides) must be less than 1/3 of the total length of the cable under test. If you cannot avoid longer interface cables, or if you cannot maintain the same twisted pair pattern in your interface cable, a coaxial cable can be used instead. In this case, all points that must be tested for twisted pairs must be connected through coax cable and the shields of all the coax wires must be connected together and grounded to the tester chassis.

- You may not be able to test poor-quality twisted pair cabling shorter than 20 feet. In poor-quality twisted pair cabling each pair is not shielded, the wires have less than 2 twists per inch and there is a general twisting lay to the bundle every foot or so for the length of the cable. For best results with this type of poor-quality cable it is even more important to keep all adapting cables short and to use high quality twisted pair wiring, or shielded wiring in your fixturing.

- Very short cables (less than 2 ft.) have little chance of being properly tested for split pairs. If you have a cable under 6 feet long or a poor quality twisted pair cable as outlined above, you may have success testing this type of cable by adding an *extender cable*. By using a couple of feet of high quality twisted pair cabling matching the twist pattern of the cable to be tested you can increase the length of the whole assembly being tested thus allowing the tester to get a "better read" on the cable. Keep in mind however, if you exceed the length of the cable under test with the extender cable you will be testing the extender cable for split pairs rather than the cable you really want to test.

- Some other techniques you can use to test short cables are to build the cables twice as long as required, test them, then cut the cable in half and terminated the cut ends. Remember, the twisted pair test can be performed on a cable from one end only! Another simple approach is to terminate one end of your cable while the other end is still attached to the reel. After testing for twisted pairs, cut the cable to length right from the reel and terminate the second end.

Wire Fixturing Issues

If you will be testing using 4-wire fixturing adapter cables that are longer than a few inches:

- Each pair of wires that goes to a single test point must be shielded, either individually or as pairs within one shield. These shields in the adapting cable must be tied to the tester chassis.

Wiring Your Network With Bulk Fiber Optic Cables

FIGURE 69FIBER OPTICS

A majority of networks in America are wired using copper network cable, often using Cat5e or Cat6. With the development and growing availability of fiber optics, many people are starting to convert to this newer, slimmer, faster, and less expensive medium.

Optical fiber cable is made of thin reflective tubing that sends light particles that can contain data from one end to the other. The tubing has a mirror-like interior that literally bumps the particle around the microscopic tube until it arrives at its destination.

Because of a resin buffer layer, the light typically does not escape the fiber cable or cause "cross-talk" between individual strands. Also, you don't have to worry about interference or heavy shielding like you would with Cat5 copper cable, so the cables end up being a lot less bulky and lighter.

Different Connectors for Different Uses

Some of the more common connectors on fiber cable include LC, , ST, , SC, , MTRJ, , and Toslink (used in audio applications). Don't let all of these connectors of different shapes and sizes fool you. Fiber is fiber, but different devices choose to use different connector types.

MULTI-MODE FIBER OPTIC CABLE VS. SINGLE MODE FIBER OPTIC CABLES

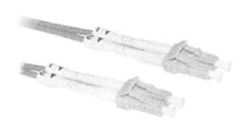

Multi-Mode is mostly used for shorter distance applications, such as wiring the networking backbone of a building. It has transmission speeds ranging from 10 Megbits to approaching 10 gigabits depending on the equipment that is transmitting the data, and generally supports transmission distances up to 550 meters. Generally speaking, the equipment used for multi-mode purposes is far less expensive than for single-mode.

Single-mode optical fiber sends only a single ray of light, but it can non-intuitively travel father and deliver higher bandwidth. The reason for this is that the tighter "tube" is actually better at retaining the fidelity of each individual light pulse. Although equipment for transmitting single mode signals is generally more expensive, buying single-mode fiber in bulk is generally less expensive. Single mode cable can transmit a solid 10 gigabit per second stream to locations 60 kilometers away.

Applications

Generally, multi-mode cable is ideal for short distance networking situations, like wiring a building or a campus. In order to use fiber, you'll need a media converter. Media Converters don't only help you integrate fiber into your network, it can also help you extend your A/V or other digital signals with distance limitations.

THE TWO TYPES OF LOCAL AREA NETWORKS

There are two main types of local network architecture:

1. Wired networks, based on the Ethernet technology, which represent almost all local area networks. Given that Ethernet networks generally use RJ45 cables, people often talk of RJ45 networks;

2. Wireless networks, which generally use the Wi-Fi technology.

NECESSARY HARDWARE

To create an RJ45 local area network in Windows, for example, you will need:

*   Several computers running Windows (computers running two different versions of Windows can be part of the same network);

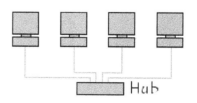

FIGURE 70 A HUB

- Ethernet cards on a PCI or ISA port (with an RJ45 plug) or built into the motherboard. When applicable, make sure the diodes on the back of the network card light up when the computer is on and that a cable is plugged in! There are also network adapters for USB ports, particularly in the case of wireless network adapters;

- RJ45 cables in the case of wired networks;

- A hub, a device you can connect the RJ45 cables from the network's various computers to, which are fairly inexpensive (expect to pay around â,¬50), or a switch, or, as an alternative option, a crossover cable if you want to connect just two computers.

The structure of such a network looks like this:

QUIZ

1. Mention three necessary hardware to create a local area network (LAN):

- Ethernet cards on a PCI or ISA port.

- RJ45 cables.

- A hub, a device you can connect the RJ45 cables.

2. Which are the two main local area networks architecture that exist?

- Wired networks, based on the Ethernet technology.

- Wireless networks, which generally use the Wi-Fi technology.

3. Mention three physical connection medium used to link the computers together:

- Coaxial cable.

- Twisted pair.

- Fibre optics.

Communication standards for networks.

DSL - Digital subscriber line (DSL) Technology is one of the most promising for supporting high-speed digital communication over the existing local loops. DSL technology is the set of technologies each differing in the first letter ADSL, VDSL, DSI and SDSL.

CCITT: Acronym for comité consultatif internationale de telephonic et de telegraphic.

An organization, based in Geneva that develops world-wide data communication standards. CCITT is part of the ITU (International telecommunication Union).

Three main sets of standards have been established CCITT group 1-4 standards apply to facsimile transmissions the CCITT V series of standards apply to modems and error detection and correction methods and series CCITTX standards apply to local area networks.

CABLE MODEM: A cable modem is a type of modem that provides access to a data signal sent over the cable television infrastructure. Cable modems are primarily used to deliver broadband Internet access in the form of cable Internet, taking advantage of unused bandwidth on a cable television network.

MODEM: Contraction of modulator/Demodulator a device that allows a computer to transmit information over a telephone line. The modem translates between the digital signals that the computer uses and analog signals suitable for transmission over a telephones line.

When transmitting the modem modulates the digital data onto a carrier signal on the telephone line. When receiving the modem performs the reverse process and demodulates the data from the carrier signal.

VDSL: The very high bit rate digital subscriber line (VDSL) an alternate approach similar to ADSL, uses coaxial fiber optics or twisted-pair cable for short distances (300 to 1800m).

APPLICATIONS FOR SIMPLEX AND DUPLEX are as follows:

Simplex

1. AM and FM broadcasting

2. TV broadcasting

3. Cable IV

4. Facsimile (Fax)

Duplex

1. Telephones

2. Two-way radio

3. Radar

4. Sonar

5. Local Area Network.

The advantages and disadvantages of RS-232 Interface?

Ans. Advantages.

1. The RS-232 interfaces provides a reliable means of communication. It is a low c interface.

2. It is suitable for low band rate slow system typically up to 20,000 bands.

Disadvantages: RS-232 specifications are for distances less than 50 ft. To increase the distance, the band rate has to be reduced.

What are two components used to utilize the cable network?

Ans. in order to utilize the cable networks for data transmission we have to use two devices namely CM (Cable Modem) and CTMS (Cable modem transmission system).

Q. 13. What is CM (Cable modem)?

Ans.

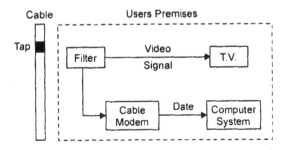

Fig shows the block schematic of cable modem. It is similar to ADSL modem and it is installed at the user premises. The filter separates out video and data in the incoming signal from the cable. [Video signal is applied to T.V. whereas the data signal is applied to the computer via the cable modem.

Q. 14. What is cable modem transmission system (CMTS)?

Ans. The cable companies install the CMTS inside the distributions as shown in fig.

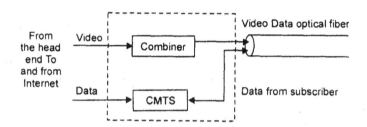

The data from internet is passed through the CMTS to the combiner. The video signal from the head and also is applied to the combiner. The combiner output contains video as well as data from the Internet. This signal is put on the fiber for routing it to the subscribers. The data from the subscribers coming via the optical fiber is applied to the CMTS and the CMTS passes it to the internet.

Q. 15. What is 4 wire modem?

Ans. 4 wires of modems are modems in which one pair of wires is used for the outgoing carrier and other is used for the incoming signal.

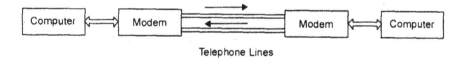

Telephone Lines

Q. 16. What are the advantages of X-21?

Ans.1. The advantages of X.21 standard over RS-530 standard is that X.21 signals are encoded in the serial digital form.

2. This allows the provision of special new services in computer communication.

Q. 17. What is point-to-point connection?

Ans. Point to point—A point to point connection provides a dedicated link between two devices. Entire capacity of the link is reserved for transmission between these two devices only.

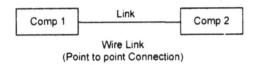

Wire Link
(Point to point Connection)

Multipoint: A multipoint connection is also called as a multidrop connection. In such a connection more than two devices share a single link.

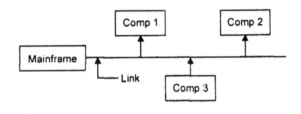

Multipoint Configuration

Q. 18. What are the disadvantages of DSL?

Ans. Disadvantages

1. Availability—Because DSL is distance sensitive availability is determined by the distance from the provider's central office.

2. Distance sensitivity limitations—because service may be limited to within 18,000 net of the DSL provides local office, or point of presence though there are usually several such limitations in given area.

Q 19. What is RS-530?

Ans. RS-530 is a differential communication interface with some single-ended link management signals, typically limited to a maximum though put of 10 Mbps. It uses DB-25 connector and differential equivalents of the V-24 signals.

Q. 20. What is the difference between DSL and cable?

Ans. DSL and Cable- Comparison and Contrast

1. Speed (advantage—Cable) — Cable boasts faster speed than DSL internet in theory. However, cable does not always deliver on the promise in everyday practical use.

2. Popularity—(advantage—both) —In the world, cable internet enjoys significantly greater popularity than DSL, although DSL has been closing the gap recently.

3. Customer satisfaction advantage — DSL)—Even if a technology is popular, customers may be unhappy with it whether   due to cost, reliability or other factors.

4. Security (Advantage—Both)—Cable and DSL implement different network security models. Historically, more concerns have existed with cable security, although cable providers have definitely taken steps to improve security over the past few years. It's likely both DSL and cable are "Secure enough" for most people's needs.

Q. 21. What is DSL and explain various types for that?

Ans. Digital Subscriber Line (DSL) service is one of the most exciting technologies to come to market in the area of information access. The concept is as elegant as it is simple-DSL achieves broadband speeds over ordinary phone lines. That elegance and simplicity has attracted significant attention from a wide variety of customers, and DSL is one of the fastest growing high-speed access technologies for both business and personal use on the market.

Of all of the new telecommunications technologies, DSL is the most powerful, straightforward and flexible solution for high-speed access and information transfer— and the supporting network is already in place.

Digital subscriber Line is a telecommunications service that makes it possible to transform an ordinary phone line into a high-speed conduit for data, voice and video. As long as your home or business is close enough to your service providers central office (a local office with switching equipment which connects everyone in a certain area to the company's net-work, you'll be able to subscribe to DSL service. Typical connections allow users to receive data at 1.5 Mbps and send data at approximately 256 Kbps, though actual speed is determined by the proximity to the provider's central office. DSL service is always on—users don't need to dial a connection to gain access to the internet—and some services even allow users to use the same line for voice and data traffic. There are wide arrays of DSL technologies available, depending on your location and your bandwidth needs. In brief they are

1. IDSL (ISDN Digital Subscriber Line) is a form of DSL that uses ISLJN provisioning and testing, and can coexist with current analog and ISDN services. IDSL is usually limited to 144 Kbps upstream and downstream, but can sometimes provide further reach than other DSL solutions because it does not have the same distance limitations.

2. ADSL (Asymmetric Digital Subscriber Line) employs two different transmission speeds, with the downstream speed (from the provider to the user) usually being much higher than the upstream speed (from the user to the corporate host). ADSL can achieve downstream data rates up to 8 Mbps and upstream rates to I Mbps.

3. VDSL (Very High Speed Digital Subscriber Line) promises even higher speeds than ADSL, although over much shorter distances. Standardization on speeds and technology specifications are currently in progress.

4. RADSL (Rate Adaptive Digital subscriber Line) adjusts the data transmission rate to match the quality of the phone line. RADSL users get the very best performance their telephone line is conditioned to provide, providing transmission rates of up to 7 Mbps downstream and 1 Mbps upstream.

5. HDSL/SDSL (High Data Rate Digital subscriber Line/Symmetric Digital Subscriber Line) utilize two standard phone lines for 1.5 Mbps transmission speeds and offer the capability to combine three phone lines for 2.0 Mbps speeds. HDSL and SDSL are intended as lower cost replacements for dedicated and fractional T-l lines 2.

Q. 22. What is X.21? What are the various signals provided by it?

Ans. X.21 Overview—X.21 is a state-driven protocol running full duplex at 9600 bps to 64 Kbps with subscriber networks. It is a circuit-switching Protocol using Synchronous ASCII with odd parity to connect and disconnect a subscriber to the public- switching network.

The data-transfer phase is transparent to the network. Any data can be transferred through the network after Call Establishment is made successfully via the X. 21 protocol. The call control phases which are used were defined in the CCITT (now ITU) 1988 Blue Book" Recommendations X.l-X.32.

Signals provided: The signals of the X.21 interface are presented on a 15—pin connector defined by ISO Document 4903. The electrical characteristics are defined in CCITT Recommendations X.26 and X.27, which refer to CCITT Recommendations V.10 and V.11.

X.21 PROVIDES EIGHT SIGNALS

1. Signal Ground (G): This provides reference for the logic states against the other circuits. This signal may be connected to the protective ground (earth).

2. DTE Common Return (Ga): Used only in unbalanced-type configurations (X.26), this signal provides reference ground for receiver in the DCL interface.

3. Transmit (T): This carries the binary signals which carry data from the DTE to the I)CL. this circuit can be used in data-transfer phases or in call-control phases from the DIE to DCL (during Call Connect or Call Disconnect).

4. Receive (R): This carries the binary signals from DCE to DTE. It is used during the data transfer or Call Connect/Call Disconnect phases.

5. Control (C): Controlled by the DTE to indicate to the DCE the meaning of the data sent on the transmit circuit. This circuit must be ON during data-transfer phase and can be ON or OFF during call-control phases, as defined by the protocol.

6. Indication (I): The DCE controls this circuit to indicate to the DIE the type of data sent on the Receive line. During data phase, this circuit must be ON and it can be ON or OFF during call control, as defined by the protocol.

7. Signal Element Timing (S): This provides the DTE or DCE with timing information for sampling the Receive line or Transmit line. The DTE samples at the correct instant to determine if a binary I or 0 is being sent by the DCL. The DCE samples to accurately recover signals at the correct instant. This signal is always ON.

8. Byte Timing (B): This circuit is normally ON and provides the DTE with 8 bit byte element timing. The circuit transitions to OFF when the Signals Element Timing circuit samples the last bit of an 8-bit byte. Call-control characters must align with the 13 lead during call-control phases. During data-transfer phase, the communicating devices bilaterally agree to use the B lead to define the end of each transmitted or received byte. The C and I leads then only monitor and record changes in this condition when the 13 lead changes from OFF to ON, although the C and I leads may be altered by the transitions on the S lead. This lead is frequently not used.

Q. 23. What are DCE and DTE for Ethernet?

Ans. Most data communication protocols specify communications between two types of equipment. Typically, one is called DTE (Data Terminal Equipment) and the other is called DCE (Data Circuit-Terminating Equipment). For instance, in EIA 232 communications, DTE devices (terminals, PCs, mini-computers) are quite stubborn and only want to talk to DCE devices (modems, multiplexers), and vice versa. For this reason, you may connect a PC COM port to a modem using a "straight through" EIA 232 cable. However, when you must connect a PC COM port to another PC COM PORT, you must use a "null modem" cable. The function of the null modem cable is to "trick" the DTE device into believing that it is talking to a DCE device by cross-wiring the data and control pins in the cable. Ethernet AUI (Attachment Unit interface) also uses the DTE/DCE convention; however, it's not as simple as it is with EIA-232. The AUI port of a workstation's NIC (Network Interface Card) is a female DB-15 DTE. So is the AU! Port on a multiport hub/repeater such as Patton's Model 2108. The AUI port of a Transceiver like the Model 2100 is a male D13-15 configured DCE. Therefore, it can plug directly into AUI port of the NIC or to the Model 2108. The problem comes with the need to connect a DTE to another DTE, or a DCE to another DCE. The answer is simple: Unlike RS-232, it can't be done with just a cable.

If it were simply a matter of crossing the DI (Data In) pins to the D0 (Data Out) pins via a null modem cable, the matter could be solved simply. However, the CI (Control In) Signals are used specifically by the DCE to indicate to the DTE that a collision has been detected or during a Signal Quality Error. If one were to connect a DTE device to another DTE device with a null modem cable, there would be no provision for this signal. Similarly, connection between two DCEs would cause these signals to conflict with one another. There are CO (Control Out) signals in Ethernet, but these signals are used for another function and are almost never used. So what's the solution when connecting two DTEs together? In order to connect two DTEs together, such as a workstation to a model 2108 hub, two model 2100s may be used, one connects to the workstation's AUI Port and the other to the AUI port of the model 2108 with 10 Base T twisted pair connections in between. The model 2108 also allows up to 8 additional 10 Base-T connections at UTP connections up to 330 ft.

Q. 24. What is a modem? Explain the types.

Ans. A modem provides the communication interface. It transports device protocols transparently over the network through a serial interface. A modem adapts the machine to communicate over various networks in order to gain access to the machine including—

1. PSTN-a wire line dial-up network

2. GSM-.a wireless dial-up network

3. GPRS— a wireless "always on" network.

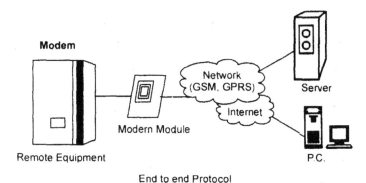

End to end Protocol

Moderns are traditionally associated with PC's in the form of box/PC modems,

However this technology is not suited to non-PC equipment or "machines", which have specialized needs

1. Size—there is little space within many embedded devices for a modem box

2. Power consumption- some devices are battery powered and need low power modems

3. Environment—machines can be deployed and need wide temperature range.

4. Integration— modems need to be integrated within the machine and not external Modems provide remote access to machines in the field to eliminate unnecessary site visits and provide fast access to information in the machine. However, integrating moderns.

1. Moderns are "black art" products, surrounded by complex compliance and regulatory issues. Designing your own modem solutions requires specialized skills. Using off-the-shelf modems enables designers to focus on their core application strengths and not be drawn into solving issues that are not related to core competency yielding potentially unreliable products.

M2M moderns are embedded with the machine and transport higher level protocols between the machine and central location via the network.

2. Point to Point "polled" networks where proprietary or industry specific protocols to communicate with central servers.

3. TCP/IP enabled remote machines such as Embedded PC's, where modems provide the physical network connectivity.

        M2M Modems are Al-command compatible at the serial interface to the machine and common between many modems.

4. Driven and controlled by the remote machine processor using industry standard Commands.

5. Fast time to market.

Q. 25. Explain with pin diagrams of EIA-449 interface.

Ans. EIA 449 interface Standard in case of EIA 232 the data rate is restricted to 20kbps and the cable length to 50 feet. The EIA and ITU-T have introduced the EIA 449 standard for users who require speed and distance.

Mechanical Specifications

1. The mechanical specification of EIA-449 defines a combination of two connectors, one with 37 pins and with 9 pins, for a combined 46 pins as shown in Fig.

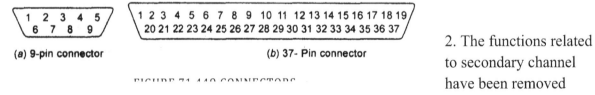

(a) 9-pin connector   (b) 37- Pin connector

FIGURE 71 449 CONNECTORS

2. The functions related to secondary channel have been removed from the DB 37 connector since they are very rarely used.

3. The EIA separates the secondary functions out and has puts them in the second 9 pin connector (DB-9). In this way a second channel is available to systems that need it.

4. To maintain compatibility with EIA-232, EIA-449 defines two categories of pins to be used in exchanging data, control and timing information.

5. The category I pins are those pins whose functions are compatible with those of   EIA-232. Category II pins are those that have no equivalent in EIA-232 as shown in Table 19.

Table 19 pin functions

TABLE-1

Pin	Function	Category	Pin	Function	Category
1.	Shield		20	Receive common	II
2.	Signal rate Indicator		21	Unassigned	I
3.	Unassigned		22	Send data	I
4.	Send data	I	23	Send timing	I
5.	Send timing	I	24	Receive data	I
6.	Receive data	I	25	Request to send	I
7.	Request to send	I	26	Receive timing	I
8.	Receive timing	I	27	Clear to send	I
9.	Clear to send	I	28	Terminal in service	II
10.	Local loopback	II	29	Data mode	I
11.	Data mode	I	30	Terminal ready	I
12.	Terminal ready	I	31	Receive ready	I
13	Receive ready	I	32	Select standby	II
14.	Remote loopback	II	33	Signal quality	
15.	Incoming call		34	New signal	II
16.	Select frequency	II	35	Terminal timing	I
17.	Terminal timing	I	36	Standby indicator	II
18.	Test mode	II	37	Send common	II
19.	Signal ground				

Table 20 gives the pin functions of the DB-9 connector.

TABLE—2

PIN	FUNCTION
1.	Shield
2.	Secondary receive ready
3.	Secondary send data
4.	Secondary receive data
5.	Signal ground
6.	Receive ground
7.	Secondary request to send
8.	Secondary clear to send
9.	Send common

Table 20 Pin functions

Q. 26. How fast is DSL? What are the various fields DSL use with some advantages and disadvantages of DSL?

Ans. DSL services transfer data at speed ranging from 128 Kbps (IDSL) to a potential 9.0 Mbps (HDSL) downstream. Up-stream speeds range from 128 Kbps to I Mbps and, in some cases even higher.

The future of DSL is very bright, as businesses and consumers increasingly move toward an information-based economy. As companies implement more sophisticated applications that require high bandwidth capability, DSL is emerging as the perfect combination of price and performance for a diverse range of applications, from workgroups in different cities across the country to teleworkers in their homes.

FIELD OF USE: DSL is used by a wide variety of companies and individuals who all who all have one thing in common - the need for reliable, always on high-speed data transmission and access. DSL service is used in the telecommunications industry by network service providers, ISPs, and local and public telephone companies. It is used by universities, hospitals and research facilities where high-speed data transmission is essential. In the business environment, DSL services are used for telework programs, workgroup solutions, companies with campuses, and corporate networks in single and multiple locations on a regional or nationwide basis.

ADVANTAGES: There are many advantages to DSL. The most significant advantage is the fact that DSL is more cost-effective because it eliminates the need for extensive and expensive infrastructure upgrades. DSL service requires no new phone lines and little new equipment.

Another advantage that is equally important is DSL's blazing speed. DSL technology transforms the nearly 700 million phone lines installed worldwide into multi-megabyte data pipes capable of speeding digital video and data to homes and businesses.

Additionally DSL is:

1. Easy to use, and requires no additional training

2. Rapidly being deployed and accepted as the emerging standard for high-speed connectivity

3 An always on service that does not require unreliable dial up connections

4. The fastest solution available for telework programs

DSL solves many of the problems associated with alternate access technologies by using the existing telecommunications system to remove the bottlenecks often associated with the last mile between the network service provider and the users of those services.

DISADVANTAGES: There are some disadvantages to the use of DSL service. The greatest disadvantage at the present time is availability—because DSL is distance sensitive, availability is determined by the distance from the provider's central office. Although DSL service is widely available in most metropolitan areas, is often not available in non-metropolitan or rural areas because the distance sensitivity limitation. Service may be limited to within 18,000 feet of the DSL providers local office, or point of presence, though there are usually several such locations in a given urban area. Additionally, DSL operates on traditional copper telephone lines, and is incompatible with fiber optic lines

Q. 27. What is Null modem? Explain the pin configuration of null modem.

Ans. Serial communications with RS232. One of the oldest and most widely spread communication methods in computer world. The way this type of communication can be performed is pretty weil defined in standards i.e. with one exception. The standards show the use of EYI'E/l) CE communication, the way a computer should communicate with a peripheral device like a modem. For your information, DTE means data terminal equipment (Computers etc.) where DCE is the abbreviation of data communication equipment (modems). One of the main uses of serial communication today where no modem is involved—a serial null modem configuration with DTE/DTE communication— is not so well defined, especially when it comes to flow control. The terminology null modern for the situation where two computers communicate directly is so often used nowadays, that most people don't realize anymore the origin of the phrase and that a null modern connection is an exception, not the rule.

In most situations, the original modem sign lines are reused to perform some sort of handshaking. Handshaking can increase the maximum allowed communication speed because it gives the computers the ability to c the flow of information. High amounts of incoming data are allowed if the computer is capable to handle it, but not if it is busy performing other tasks. If no flow control is implemented in the null modem connection, communication is only possible at speeds at which it is sure the receiving side can handle the amount information even under worst case conditions.

Use of RS232 When we look at the connector pin out of the RS232 port, we see two pins which are certainly used for flow control. These two pins are RTS, request to send and CTS, clear to send. With EYI'E/DCE communication (i.e. a computer communicating with a modem device) RTS is an output on the IJTE and input on the DCE. CTS are the answering signal coming from the DCE.

Before sending a character, the DTE asks permission by setting its RTS output. No information will he sent until the DCE grants permission by using the CTS line. If the DCE cannot handle new requests, the CTS signal will go low. A simple but useful mechanism allowing flow control in one direction. The assumption is that the DTE can always handle incoming information faster than the DCE can send it in the past, this was true. Modem speeds of 300 baud were common and 1200 baud was seen as a high speed connection.

For further control of the information flow, both devices have the ability to signal their status to the other side. For this purpose, the DTR data terminal ready and DSR data set ready signals are present. The DTE uses the DTR signal to signal that it is read to accept information, whereas the DCE uses the DSR signal for the same purpose. Using these signals involves not a small protocol of requesting and answering as with the RTS/CTS handshaking. These signals are in one direction only.

The last flow control signal present in DTE/DCE communication is the CD carrier detect. It is not used directly for flow control, but mainly an indication of the ability of the modem device to communicate with its counter part. The Signal indicates the existence of a communication link between two modem devices.

Null modem without handshaking: Flow to use the handshaking line in a null modem configuration? The simplest way is to don't use them at all. In that situation, only the data lines and signal ground are cross connected in the null modem communication cable. All other pins have no connection. An example of such a null modem cable without handshaking can be seen in the figure below.

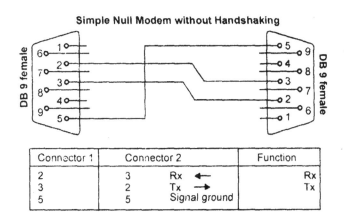

Simple Null Modem without Handshaking

Connector 1	Connector 2		Function
2	3	Rx ←	Rx
3	2	Tx →	Tx
5	5	Signal ground	

Q. 28. What is RS-530 standard explain pins for this standard?

Ans. Interface Standards: RS-530 (often written as RS530) is a specification for differential communication interface that uses a DB-25 connector and differential equivalent of the \'-24 (RS-232) signals. The majority of the signals conform to the RS 422 standard and for the majority of requirements requiring RS-422 signaling the RS530 cable is suitable. Some of the link management controls signals are implemented using V.10 (RS-423) single ended interfaces, and a variant of this standard called RS53OA/ElA-530A also uses V.10 for the DTR signal. Note that the EIA standards have effectively replaced the RS standards.

Interface Characteristics: RS-530 is a differential communications interface with some single-ended link management signals, typically limited to a maximum throughput of 10Mbps. Communications over distance exceeding l000m is possible at low hit rates, actual performance being mostly dependent on cable specification. Separate clock lines are used for receiving and transmitting data.

Interface Applications: E1A530 interfaces are commonly found on communications equipment in some parts of the world where high throughput and /or long distances are required. The interface also offers good noise immunity enabling reliable communications in environments where there are high levels of EM1 (electromagnetic interference).

Applications include high-speed connections between satellite modems and host computer systems.

Interface Connector types and Pinouts: The signals used by the overwhelming majority of applications are marked in bold.

DB25 Connector Pinouts

Signal Name	DB 25 Contact	Supported on Far Sync cards
Shield	1	Yes
Transmit Data (A)	2	Yes
Receive Data (A)	3	Yes
Request to send (A)	4	Yes
Clear to Send (A)	5	Yes
DCE Ready (A)	6	
Signal Ground	7	Yes
Receive Line Signal Detector (A)	8	
Receive Signal Element Timing (B)	9	Yes, see Note
Receive Line Signal Detector (B)	10	
Ext. TX signal Element Timing (B)	11	
Transmit Signal Element Timing (B)	12	Yes
Clear to Send (B)	13	Yes
Transmit Data (B)	14	Yes
Transmit Signal Element Timing (A)	15	Yes
Receive Data (B)	16	Yes
Receive Signal Element Timing (A)	17	Yes, see Note
Local Loopback	18	
Request To Send (B)	19	Yes
DTE Ready (A)	20	
Remote Loopback	21	
DCE Ready (B)	22	
DTE Ready (B)	23	
Ext. TX signal Element Timing (A)	24	
Test Mode	25	

WAN systems.

Is a computer network that spans a relatively large geographical area. Typically, a WAN consists of two or more local-area networks (LANs).

Computers connected to a wide-area network are often connected through public networks, such as the telephone system. They can also be connected through leased lines or satellites. The largest WAN in existence is the Internet.

ADSL: Asymmetric Digital Subscriber Line (ADSL) technology is a modem technology that uses existing twisted-pair telephone lines to transport high-bandwidth data, such as multimedia and video service subscriber.

A **Wide Area Network (WAN)** is a network that covers a broad area (i.e., any telecommunications network that links across metropolitan, regional, or national boundaries) using private or public network transports. Business and government entities utilize WANs to relay data among employees, clients, buyers, and suppliers from various geographical locations. In essence, this mode of telecommunication allows a business to effectively carry out its daily function regardless of location. The Internet can be considered a WAN as well, and is used by businesses, governments, organizations, and individuals for almost any purpose imaginable.

Related terms for other types of networks are personal area networks (PANs), local area networks (LANs), campus area networks (CANs), or metropolitan area networks (MANs) which are usually limited to a room, building, campus or specific metropolitan area (e.g., a city) respectively.

WANs are used to connect LANs and other types of networks together, so that users and computers in one location can communicate with users and computers in other locations. Many WANs are built for one particular organization and are private. Others, built by Internet service providers, provide connections from an organization's LAN to the Internet. WANs are often built using leased lines. At each end of the leased line, a router connects the LAN on one side with a second router within the LAN on the other. Leased lines can be very expensive. Instead of using leased lines, WANs can also be built using less costly circuit switching or packet switching methods. Network protocols including TCP/IP deliver transport and addressing functions. Protocols including Packet over SONET/SDH, MPLS, ATM and Frame relay are often used by service providers to deliver the links that are used in WANs. X.25 was an important early WAN protocol, and is often considered to be the "grandfather" of Frame Relay as many of the underlying protocols and functions of X.25 are still in use today (with upgrades) by Frame Relay.

Features:

- Have machines dedicated to running user programs (hosts).

- A subnet, which connect multiple hosts.

- Division between transmission lines and switching elements (routers).

- It is a system interconnects geographically dispersed computers, which may be even continents. The docking system involves those networks to public data.

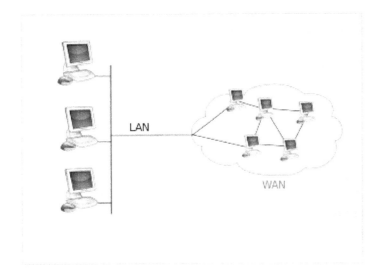

Topologies routers in a wide area network:

- Star.

- Ring.

- Tree.

- Full Mesh.

- Intersection of rings.

- Irregular Mesh.

QUIZ

1. Name at least two topologies for a wide area network:

- Star.

- Ring.

2. The mnemonic WAN stands for the following description:

- Wide Area Network.

3. With your own words define briefly what a WAN consists:

- Consists of two or more local-area networks (LANs).

What is Network Security?

The increasing number of internet threats has caused the need of defense against such threats to become a major demand of common computer users and industries. These threats include various types of viruses, worms, malware, and Trojan horses that are operated by computer hackers (also known as intruders). An intruder can be anyone from a random person trying to compromise your confidential data just for the sake of fun or hobby, to a person who is actually your enemy (either a personal nemesis or part of business rivalry). Hence various techniques and policies are adopted to prevent these threats from intruding into ones' privacy and confidential data. The act of implementing such techniques and policies are called "Network Security".

The prime goal of network security is to protect the usability, integrity, safety and reliability of a network. It detects for possible threats and prevents them from damaging a single machine or entire network from gaining unauthorized privilege. All the network traffic is filtered through the network security policies, these policies can be anything from a set of packet filtering rules (deployed by a network administrator in to the gateway firewall *see figure 72)* to an encrypted transmission that conveys the messages in encrypted format (known as cryptography).

Figure 72 example of gateway firewall

So there are certain measurements that are commonly deployed by network administrator to implement network security which involves cryptography/encryption, improving authentication system, filtering services and ports, using traffic analyzers and intrusion prevention systems such as SNORT, performing vulnerability assessments and a lot more. We will be covering all this and a lot more in this entire course of Network Security, and that will help not only individuals but it specifically protects a business from being disrupt and employees can be kept productive.

All the data of your customers will be safe, and they will have enough trust in you. All of this can be achieved by implementing security to your network. So let's go deep inside this course and explore how these goals are achieved, and let's hope that we will benefit from it as much as possible.

The networks are computer networks, both public and private, that are used every day to conduct transactions and communications among businesses, government agencies and individuals. The networks are comprised of "nodes", which are "client" terminals (individual user PCs) and one or more "servers" and/or "host" computers. They are linked by communication systems, some of which might be private, such as within a company, and others which might be open to public access. The obvious example of a network system that is open to public access is the Internet, but many private networks also utilize publicly-accessible communications. Today, most companies' host computers can be accessed by their employees whether in their offices over a private communications network, or from their homes or hotel rooms while on the road through normal telephone lines.

Network security involves all activities that organizations, enterprises, and institutions undertake to protect the value and ongoing usability of assets and the integrity and continuity of operations. An effective network security strategy requires identifying threats and then choosing the most effective set of tools to combat them.

Threats to network security include:

Viruses : Computer programs written by devious programmers and designed to replicate themselves and infect computers when triggered by a specific event
Trojan horse programs : Delivery vehicles for destructive code, which appear to be harmless or useful software programs such as games
Vandals : Software applications or applets that cause destruction
Attacks : Including reconnaissance attacks (information-gathering activities to collect data that is later used to compromise networks); access attacks (which exploit network vulnerabilities in order to gain entry to e-mail, databases, or the corporate network); and denial-of-service attacks (which prevent access to part or all of a computer system)
Data interception : Involves eavesdropping on communications or altering data packets being transmitted
Social engineering : Obtaining confidential network security information through nontechnical means, such as posing as a technical support person and asking for people's passwords

Other threats could be any of the following:

- Web Worms
- Rootkits
- Honeypots

- Identity lost

- Sniffers

- Physical Threats

- Dangerous Macros

- Eavsdropping

- Security Vulnerabilities

- Risks from the Naive employees.

- Denial of service attacks.

- Data Interception.

Network security tools include

Antivirus software packages : These packages counter most virus threats if regularly updated and correctly maintained.

Secure network infrastructure : Switches and routers have hardware and software features that support secure connectivity, perimeter security, intrusion protection, identity services, and security management.

Dedicated network security hardware and software-Tools such as firewalls and intrusion detection systems provide protection for all areas of the network and enable secure connections.

Virtual private networks : These networks provide access control and data encryption between two different computers on a network. This allows remote workers to connect to the network without the risk of a hacker or thief intercepting data.

Identity services : These services help to identify users and control their activities and transactions on the network. Services include passwords, digital certificates, and digital authentication keys.

Encryption : Encryption ensures that messages cannot be intercepted or read by anyone other than the authorized recipient.

Security management : This is the glue that holds together the other building blocks of a strong security solution.

A computer network can be kept secured by implementing the following techniques and using the tools.

- Install an up-to-dated antivirus program on all the computers and regularly scan them.

- Install an up-to-dated anti spyware program.

- Configure a software or hardware firewall on the gateway computer.

- Limit the rights of the users in your network.

- Use monitoring, diagnosing, troubleshooting and network management tools.

- Implement an intrusion detection system as it will determine that if your network is under attack or not.

- Use strong password, digital authentication keys, and security certifications to identify the users and control their activities.

- Monitory the online activities of the users through he monitoring software and block the suspicious and potentially risky online applications and the websites.

- Encrypt your messages and data while transmitting over the network. Encryption ensures that your data cannot be intercepted or read by the unauthorized users.

- Apply security patches against the known vulnerabilities.

- Update your operating system regularly.

- Lock your server room and no unauthorized user should be allowed to enter in the server room.

- Keep inventory of all the devices including computers, hubs, switches, routers, cables, printers and scanners etc.

- Block the unwanted ports and services.

- Increase the security of your web browsers.

- Regularly take backup of your critical data.

Wireless Network Security

Wireless security is the prevention of unauthorized access or damage to computers using wireless networks. The most common types of wireless security are Wired Equivalent Privacy (WEP) and Wi-Fi Protected Access (WPA). WEP is one of the least secure forms of security. A network that is secured with WEP has been cracked in 3 minutes by the FBI. WEP is an old IEEE 802.11 standard from 1999 which was outdated in 2003 by WPA or Wi-Fi Protected Access. WPA was a quick alternative to improve security over WEP. The current standard is WPA2; some hardware cannot support WPA2 without firmware upgrade or replacement. WPA2 uses an encryption device which encrypts the network with a 256 bit key; the longer key length improves security over WEP.

Many laptop computers have wireless cards pre-installed. The ability to enter a network while mobile has great benefits. However, wireless networking is prone to some security issues.

Crackers have found wireless networks relatively easy to break into, and even use wireless technology to crack into wired networks. As a result, it's very important that enterprises define effective wireless security policies that guard against unauthorized access to important resources. Wireless Intrusion Prevention Systems (WIPS) or Wireless Intrusion Detection Systems (WIDS) are commonly used to enforce wireless security policies.

The risks to users of wireless technology have increased as the service has become more popular. There were relatively few dangers when wireless technology was first introduced. Crackers had not yet had time to latch on to the new technology and wireless was not commonly found in the work place. However, there are a great number of security risks associated with the current wireless protocols and encryption methods, and in the carelessness and ignorance that exists at the user and corporate IT level. Cracking methods have become much more sophisticated and innovative with wireless. Cracking has also become much easier and more accessible with easy-to-use Windows or Linux-based tools being made available on the web at no charge.

Types of Wireless Network Security and their Standards

1. **WPA**

   o "WPA," or "Wi-Fi Protected Access," is a type of wireless network security that relies on encryption. This means that all digital data sent over a wireless network is coded in a way that is extremely difficult to decipher. In addition to encrypting data, WPA security provides user authentication. Authentication means that only permitted computer users are allowed access to the network.

Two versions of WPA, known as WPA and WPA2, are available. The first version is commonly used in corporate or organization situations where many different users must connect to a single network. It is designed to use a pre-shared security key, which is the same for every user. The second version, WPA2, is compatible with fewer networks, but is more secure. WPA2 is typically used whenever possible, with WPA as a backup option for older systems.

2. **WEP**

   o "WEP," which is short for "Wired Equivalent Privacy," was introduced earlier than WPA and was one of the first wireless security protocols available. While outdated, WEP is still available on many older network devices. When WEP is used, a security password is created and wireless data is encrypted. Unfortunately, because this encryption is not very sophisticated, it can be bypassed by somebody intent on stealing data.

Because of this potential security vulnerability, using WEP is usually not recommended. Wireless devices such as routers and access points that rely on WEP should be upgraded to the more secure WPA security type if possible. However, if there is no alternative, WEP security is still preferable to a completely unsecure wireless network.

o

802.1X

    o   The 802.1X wireless security type is used as an additional layer of security that can be used with both WEP and WPA networks. Under this security, a special server is used to validate network users. Essentially, this server contains a list of users who are authorized on the network. Users with the proper permission are allowed to connect, while unauthorized outside users are blocked.

Using the 802.1X security type in conjunction with an additional encryption type, such as WPA, is usually very secure. In this setup, not only is wireless data encoded, but only pre-screened users are allowed to share data. This high level of wireless network security is common in business or government settings where sensitive data is present.

Principles of cryptography

Cryptography is one of the essential components of the network security. It is the process of sending encrypted data and decrypting it upon reception using a pair of keys. Both the sender and receiver use the key to encrypt and decrypt the data. The purpose of cryptography is to disguise the information inside the data in to something that can not be understood by an interceptor even if he has successfully intercepted the transmission. Only authorized parties who has the key will be able to decrypt the information inside the received data. Now upon reading, this sounds an easy job but practically it involves more than just one or two process (which we will learn in this chapter).

For our better understanding let's assume that there are two parties talking to each other and they want make their chat private (so no one else can read it). They will use cryptography to encrypt their message transmission. *(see figure 54)*. Let us say Alice said "meet me at 5" to Bob, in this scenario "meet me at 5" is the data in plain-text (or clear-text) form. Without encryption anyone can read it if they are successfully able to intercept the transmission. If the transmission has cryptography enabled; intruder should only be able to receive something like this "*?b64ICjEwsYgwtJ8W69 MbkuCT165KLuk Z4aXB619K HOpG07VAh4Q9zzUW xn7HOHOB619KAkxn7HOHOpG07VAh4Q9zzUW bkuCT165*" (which is an example of encrypted text also known as cipher-text) instead of the original message "meet me at 5" (which will be sent to its destined recipient only, which the receiver will read it in clear-text when he will provide the right key).

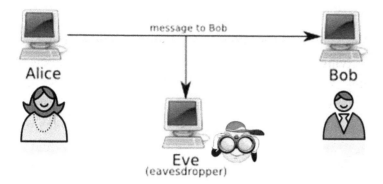

Figure 73 eve (eavesdropper)

Now there's a little more to this than just using keys to encrypt and decrypt data. There are two types of key algorithm:

1. **Symmetric Key Cryptography**

2. **Public Key Cryptography**

Both of these algorithms have their own usage and advantages. Let's go in a little more detail to this subject and let's learn more about these types of keys.

SYMMETRIC KEY CRYPTOGRAPHY

In symmetric-key cryptography, a single key is shared between both sender and receiver, so encrypting and decrypting requires same key. The key in symmetric cryptography is kept secret between sender and receiver only. So literally speaking it is something like a person is sending a written message on a paper to the recipient in a secret code words pattern that only your recipient knows about. For example, "tomorrow dinner at five" is coded in to something like "vqottqy fkppgt cv hkxg" and sender has used coding pattern of reverting back 2 steps on each alphabet (i.e. tomorrow's T is two alphabets before V, so you see it's starting with vqottqy and the same pattern is applied to rest of the message). This is just a practical life example of how the symmetric key cryptography works as part of network security. Even if an intruder has gained access to the message, he will not be able to understand the message unless he has the required key. *(see figure 55)*

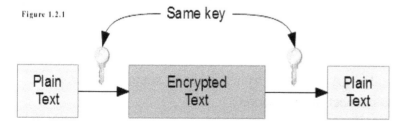

Figure 74 symmetric key crytography

PUBLIC KEY CRYPTOGRAPHY

This type of cryptography is also known as asymmetric cryptography, as this technique requires two different keys at both sending and receiving points. Both parties will have one private key and one public key, in which the private key is kept secret and not shared whereas the public key is published publicly and can be viewed by anyone. The mechanism of this cryptography is to encrypt the message using a symmetric key that is further encrypted by symmetric public key of the

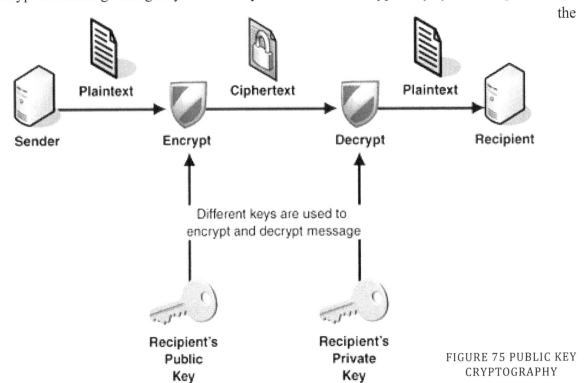

FIGURE 75 PUBLIC KEY CRYPTOGRAPHY

receiving party. The receiver will use its private key to decrypt
the symmetric key first and then the symmetric key inside will decrypt the entire message. *(see figure 75)*

AUTHENTICATION

In terms of cryptography, authentication is slightly different from what a normal authentication process is. That is to say, in a normal authentication process, when Host A communicates with Host B, and Host A will be asked a password in order to gain access to Host B (i.e. a username and its corresponding password) and Host A will response to request of Host B by providing the required credentials and then finally we have a connection established between both the Host A and Host B. (Usually in such scenarios, Host A is a client trying to access some service running on Host B i.e. SSH client attempting to connect to SSH server).

In cryptography, the transmission is based upon both the encrypted message and signature (to prove authenticity). Sender is bound to send recipient with a secret and authenticated message (known as) M, so the recipient can be assured that it was indeed sent by the true sender and not by some intruder (i.e. Bob needs to be assured that message was indeed sent by Alice and not by some intruder). *(see figure 1.3)*

As we can see in the above illustration that there are total four keys used for encrypted transmission. Both the sender and receiver require a pair of keys. If sender has to send a message to recipient then sender will use recipient's public key to encrypt the message and then the encrypted message will be further encrypted using the sender's own private key. After transmission has established, the recipient will authenticate the message by using the public key of sender, and then just like in the sending procedure -recipient will further decrypt it using its own private key and then it will be opened to its original form (clear-text). This secure transmission of cryptography, guarantees the authenticity of sender to the recipient.

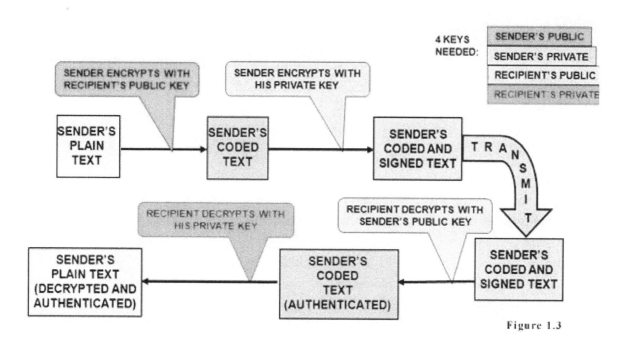

Figure 76 example of authentication

MESSAGE AUTHENTICATION CODE (MAC)

Message Authentication Code (or MAC) is a small component of authentication procedure in cryptography mechanism. Its function is to provide integrity and authenticity to the message during an encrypted transmission. While the goal of integrity is to ensure accidental or intentional message changes by intruder, the goal of MAC is to ensure the sender's identity in the transmission so that receiver can verify the origin.

INTEGRITY

Even with the powerful encryption scenario explained previously, there are still chances of integrity failure in an encrypted transmission between sender and receiver. That is to say, cryptography's responsibility is to ensure that the messages being sent to its destination are not by any mean altered in the middle by the intruder. To keep the integrity of transmission the method of cryptographic hashes is used to prevent intruder from altering the messages.

HASH FUNCTIONS

Hash functions do not require any sort of key, neither public nor private. It utilizes an algorithm to produce a fixed length hash value by taking an arbitrary block of data from the originated clear-text message. *(see figure 58)*

Figure 77 Hash Function

As you can see in the illustration above, we have explained that the hash function has generated some hexadecimal values (called digest/hash sum). These sums are generated when a message is dispatched from its origin. They are verified at the receiving end to make sure the sums are same or not. Once verified it will ultimately prove the integrity of the message that it has not been altered or compromised by the intruder in the middle. Even a single bit of alphanumeric changes in the clear-text message will create entirely different hash sum. This is the proof of strong strength of hash function and how it can secure a transmission.

So the goal of hash functions is to check for the integrity of the message whether the message has been altered/compromised or not by the intruder or virus. And this along other function of cryptography as explained previously put together a strong privacy barrier to the transmission between sender and receiver.

Now let us review entire encryption procedure with hash function in the illustration below:

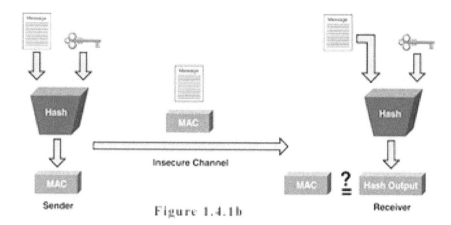

Figure 78 example of a hash function

Therefore, this is the wonders of cryptography to the world of data transmission and we feel very blessed and secured with such incredible feature provided by the cryptography.

KEY DISTRIBUTION AND CERTIFICATION

Now at this point everything seems so secure and confidential to you after reading about how cryptography can secure a message or data transmission. But let's go more in detail of the topic and let's discuss how the key distribution takes place and what certification is. Even though symmetric key cryptography is a fine cryptographic method of communication but it has its own little drawback. Both the sending and receiving party will have to share a single key for encryption and decryption. While with asymmetric cryptography the hassle of sharing single key is eliminated, but still the fact that the encryption method for this cryptography is quite complicated because it requires obtaining of sender's genuine public key. So both these issues can be resolved when we use a trusted intermediary.

To make things more flexible in symmetric cryptographic, the trusted intermediary, called "Key Distribution Center (KDC) is used. It is a stand-alone trusted entity over the network to which sender will establish its shared secret key for the receiver to obtain it for decryption the information. With Asymmetric cryptography, the trusted intermediary is "Certification Authority (CA)". Its responsibility is to certify that a public key belongs to a certain entity. After the concerned parties have trusted the CA that it certifies the key, then they can be sure to whom the public key belongs. Once public key is certified, it will be distributed from anywhere, whether it's a public key server, website or any storage location over the network.

THE KEY DISTRIBUTION CENTER

Let's explore KDC in a little more detail. If we make a scenario in which Alice and bob are two participant of a conversion and they have never met before but want to establish a shared secret key in advance. Now the question is how they can communicate and agree upon a common secret key for encrypted message transmission. Here is when KDC play a major role in resolving this issue. KDC is a server that shares a different secret symmetric key amongst its registered users. This key can be manually installed at the KDC when a user registers.

Now let us see how KDC allow a user to securely obtain a key from it for communication. Let us say that Alice and bob are registered at KDC; they only know each other's key respectively, KA-KDC and KB-KDC, for both respectively. Alice initiates the procedure as illustrated in *figure 79*

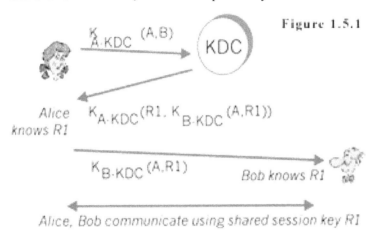

Figure 79 Example of key distribution

- Using $K_{A\text{-}KDC}$ to encrypt her transmission with the KDC, Alice has send the message to KDC stating (*A*) is trying to communicate with Bob (*B*). We denote this transmission, $K_{A\text{-}KDC}$ *(A,B)*. As part of this transmission, Alice should authenticate the KDC and the shared key $K_{A\text{-}KDC}$.

- The KDC, knowing $K_{A\text{-}KDC}$, decrypts $K_{A\text{-}KDC}$ *(A,B)*. The KDC has authenticated Alice. The KDC then generates a random number, which we have denoted as *R1*. This is used as shared key value that Alice and Bob are using to perform symmetric key cryptography during the transmission. This key is known as a **one-time session key** *(see section 1.5.3)*. The KDC will now inform Alice and Bob of the value of *R1*. The KDC therefore sends back an encrypted message to Alice which contains following:

  o *R1,* the one-time session key that Alice and Bob will use for transmission;

  o a pair of values: A, and *R1,* encrypted by the KDC using Bob's key, $K_{B\text{-}KDC}$. We now denote this $K_{B\text{-}KDC}(A,R1)$. It is necessary to note that KDC is sending Alice not just the value of *R1* for her own usage, but also an encrypted variation of *R1* and Alice's name encrypted using Bob's key. Alice can't decrypt this pair of values in the message.

These items are put into a message and encrypted using Alice's shared key. The message from the KDC to Alice is thus $K_{A\text{-}KDC}(R1,K_{B\text{-}KDC}(R1))$.

- Alice receives the message from the KDC, verifies the nonce, extracts *R1* from the message and saves it. Alice now knows the one-time session key, *R1*. Alice also extracts $K_{B-KDC}(A,R1)$ and forwards this to Bob.

- Bob decrypts the received message, $K_{B-KDC}(A,R1)$, using K_{B-KDC} and extracts A and *R1*. Bob is now aware of the one-time session key, *R1,* and the person with whom he is sharing this key.

Certification Authority (CA)

Now let's learn about Certification Authority (CA) in detail. Just like KDC is for symmetric key cryptography, CA is an entity that generates digital certificates in asymmetric key cryptography. This allows the communicating parties to rely on signatures made by the private key which corresponds to the certified public key. In this model of trust, the CA is trusted as third party by both the originator of the transmission and the receiving party which is relying on certificate. Certification Authority is part of PKI *(see section 1.5.4)*

Figure 1.5.4

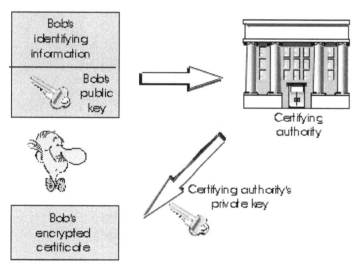

One-Time Session Keys

One-Time Session Keys is used by both KDC and in Public Key systems. For KDC, it is a single session between two communicators. By using this one-time session keys, a user is free of having to establish a priori its own shared key for any network entity with whom it wants to communicate. User just need to have a single shared secret key for communicating with the KDC, and it will receive one-time session keys from the KDC for all of its transmission with other network entities.

Public-Key Infrastructure

PKI is a complete system of software, hardware, policies, entities, and procedures required to issue, manage, distribute, store and revoke the digital certificates. PKI uses a pair of mathematically related cryptographic keys. One key is used to encrypt information, and only this related key will be able to decrypt the information. Even if you know one of the keys, you won't be able to calculate what the other one is quite easily. Therefore, in a PKI system you have the following:

- A public key

- A corresponding private key (which will be unique).

And the private key will only be used to prove your identity for the purpose of authentication.

Access control: Firewalls

A firewall is basically a type of access control mechanism which shields a network or single host with protection and security. There are two types of firewalls; hardware firewall and software firewall.

A firewall (within access control scenario) can be used to achieve very wide range of operations including preventing intruders to hack your computer, preventing your confidential data from being theft and on enterprise level it can block specific operations within the local network or external network combined. (i.e. Alice and bob on same LAN can not share files and folders to each other, OR they both can share files and folders to each other but they can not share them over the internet).

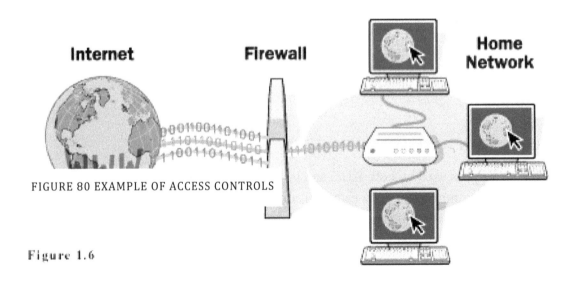

FIGURE 80 EXAMPLE OF ACCESS CONTROLS

Figure 1.6

HARDWARE FIREWALL VS. SOFTWARE FIREWALL

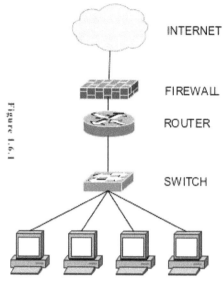

FIGURE 81 HARDWARE VS. SOFTWARE

Hardware firewalls runs independent of a PC. It is easier to maintain and manage than those firewalls that you install on your PC. Whereas software firewall is installed as a software application package on a computer system and it will share resources of the computer alongside other applications that are already running on the machine (i.e. web browsers, multimedia applications, other system utilities, etc.). While hardware firewall is based on sole operating system which in itself work as firewall and utilizes entire bandwidth of the hardware and there is nothing extra that runs on the hardware that is not part of firewall service. However hardware firewall are usually used at network gateway level and are quite expensive compared to software firewall on a home user computer. IPTables on Linux and IPFirewall on FreeBSD are most common examples of software firewalls. For hardware firewall see the example in *figure 81* Please note that all three "switch, router, firewall" in *figure 81* are hardware devices.

List of known hardware firewalls:

- Cisco PIX 535

- Netgear FVS318

- Juniper Networks SSG 550M

- Check Point Power-1 11075

- D-Link DFL-210

List of known software firewalls:

- IPTables

- IPFirewall

- Check Point Endpoint Security

- Comodo Internet Security

- ZoneAlarm

- PeerGuardian

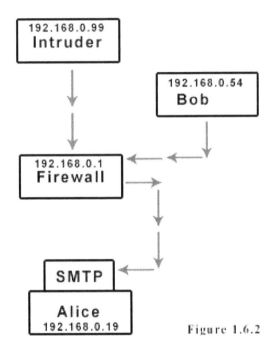

Figure 1.6.2

Figure 82 example of packet filtering

PACKET FILTERING

Packet filtering is a core feature of any firewall (especially software firewall). It intercept every traffic that passes through network interface card (both incoming and outgoing) and restricts them according to applied policies based on specific source and destination addresses, port numbers (i.e. services like smtp, http, ssh, as they run on IPv4 port numbers), or protocols (i.e. IGMP, ICMP, UDP, TCP). Suppose Alice wants her SMPT to be used only by bob and no one else then Alice will apply a packet filtering rule in which she will deny SMPT (often port 25) both incoming and outgoing to everyone else except for IP Address of Bob (in some scenario, a combination of MAC Address and IP Address both are used or just MAC Address instead of IP Address in packet filters).

ATTACKS AND COUNTER MEASURES

In cryptography, the less information intruder has, the stronger the transmission will be. First we will learn about the types of attacks that the intruder can attempt to launch, and then we will learn about possible ways of preventing them to occur. Below we will learn about different levels of attacks an attacker can use to break in to an encrypted transmission to read the cipher-text as plain-text:

CIPHER-TEXT ONLY

In "cipher-text only attack", the attacker will have only a cipher-text. This is the strongest defense of a cryptographic transmission because it is one of the most difficult for an intruder to crack.

KNOWN PLAIN-TEXT

In this attack, the attacker will capture the plaintext and its corresponding cipher-text. The attacker will now be able to easily make conclusions about the encryption key used, and will have validation once the encryption key is discovered.

CHOSEN PLAIN-TEXT

In this attack, the attacker chooses a dummy plain-text to be encrypted. This usually occurs when the original sender steps away from the computer seat and the attacker meanwhile sends a message from his/her computer and captures the resulting cipher-text. The attacker can select plain-text which will produce hints to the encryption key used.

ITERATIVE CHOSEN PLAIN-TEXT

In this attack (which is also known as batch chosen-plaintext attack), the attacker runs a network sniffer *(see section 1.7.4.1)* and sends multiple messages to capture the resulting cipher-text on his sniffer. In an adaptive chosen-plaintext attack, the attacker will use the captured results of the attack so that he can modify the plaintext and capture the resulting cipher-text to see how the changes are affecting the resulting cipher-text.

PACKET SNIFFER

Packet sniffer (also known as packet analyzer) is a program that detects and displays all the traffic that passes through the network interface on which the sniffer is installed. If it is installed at a gateway or inside a non-secure network with promiscuous mode enabled, it will capture all the traffic that passes through any source and any destination of your local network.

CHOSEN CIPHER-TEXT

In Chosen cipher-text attack, attacker compiles information, at least in chunks, by choosing a random cipher-text and obtaining its decryption through an unknown key. Thus, an adversary has a chance to enter multiple known cipher-texts into the system and acquire the resulting plain texts. From these snippets of information, the adversary can attempt to recover the hidden secret key used for decryption.

Suggested counter-measures against cryptographic attacks

We can use these countermeasures avoid cryptographic attack and strengthen the cryptosystem:

Use strong passwords

Again, we are talking about passwords that are used by MAC as part of cryptography. The length and strength of these passwords are important and they should be equally strong just like passwords of your other accounts are strong. An example of a strong password can be "N0n!.0fÿrB1x@PC" here you can see the combination of not only alpha-numeric characters but we have also demonstrated the usage of ASCII code in the password which ultimately makes your password very much stronger (almost impossible to crack).

IMPLEMENT STRONG CRYPTOSYSTEMS WITH REDUNDANT CRYPTOGRAPHY

Since cryptography is not a new technique of encrypting data transmission, a person might easily use classic methods of establishing an encrypted transmission and thus, eventually could fail to ensure strong cryptosystem. To tackle this issue it is essential to know which technology and cipher algorithm is the strongest one. Below you can see list of some of the strong cryptography mechanism and algorithms:

PGP (a program that generally considered an example of strong cryptography solution)

AES (Considered as one of the strong cipher-text algorithm)

SSL protocol (provides security for web-based transmissions)

Furthermore, as we have learned that firewall is used to prevent unwanted access to certain service or entire machine on a network, we can also use firewall to keep our transmission completely transparent for the intruder. Another great deal of encrypted transmission can be established by using Virtual Private Network and it will also make your network completely encrypted even for a packet sniffer, because there will be double encryption in this transmission. But that is really another world of Network Security.

However, there is another way of blocking the packet sniffer from reading your data transfer, which is to use a Router instead of ordinary switches or hubs in your LAN. Because a sniffer normally (if not installed at gateway) reads broadcast messages and routers are designed to work against such mechanism. Routers are intelligent enough to know the origins of a packet and its corresponding destination. They don't send broadcast packets and delivers the data uniquely to its intended destination. Even though a manageable switch (also known as layer-2 switch) is also capable of handling packet sniffing issues but obviously a router works at layer-3 and handles the traffic much more efficiently.

Exercise

Quizzes:

Q.1) what is the difference between Gateway Firewall and Personal Firewall?

Answer) A Gateway firewall is usually a hardware firewall or a particular computer system specially dedicated as a firewall machine in the middle of a network that becomes barrier between the internet traffic that passes to and by the network clients in order to restrict it, as per deployed policies. Whereas a personal firewall is similar to gateway firewall except that it is only responsible for a single machine on which it is installed and it does not take responsibility of other clients on same network (unlike gateway firewall which is held responsible for every machine on a network that has been assigned to be administer).

Q.2) Cryptography is part of packet filtering rules within firewalls. (state whether true or false)

Answer) False

Q.3) Can the receiver of encrypted message, decrypt it using his own public key in asymmetric key cryptography? (Elaborate briefly)

Answer) No, receiver's public key is used by the sender during the process of encryption, the sender will use receiver's public key to decrypt it and receiver will use his own private key to decrypt the message.

Q.4) Alice has accessed the SSH Server of Bob. While she was accessing it, she was asked for the username and password for the SSH session and once it was approved she was granted with access to SSH Server of Bob. This is a true example of cryptography authentication. (State true or false)

Answer) False

Q.5) Public-key infrastructure is only used for asymmetric cryptography? (Elaborate briefly)

Answer) PKI is generally used in asymmetric cryptographic transmission because of its sophisticated mechanism as it requires both private key and public key to ensure its two-way transmission.

Q.6) Software Firewalls are far more advanced and secured compared to Hardware Firewall. (State true or false)

Answer) False

Assignment

Learn about IPTables (from internet or through your local installation of Linux Operating system by following the instructions given in the manpage of iptables) and answer the following scenario:

Alice has a web-server running on her computer. She wants to block John, Fred, and Smith to access her web-server and only wishes to allow Bob to access the web-server. What iptables rule will accomplish this task?

Answer: let's assume john IP Address is 1.2.3.4, fred 2.3.4.5, smith 3.4.5.6, and bob 4.5.6.7

iptables -A INPUT -p tcp -s 1.2.3.4 --dport 80 -j DROP

iptables -A INPUT -p tcp -s 2.3.4.5 --dport 80 -j DROP

iptables -A INPUT -p tcp -s 3.4.5.6 --dport 80 -j DROP

iptables -A INPUT -p tcp -s 4.5.6.7 --dport 80 -j ACCEPT

PROJECT

Conduct research on section 1.7 and draw an illustration/diagram of the following cipher attacks:

Cipher-text only

Known plain-text

Chosen plain-text

Iterative chosen plain-text

Similar to chosen plain-text attack

Chosen cipher-text

Using Ethereal and TCPDUMP

Ethereal (Wireshark)

Wireshark (formerly known as ethereal) is one of the most used ntework protocol analyzer. It is used to capture and interactively browse the traffic running on a computer network's interface. It is the de facto (and often de jure) standard across many industries and educational institutions. It supports inception of more than 100 protocols and since it is an opensource project, network expert continuously contribute to this project and add more and more protocol support time after time. It is a cross-platform project and runs on Windows, Linux, OS X, Solaris, BSD and many other operating system. It comes with both GUI and CLI (compatible for TTY-mode). What makes this program superior than other is, the ability of analyzing wide rang of protocol and service which includes Rich VoIP analysis, live data can be read from Ethernet, IEEE 802.11, PPP/HDLC, ATM, Bluetooth, USB, Token Ring, Frame Relay, FDDI, and others (depending on your platform) Decryption support for many protocols, including IPsec, ISAKMP, Kerberos, SNMPv3, SSL/TLS, WEP, and WPA/WPA2 Coloring rules can be applied to the packet list for quick, intuitive analysis Output can be exported to XML, PostScript®, CSV, or plain text.

Using Ethereal/Wireshark (For GUI)

Wireshark captures packets in real time and display them in wide range of formats including human-readable format. Wireshark includes filters, color-coding and other features that explore deeply into network traffic and inspect each packet respectively.

CAPTURING PACKETS

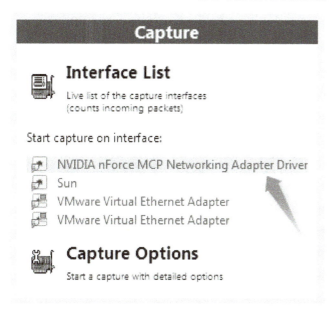

Figure 83 capturing packets

In order to capture traffic on your network, click your network interface. You can configure advanced features by clicking Capture Options.

As soon as you choose your network interface, packet capturing procedure will begin and results will start to appear in real time. Wireshark captures each packet sent TO or FROM your network interface. If you are capturing on a LAN and have promiscuous mode enabled in your capture options, you will also see other computers' packets on the network.

COLOR CODING

Figure 84 example of color coding

Wireshark usually display packets highlighted in green, blue and black colors. These colors classify the type of traffic so that you can identify the traffic at a glance without tracing the packets in detail. By default, dark blue is DNS traffic, green is TCP traffic, light blue is UDP traffic and black classify TCP packets with errors.

FILTERING PACKETS

If you want to inspect specific traffic, such as the traffic a program sends over UDP only, it helps to close down all other applications using the network so you can narrow down the traffic results. You might still have a large amount of packets to sift through. That is where we customize Wireshark's filters to display specific traffic only.

To apply a filter, type the string into the filter box at the top of the window and click Apply (or press Enter). For example, type "DNS" and you will see only DNS packets.

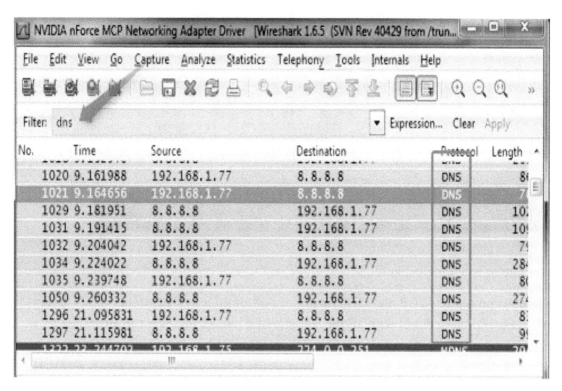

Figure 85 example of filtering packets

You can also click the Analyze menu and select Display Filters to create a customized filter.

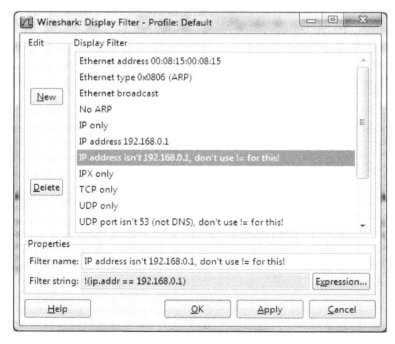

Figure 86 another example of filtering packets

INSPECTING PACKETS

Wireshark allows you to inspect each and every packet thoroughly with intense details. If you click on any packet (captured) you will see its details in window below.

Figure 87 example of ispecting packets

Most of the famous protocols (TCP and UDP) will have all of their header, trailer, body, every part of the packet explored in detail with all the statistic of a packet that went from source to destination.

TCPDUMP

TCPDUMP is a powerful network analysis tool for information security professionals. It is equally used as much as wireshark is used. Many prefer to use Wireshark (most probably because it comes with cool GUI), but TCPDUMP has its own charm and characteristics that we are going to discuss in this topic.

When using a tool that displays network traffic in raw form, the burden of analysis is placed directly on the human rather than the application. This approach cultivates continued and elevated understanding of the TCP/IP suite, and this is one of the main reason why network programmers use tcpdump instead of fancy GUI based packet analyzers.

USING TCPDUMP

Based on what kind of traffic you are inspecting, you will use a different combination of options to tcpdump, as can be seen below:

1. **Basic communication**:

This will display basic information about traffic

tcpdump -nS

2. **Basic communication (very verbose):**

It will display a good amount of traffic, with verbosity.

tcpdump -nnvvS

3. **A deeper look at the traffic:**

Add -X for payload but it won't grab any more of the packet

tcpdump -nnvvXS

4. **Heavy packet viewing:**

The final "s" increases the snap-length, which will grab entire packet

tcpdump -nnvvXSs 1514

Here's a capture of exactly two (-c2) ICMP packets using some of the options described above. Notice what detail we see about each packet.

hermes root # tcpdump -nnvXSs 0 -c2 icmp

tcpdump: listening on eth0, link-type EN10MB (Ethernet), 23:11:10.370321 IP

(tos 0x20, ttl 48, id 34859, offset 0, flags [none], length: 84)

69.254.213.43 > 72.21.34.42: icmp 64: echo request seq 0

```
0x0000:  4520 0054 882b 0000 3001 7cf5 45fe d52b  E..T.+..0.|.E..+
0x0010:  4815 222a 0800 3530 272a 0000 25ff d744  H."*..50'*..%..D
0x0020:  ae5e 0500 0809 0a0b 0c0d 0e0f 1011 1213  .^..............
0x0030:  1415 1617 1819 1a1b 1c1d 1e1f 2021 2223  .............!"#
0x0040:  2425 2627 2829 2a2b 2c2d 2e2f 3031 3233  $%&'()*+,-./0123
0x0050:  3435 3637                      4567
```

23:11:10.370344 IP (tos 0x20, ttl 64, id 35612, offset 0, flags [none],

length: 84) 72.21.34.42 > 69.254.213.43: icmp 64: echo reply seq 0

```
0x0000:  4520 0054 8b1c 0000 4001 6a04 4815 222a  E..T....@.j.H."*
0x0010:  45fe d52b 0000 3d30 272a 0000 25ff d744  E..+..=0'*..%..D
0x0020:  ae5e 0500 0809 0a0b 0c0d 0e0f 1011 1213  .^..............
0x0030:  1415 1617 1819 1a1b 1c1d 1e1f 2021 2223  .............!"#
0x0040:  2425 2627 2829 2a2b 2c2d 2e2f 3031 3233  $%&'()*+,-./0123
```

0x0050: 3435 3637   4567

2 packets captured

2 packets received by filter

0 packets dropped by kernel

hermes root #

COMMON SYNTAX

Expressions will allow you to trim out various types of traffic and find specifically what you are looking for. There are three main types of expression: type, dir, and proto.

Type options are host, net, and port. Direction is indicated by dir, and there you can have src, dst, src or dst, and src and dst. Here are a few that you should definitely be comfortable with:

- **Host**:

It looks for traffic based on IP address (also works with hostname if you're not using **-n**)

tcpdump host 1.2.3.4

(let's say if hostname is sulee then example will be)

tcpdump sulee 1.2.3.4

- **src, dst**:

It finds traffic from either source or destination

tcpdump src 2.3.4.5
tcpdump dst 3.4.5.6

- **net**:

It captures an entire network using CIDR notation .

tcpdump net 1.2.3.0/24

- **proto:**

It works for tcp, udp, and icmp. Note that you don't have to type "proto" itself.

tcpdump icmp

- **port**:

It will display only traffic TO or FROM a certain port

tcpdump port 3389

- **src, dst port**:

It will filter traffic based on the source or destination port

tcpdump src port 1025
tcpdump dst port 389

- **src/dst, port, protocol**:

We can combine all three (and more switches)

tcpdump src port 1025 and tcp
tcpdump udp and src port 53

Specialized Traffic

Just like Wireshark, TCPDUMP is also used for capturing specific and specialized traffic, such as IPv6 and malformed/likely-malicious packets.

IPv6 traffic

tcpdump ip6

Packets with both the RST and SYN flags set (why?)

tcpdump 'tcp[13] = 6'

Traffic with the 'Evil Bit' Set

tcpdump 'ip[6] & 128 != 0'

EXAMINING IP HEADER FIELDS

In this chapter, we will learn about IPv4, which has been defined in RFC 791. The Internet Protocol (IP) uses a Datagram service to transfer packets of data between end systems using routers. The IPv4 datagram is divided into two parts: the header and the payload. The header contains addressing and control fields, while the payload carries the actual data to be sent. The IPv4 packet header consists of 20 bytes of data. The full header is shown below:

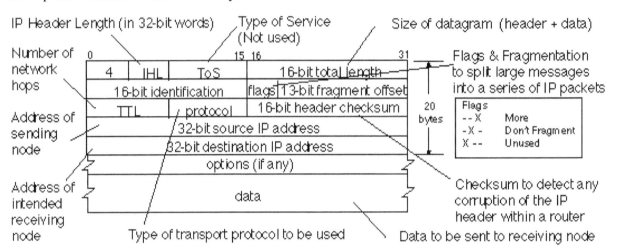

Figure 88 Examples of ip header files

The header fields are explained below:

- **Version**: Always set to the value 4 in the current version of IP.

- **IP Header Length**: Number of 32 -bit words forming the header, usually five.

- **Differentiated Services Code Point (DSCP):** Formerly known as Type of Service (ToS), it is usually set to 0, but may indicate particular Quality of Service needs from the network.

- **Size of Datagram**: It will be in bytes, this is the composite length of the header and the data.

- **Identification:** 16-bit number which together with the source address uniquely identifies this packet - used during reassembly of fragmented datagrams.

- **Flags**: A sequence of three flags used to control whether routers are allowed to fragment a packet (i.e. the Don't Fragment, DF, flag), and to indicate the various parts of a packet to the receiver.

- **Fragmentation Offset**: A byte count from the beginning of the original sent packet, set by any router which performs IP router fragmentation.

- **Time To Live (TTL)**: Number of hops which the packet may be routed over, decremented by most routers - used to prevent accidental routing loops.

- **Protocol**: It indicates the type of transport packet being carried (e.g. 1 = ICMP; 2= IGMP; 6 = TCP; 17= UDP).

- **Header Checksum**: A 1's complement checksum inserted by the sender and updated whenever the packet header is modified by a router - Used to detect processing errors introduced into the packet inside a router or bridge where the packet is not protected by a link layer cyclic redundancy check. Packets with an invalid checksum are discarded by all nodes in an IP network.

- **Source Address**: The IP address of the original sender of the packet.

- **Destination Address**: The IP address of the final destination of the packet.

- **Options**: Not normally used, but, when used, the IP header length will be greater than five 32-bit words to indicate the size of the options field.

Recognizing Attacks

Although there are plenty of attack types that an attacker utilize to manipulate or intercept transmission, but in this topic we will focus on how we can detect specific attack types using wireshark.

DETECTING WORMS AND BACKDOOR

Every worm and Trojan horse has its peculiar working (once executed or replicated). Normally your antivirus can take care of almost every threat (if it's updated regularly), but of course some customized worms/Trojan horses can trick your antivirus. Once your antivirus has been deceived there is apparently no way you can find out what exact worm or Trojan has been replicated on your computer unless you have planned to launch a packet analyzer on your machine.

In our case, we will discuss how wireshark can help you recognize a worm/Trojan. As discussed earlier, each worm or Trojan has its unique work around; we have to learn which traffic is NOT a normal traffic. With wireshark, usually black or red colored packets indicate there is something wrong going out there. But to have a precise conclusion on the nature of threat, it is necessary to analyze payload of each abnormal packet. The payload will have information about what actually the worm/Trojan is doing (sometimes even in clear-text). And sometimes you will need to search on internet to see what the payload information refers to (i.e. which specific worm acts like that, etc.). An example of Backdoor.Win32.Shiz can be seen below that we have captured using wireshark:

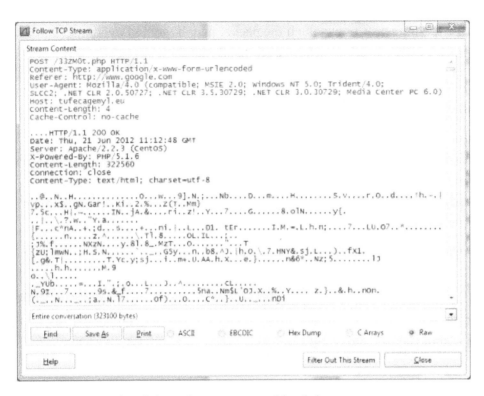

Figure 89 example of detecting worms and backdoor

DETECTING DDOS ATTACK

As most of you must have already known that a Distributed Denial of Service (DDoS) attack is an attack made towards a single service or series of port numbers of the victim. In this attack, a massive amount of data is sent to victim's machine in order to knock-out the victim from the internet. Sometimes a DDoS attack can also lead the victim's PC to entirely crash or reboot. The idea behind the attack is to overrule the bandwidth of the victim so that its network connection gets congested and eventually get disconnected. For example, victim is behind a 100 mbps network and an attack worth 1 or 10 gbps of bandwidth will knock the victim out of network in less than 5 seconds.

Preventing them is another art of network security, we will here discuss about how to detect it using wireshark. Detecting a DDoS attack can be a specialty in itself, and preventing it is a real tactical maneuver. If you experience network outages, or you expect you are being DDoS'ed – run wireshark as soon as possible. Once wireshark is launched and has started to capture packets, you will see massive buffering in the display window. You will clearly see that multiple number of IP Addresses sending large amount of packets to your IP in an unusually faster time-frame. Once detected, you are advised to follow the prevention procedure against DDoS attack (which you can obtain by researching over internet). Please have a look at the screenshot below to get an idea of how a ddos attack might look like on wireshark interface.

Figure 90 example of ddos attack

As you can see in the "Time" section, there are 15 packets sent within one second of time-frame. Also note that most of the DDoS attacks are made on "UDP" service, as this protocol do not have proper error handling and fragmentation structure.

EXAMINING EMBEDDED PROTOCOL HEADER FIELDS

In this chapter we will be examining header fields found after the IP header, namely the TCP, UDP, and ICMP headers. Hopefully, this will partition the protocols into more manageable chunks for our feasibility of understanding this topic in-depth.

TCP

TCP is a reliable protocol. It carefully take care of the exchange of data and knows when there is a possible problem by using fields such as sequence and acknowledgement numbers to order and keep track of the exchanged data. We'll examine these fields in the context of their normal and abnormal usage.

PORTS

These fields are two separate 16-bit fields in the TCP header, one for source (bytes 0 and 1 offset from the TCP header) and another for destination (bytes 2 and 3 offset from the TCP header) port. There is a range of port values in TCP service which is between 1 and 65535. When a source host establishes a connection to a destination host, a randomly chosen source port is typically selected in the range of ports above 1023. For every new connection that the host attempts that is not a retry (possibly after no ACK response from destination), a different random port should be selected.

TCP CHECKSUMS

Embedded protocols have a checksums field. These cover the embedded header and respective data for TCP, UDP, and ICMP. The embedded protocol checksums for TCP and UDP are computed using a pseudo-header in addition to the embedded protocol header and data. A pseudo-header consists of 12 bytes of data as seen in *Figure 72*. The source and destination IPs, the 8-bit protocol found in the IP header, and a repetition of the embedded protocol length (this is the protocol header length plus the number of data bytes).

Figure 2.4.1.3

4 byte source IP		
4 byte destination IP		
1 byte zero-pad	1 byte protocol	2 byte TCP length

Figure 91 example of TCP Checksums

ECN FLAG BITS

Normally the two high-order bits of the TCP byte are known as the reserved bits. They have no purpose, and the value found in this field is 0. However, if we use tools such as nmap, we can use these bits acquire OS fingerprint of a remote operating system. Different operating system TCP/IP stacks responds uniquely when these bits are set. Hence, some insight could be made of the remote host's operating system TCP/IP stack. However, this alone trace method is sometimes not enough to inform the scanner of the operating system, so we use it in conjunction with several other tests, the operating system could be conjectured with a high probability.

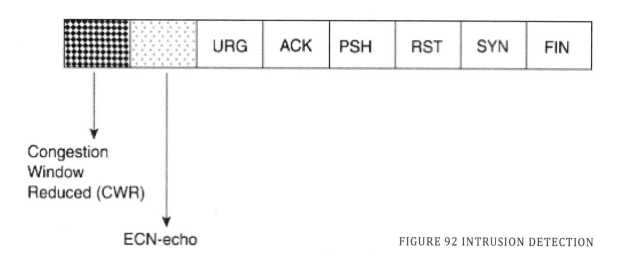

Congestion Window Reduced (CWR)

ECN-echo

FIGURE 92 INTRUSION DETECTION

UDP

UDP is a much less complicated protocol compared to TCP because it doesn't have any of the fields that ensure reliable delivery of data. UDP does guarantees that data will be delivered and leaves this function to applications to handle.

Ports

Figure 2.4.2.1

Source Port (16 bits)	Destination Port (16 bits)
Length (16 bits)	Checksum (16 bits)
Data....	

FIGURE 93 UDP PORTS

Just like TCP ports, UDP port fields are two separate 16-bit fields in the UDP header — one for source and another for destination. The valid range of values is between 1 and 65535; the use of port 0 is typically a signature of unusual activity.

INTERNET CONTROL MESSAGE PROTOCOL (ICMP)

ICMP is another fairly simple protocol as far as the fields found in the header are concerned. Like UDP, ICMP does not guarantee delivery of the message, so its structure and fields are very simple.

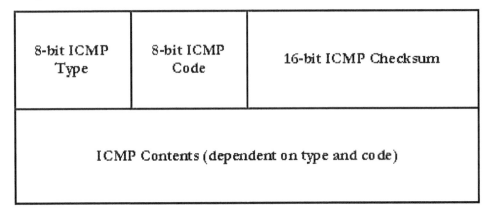

Figure 94 ICMP

ICMP TYPE AND CODE

Considering the fact that ICMP has no ports, there are methods indicating what type of ICMP message is being sent or received. The initial two bytes of the ICMP message are the ICMP message type and code, respectively. The message code is a subcategory under the message type. Following are the ICMP message types and their description:

Type	Message
0	Echo reply
3	Destination unreachable
4	Source quench
5	Redirect
8	Echo request
11	Time exceeded
12	Parameter unintelligible
13	Time-stamp request
14	Time-stamp reply

15	Information request
16	Information reply
17	Address mask request
18	Address mask reply

REAL-WORLD ANALYSIS

In this topic we will analyze traffic from many different viewpoints. We've evolved from bits and fields in previous topics to inspecting one or more packets for their intent and explaining some actual events of interest that were captured by Shadow from sites. It will take time and exposure to some interesting traffic before you gain the confidence and experience to make this transition. The examples shown in this topic should help you get started.

Suppose you've been hacked!

In this topic we will demonstrate some real-life packet captures of some abnormal (illegal) network traffic. This will help you understand more about abnormal behavior and how could you take prompt actions against it. Just like we used wireshark earlier to demonstrate some of the internet threats, we will now demonstrate how tcpdump can come handy in such scenario.

NETBUS SCAN

Even though Netbus is nowadays very outdated backdoor program, but we will demonstrate its malicious traffic to you so that you have at least basic idea about how a common backdoor program works. Netbus (once launched) will open its service on port 12345 of victim. So if you have this port opened on your system you should examine a scan to port 12345. This particular scan was launched against a Class C subnet so that it set off all kinds of alarms. The network that was scanned had some high-numbered port access open through the packet-filtering devices. It is important to note that this traffic was collected on a sensor located behind (inside) the packet-filtering device. However, this is inside the packet-filtering device making it more than a curiosity, as we will later see. Here are the records:

bigscan.net.1737 > 192.168.7.0.12345: S 2299794832:2299794832(0) win 32120

<mss 1380,sackOK,timestamp 120377100[|tcp]> (DF)

 bigscan.net.1739 > 192.168.7.2.12345: S 2299202490:2299202490(0) win 32120

<mss 1380,sackOK,timestamp 120377100[|tcp]> (DF)

 bigscan.net.1741 > 192.168.7.4.12345: S 2293163750:2293163750(0) win 32120

<mss 1380,sackOK,timestamp 120377100[|tcp]> (DF)

bigscan.net.1743 > 192.168.7.6.12345: S 2298524651:2298524651(0) win 32120

<mss 1380,sackOK,timestamp 120377100[|tcp]> (DF)

bigscan.net.1745 > 192.168.7.8.12345: S 2297131917:2297131917(0) win 32120

<mss 1380,sackOK,timestamp 120377100[|tcp]> (DF)

bigscan.net.1747 > 192.168.7.10.12345: S 2291750743:2291750743(0) win 32120

<mss 1380,sackOK,timestamp 120377100[|tcp]> (DF)

bigscan.net.1749 > 192.168.7.12.12345: S 2287868521:2287868521(0) win 32120

<mss 1380,sackOK,timestamp 120377100[|tcp]> (DF)

We see the scanning host bigscan.net methodically moving through the 192.168.7 subnet with a unique scan search pattern of looking at the .0 address and even final octets thereafter.

Not All That Runs on Port 12345 Is Associated to Netbus

Below is a list of some applications that use port 12345 other than Netbus:

- Trend Micro's OfficeScan products use port 12345 as well.

- Italk Chat System

- TrendMicro OfficeScan TMListen

Therefore, it is important to monitor the network traffic carefully even if you see a suspicious port opened on your system.

BOTTOM LINE

The events described in this topic have demonstrated the added value of having TCPdump running at a machine to capture the background traffic. TCPdump was used in the scan incident to assess the reaction of hosts on the monitored network to the scan.

WRITING TCPDUMP FILTERS

By default, TCPdump examines all of the network traffic from either the network or from a file. But often you will want to examine only records with specific values set in identified fields in the IP datagram to look for signs of malicious activity directed at your network. TCPdump filters can be used to specify your criteria of traffic examination, such as a field in the IP datagram for record selection. Such items might be part of the IP header (the IP header length, for example), the TCP header (TCP flags, for example), the UDP header (the destination port, for example), or the ICMP message (message type, for example).

TCPdump provides some macros for commonly used fields, such as "port" to indicate a source or destination port, or "host" to indicate an IP number or name of a source or destination host. TCPdump assigns a designated name for each type of header associated with a protocol. for example, "ip" is used to denote a field in the IP header or data portion of the IP datagram, "tcp" for a field in the TCP header or data of the TCP segment, "udp" for a field in the UDP header or data of the UDP datagram, and "icmp" for a field in the ICMP header or data of the ICMP message.

Figure 2.6 is the standard layout of the IP header. Notice that each of the rows has 32 bits, ranging in value from 0 through 31. Essentially, each row is composed of 4 bytes—and don't forget that counting starts with 0. That is one of the hardest things to commit to memory.

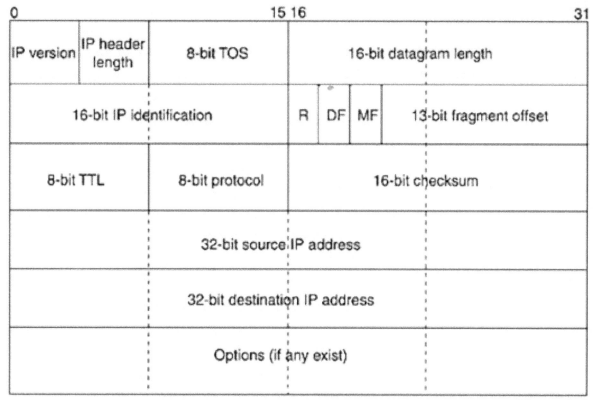

Figure 2.6

Figure 95 Standard layout of IP header

Examples

Now we will have a look at some examples of tcpdump filters, which will help you write your own filters:

tcpdump host sundown

To print all packets arriving at or departing from sun down.

tcpdump host helios and \(hot or ace \)

To print traffic between helios and either hot or ace.

tcpdump ip host ace and not helios

To print all IP packets between ace and any host except helios.

tcpdump net ucb-ether

To print all traffic between local hosts and hosts at Berkeley.

tcpdump 'gateway snup and (port ftp or ftp-data)'

To print all ftp traffic through internet gateway snup (note that the expression is quoted to prevent the shell from (mis-)interpreting the parentheses).

tcpdump ip and not net localnet

To print traffic neither sourced from nor destined for local hosts (if you gateway to one other net, this stuff should never make it onto your local net).

tcpdump 'tcp[tcpflags] & (tcp-syn|tcp-fin) != 0 and not src and dst net localnet'

To print the start and end packets (the SYN and FIN pack ets) of each TCP conversation that involves a non-local host.

tcpdump 'gateway snup and ip[2:2] > 576'

To print IP packets longer than 576 bytes sent through gateway snup.

tcpdump 'ether[0] & 1 = 0 and ip[16] >= 224'

To print IP broadcast or multicast packets that were not sent via ethernet broadcast or multicast.

tcpdump 'icmp[icmptype] != icmp-echo and icmp[icmptype] != icmp-echoreply'

To print all ICMP packets that are not echo requests/replies (i.e., not ping packets).

Exercise

Quizzes:

Q.1) What is the difference between wireshark and tcpdump ?

Answer) Wireshark is very similar to tcpdump, but has a graphical front-end, plus some integrated sorting and filtering options.

Q.2) Internet Protocol version 6 is commonly used as communication medium in every industry or organization.

Answer) False

Q.3) what are the functions of IP Header field "Flags"?

Answer) Flags are used to control whether routers are allowed to fragment a packet (i.e. the Don't Fragment, DF, flag), and to indicate the various parts of a packet to the receiver.

Q.4) Distributed Denial of Service Attack and bandwidth attack are same thing. (State true of false)

Answer) True

Q.5) In TCPDUMP, what is the command to display traffic with the "Evil Bit" set ?

Answer) tcpdump 'ip[6] & 128 != 0'

Q.6) In TCP Checksum, fields that are responsible for source and destination IP are of 16-bit (State true or false)

Answer) False

Assignment

Research about conficker worm, and how we can prevent it from spreading.

Answer) Information can be found here: http://www.microsoft.com/security/pc-security/conficker.aspx

PROJECT

With reference to section 2.4.1.4. Please conduct a research or experiment yourself of sending OS Fingerprint request and show different response from FreeBSD, Linux and Windows 7 operating systems.

Answer) Reference to this can be found here: http://en.wikipedia.org/wiki/Explicit_Congestion_Notification#Implementations this link will give you an idea , what the students should be presenting with and how to evaluate it.

Intrusion Detection System

Intrusion Detection Systems help information systems to deal with attacks. They accomplish this by gathering information from a variety of systems and network sources, and then analyzing it for possible security problems.

Following are the main features of Intrusion Detection Systems:

- Monitoring and analysis of user and system activity

- Auditing of system configurations and vulnerabilities

- Assessing the integrity of critical system and data files

- Statistical analysis of activity patterns based on the matching to known attacks

- Abnormal activity analysis

- Operating system audit

See below illustration to have an idea about where the IDS lay down within your network:

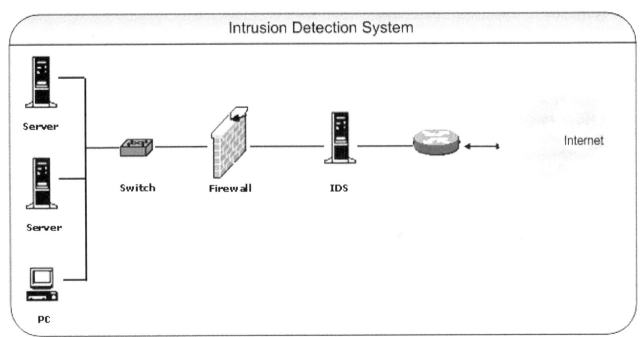

Figure 96 Intrusion detection system

There are three main components to the Intrusion detection system

1. Network Intrusion Detection system (NIDS) – performs an analysis of entire network traffic. It works in a promiscuous mode, and matches the traffic that is passed on the subnets to the library of knows attacks. Once the attack is detected, or abnormal behavior is observed, the alert can be send to the administrator.

2. Network Node Intrusion detection system (NNIDS) – performs the analysis of the traffic that is passed from the network to a specific host. The difference between NIDS and NNIDS is that the traffic is monitored on the single host only and not for the entire network.

3. Host Intrusion Detection System (HIDS) – takes a snap shot of your existing system files and matches it to the previous snap shot. If the critical system files were modified or deleted, the alert is sent to the administrator for further investigation.

Benefits of Keeping IDS in your Network

It's always handy to keep an IDS installed in your network. Although a gateway firewall and an enterprise level antivirus solution provides pretty much of the security to entire network, but IDS has its own advantages which are listed below:

- IDS can add a greater degree of integrity to the rest of you infrastructure.

- IDS can trace user activity from point of entry to point of impact.

- IDS can recognize and report alterations to data.

- IDS can automate a task of monitoring the Internet searching for the latest attacks.

- IDS can detect when your system is under attack.

- IDS can detect errors in your system configuration.

- IDS can guide system administrator in the vital step of establishing a policy for your computing assets.

- IDS can make the security management of your system possible by non-expert staff.

The Alarm Problem

A false alarm (or false positive) is any normal or expected behavior that is identified as malicious. This can be divided into several categories. Some legitimate software programs do not strictly follow RFCs. Signatures written to the RFC may trigger when such software runs.

A software program is not seen in the training stage of an abnormal detection system will likely trigger an alert when the application attempts to run. A signature can be written too broadly and thus include both legitimate and illegitimate traffic.

Abnormal behavior in some criteria may be acceptable while highly suspect in another. For example, NBT traffic is normal in a Windows LAN environment but not generally expected on the Internet. This is not an exhaustive list but the most common places that IDSes can have false positives. Below is an illustration of how IDS can produce a false alarm:

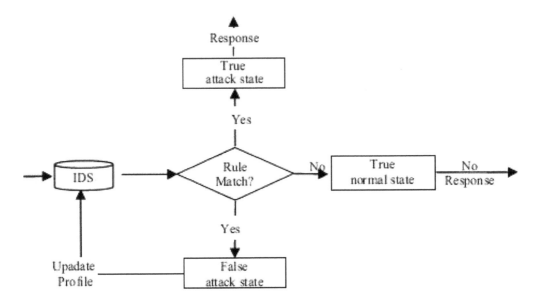

Figure 97 False alarm

Classification of False Alarms

False alarms can be classified into several more meaningful and specific categories. Common categories include:

- **Reactionary Traffic alarms:** Traffic that is caused by another network event, often non-malicious. An example of this would be a NIDS device triggering an ICMP flood alarm when it is really several destination unreachable packets caused by equipment failure somewhere in the network.

- **Equipment-related alarms:** Attack alerts that are triggered by odd, unrecognized packets generated by certain network equipments. Load balancers often trigger these types of alarms.

- **Protocol Violations:** Alerts that are caused by unrecognized network traffic often caused by poorly or oddly written client software.

- **True False Positives:** Alarms that are generated by an IDS for no apparent reason. These are often caused by IDS software bugs.

- **Non-Malicious alarms:** Generated through some real occurrence that is non-malicious in nature, possibly like our Code Red web page example above.

Prevention of False Alarms

We won't go in to detail as it could require a whole chapter specially assigned to this topic but we will discuss some basics of how one can prevent IDS to generate false alarms. Practically an IDS can not be configured to generate 100% positive reports, there will always be at least 10% of false alarms generated by an IDS. As we have discussed earlier, we can judge that there are certain traffic that will always be considered as false alarm (i.e. if it's mandatory for a network to have at least one file-sharing server on the network, IDS may see some of the packets as malicious packets). We can however choose to ignore such traffic pattern, but that really isn't recommended since even if a malicious traffic will occur on such service, it will also go ignored.

The best can be done here; we can set priority for false alarms. Let's say, if a file-server is mandatory for a network, then we will investigate its traffic later and set priority high for those traffic that seems unusual.

Introduction to SNORT

Snort is a free open source network intrusion prevention and detection system (IDS/IPS). It is composition of benefits of signature, protocol, and anomaly-based inspection. Snort is one of the most widely deployed IDS/IPS technology worldwide (specially in organizations where OpenSource environment is encouraged). Snort was first released back in 1998 by Sourcefire founder and CTO Martin Roesch. Snort is capable of performing real-time traffic analysis and packet logging on IP networks. It is feature-rich IPS technology that has become the de facto standard in intrusion detection and prevention. Snort can perform protocol analysis and content searching/matching. It can be used to detect a variety of attacks and probes, such as buffer overflows, stealth port scans, CGI attacks, SMB probes, OS fingerprinting attempts, and much more.

Just like wireshark, Snort has a real-time alerting capability as well by incorporating alerting mechanisms for syslog, a user specified file, a UNIX socket, or WinPopup messages to Windows clients. Snort has three primary uses: a straight packet sniffer like tcpdump, a packet logger (useful for network traffic debugging, etc), or a full-blown network intrusion prevention system. Best thing about snort is that it can adjust with existing firewalls like a charm *(see figure 79)*.

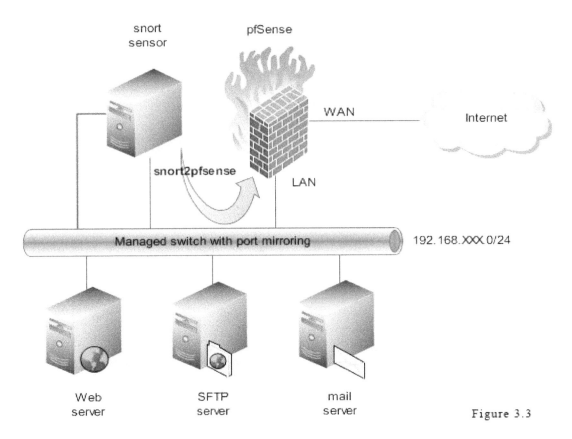

Figure 3.3

Figure 98 example of snort

In above illustration, we can see that snort is used parallel to pfSense (a gateway firewall). We can also see where it lies in a network and how it can examine network traffic.

Snort modes

Snort can be configured to run in three modes:

1. **Sniffer mode**, which simply reads the packets off of the network and displays them for you in a continuous stream on the console (screen).

2. **Packet Logger mode**, which logs the packets to disk.

3. **Network Intrusion Detection System (NIDS) mode**, the most complex and configurable configuration, which allows Snort to analyze network traffic for matches against a user-defined rule set and performs several actions based upon what it sees.

SNORT Filtering Rules

Snort uses a simple, lightweight rules description language that is flexible and quite powerful. There are a number of simple guidelines to remember when developing Snort rules that will help safeguard your sanity. Rules may span multiple lines by adding a backslash \ to the end of the line. Snort rules are divided into two logical sections, the rule header and the rule options. The rule header contains the rule's action, protocol, source and destination IP addresses and netmasks, and the source and destination ports information. The rule option section contains alert messages and information on which parts of the packet should be inspected to determine if the rule action should be taken. *Figure80* illustrates a sample Snort rule.

```
alert tcp any any -> 192.168.1.0/24 111 \
     (content:"|00 01 86 a5|"; msg:"mountd access";)
```

Figure 3.4

Figure 99 example of snort rule

Rules Headers

The rule header contains the information that defines the who, where, and what of a packet, as well as what to do in the event that a packet with all the attributes indicated in the rule should show up.

Rule Actions

The first item in a rule is the rule action. The rule action tells Snort what to do when it finds a packet that matches the rule criteria. There are five available default actions in Snort, alert, log, pass, activate, and dynamic. In addition, if you are running Snort in inline mode, you have additional options which include drop, reject, and sdrop.

1. alert – it generates an alert using the selected alert method, and then logs the packet.

2. log - logs the packet.

3. pass - ignores the packet.

4. activate – it will alert and then turn on another dynamic rule.

5. dynamic - remains idle until activated by an activate rule, then acts as a log rule.

6. drop - blocks and logs the packet.

7. reject - blocks the packet, logs it, and then send a TCP reset if the protocol is TCP or an ICMP port unreachable message if the protocol is UDP.

8. sdrop - blocks the packet but do not log it.

You can also define your customized rule types and associate one or more output plugins with them. You can then use the rule types as actions in Snort rules.

Below is an example which creates a type that will log to just tcpdump:

ruletype suspicious

```
{

type log

output log_tcpdump: suspicious.log

}
```

This example will create a rule type that will log to syslog and tcpdump database:

```
ruletype redalert

{

type alert

output alert_syslog: LOG_AUTH LOG_ALERT

output log_tcpdump: suspicious.log

}
```

Protocols

The next field in a rule is the protocol field. There are four protocols that Snort currently analyzes for suspicious behavior – TCP, UDP, ICMP, and IP. In the future there may be more, such as ARP, IGRP, GRE, OSPF, RIP, IPX, etc.

IP Addresses

The next portion of the rule header deals with the IP address and port information for a rule specified. The keyword any may be used to define any address. Snort does not have a mechanism to provide host name lookup for the IP address fields in the config file. The addresses are formed by a straight numeric IP address and a CIDR block. For example, the address/CIDR combination 192.168.1.0/24 would signify the block of addresses from 192.168.1.1 to 192.168.1.255. Any rule that used this designation for, say, the destination address would match on any address in that range. The CIDR designations give us a nice short-hand way to designate large address spaces with just a few characters.

```
alert tcp !192.168.1.0/24 any -> 192.168.1.0/24 111 \
    (content:"|00 01 86 a5|"; msg:"external mountd access";)
```

Figure 3.4.1.4

Figure 100 negation operation

There is an operator called, "the negation operation" which can be applied to IP addresses. This operator tells Snort to match any IP address except the one indicated by the listed IP address. The negation operator is indicated with a !. For example, an easy modification to the initial example is to make it alert on any traffic that originates outside of the local net with the negation operator as shown in *Figure 100*

This rule's IP addresses indicate any tcp packet with a source IP address not originating from the internal network and a destination address on the internal network.

Rules Options

Rule options are core component of Snort's intrusion detection engine, combining ease of use with power and flexibility. All Snort rule options are separated from each other using the semicolon (;) character. Rule option keywords are separated from their arguments with a colon (:) character.

There are four main categories of rule options.

1. **general** These options provide information about the rule but do not have any affect during detection.

2. **payload** These options all look for data inside the packet payload and can be inter-related.

3. **non-payload** These options look for non-payload data

4. **post-detection** These options are rule specific triggers that happen after a rule has "fired."

Examples

*alert tcp any any -> any 7070 (msg:"IDS411/dos-realaudio"; *

flags:AP; content:"\fff4 fffd 06|"; reference:arachnids,IDS411;)

*alert tcp any any -> any 21 (msg:"IDS287/ftp-wuftp260-venglin-linux"; *

*flags:AP; content:"|31c031db 31c9b046 cd80 31c031db|"; *

*reference:arachnids,IDS287; reference:bugtraq,1387; *

reference:cve,CAN-2000-1574;)

REAL-WORLD ANALYSIS

We have already discussed about real-world analysis in previous chapters and further topics, so in this topic we will specifically focus on how we can read traffic from pcap files. Once you will open a pcap file with snort, it will read and analyze the packets as if they came off the wire. This can be useful for testing and debugging Snort.

COMMAND LINE ARGUMENTS

As seen in *figure 3.5.1*, any of these can be specified multiple times on the command line (-r included) and in addition to other Snort command line options. Note, however, that specifying --pcap-reset and --pcap-show multiple times has the same effect as specifying them once.

Option	Description
-r <file>	Read a single pcap.
--pcap-single=<file>	Same as -r. Added for completeness.
--pcap-file=<file>	File that contains a list of pcaps to read. Can specify path to pcap or directory to recurse to get pcaps.
--pcap-list="<list>"	A space separated list of pcaps to read.
--pcap-dir=<dir>	A directory to recurse to look for pcaps. Sorted in ASCII order.
--pcap-filter=<filter>	Shell style filter to apply when getting pcaps from file or directory. This filter will apply to any --pcap-file or --pcap-dir arguments following. Use --pcap-no-filter to delete filter for following --pcap-file or --pcap-dir arguments or specify --pcap-filter again to forget previous filter and to apply to following --pcap-file or --pcap-dir arguments.
--pcap-no-filter	Reset to use no filter when getting pcaps from file or directory.
--pcap-reset	If reading multiple pcaps, reset snort to post-configuration state before reading next pcap. The default, i.e. without this option, is not to reset state.
--pcap-show	Print a line saying what pcap is currently being read.

Figure 3.5.1

Figure 101commandline arguments

Examples

Reading from a single pcap file

snort -r foo.pcap

snort --pcap-single=foo.pcap

Read pcaps from a file

cat foo.txt

foo1.pcap

foo2.pcap

/home/foo/pcaps

snort --pcap-file=foo.txt

This will read foo1.pcap, foo2.pcap and all files under /home/foo/pcaps. Note that Snort will not try to determine whether the files under that directory are really pcap files or not.

Read pcaps from a command line list

snort --pcap-list="foo1.pcap foo2.pcap foo3.pcap"

This will read foo1.pcap, foo2.pcap and foo3.pcap.

Read pcaps under a directory

snort --pcap-dir="/home/foo/pcaps"

This will include all of the files under /home/foo/pcaps.

Using filters

cat foo.txt

foo1.pcap

foo2.pcap

/home/foo/pcaps

snort --pcap-filter="*.pcap" --pcap-file=foo.txt

snort --pcap-filter="*.pcap" --pcap-dir=/home/foo/pcaps

The above will only include files that match the shell pattern "*.pcap", in other words, any file ending in ".pcap".

snort --pcap-filter="*.pcap --pcap-file=foo.txt \

> --pcap-filter="*.cap" --pcap-dir=/home/foo/pcaps

In the above, the first filter "*.pcap" will only be applied to the pcaps in the file "foo.txt" (and any directories that are recursed in that file). The addition of the second filter "*.cap" will cause the first filter to be forgotten and then applied to the directory /home/foo/pcaps, so only files ending in ".cap" will be included from that directory.

snort --pcap-filter="*.pcap --pcap-file=foo.txt \

> --pcap-no-filter --pcap-dir=/home/foo/pcaps

In this example, the first filter will be applied to foo.txt, then no filter will be applied to the files found under /home/foo/pcaps, so all files found under /home/foo/pcaps will be included.

snort --pcap-filter="*.pcap --pcap-file=foo.txt \

> --pcap-no-filter --pcap-dir=/home/foo/pcaps \

> --pcap-filter="*.cap" --pcap-dir=/home/foo/pcaps2

In this example, the first filter will be applied to foo.txt, then no filter will be applied to the files found under /home/foo/pcaps, so all files found under /home/foo/pcaps will be included, then the filter "*.cap" will be applied to files found under /home/foo/pcaps2.

snort --pcap-dir=/home/foo/pcaps --pcap-reset

The above example will read all of the files under /home/foo/pcaps, but after each pcap is read, Snort will be reset to a post-configuration state, meaning all buffers will be flushed, statistics reset, etc. For each pcap, it will be like Snort is seeing traffic for the first time.

Printing the pcap

snort --pcap-dir=/home/foo/pcaps --pcap-show

The above example will read all of the files under /home/foo/pcaps and will print a line indicating which pcap is currently being read.

Exercise

Quizzes:

Q.1) what is the difference between IDS and IPS?

Answer) IDS is a passive implementation where as IPS is an active implementation. Therefore, IDS only attempts to detect and report about abnormal traffic and on the other hand IPS does the very same but it also attempt to prevent the intrusion

Q.2) Intrusion Detection System and Firewall are same in nature. (State true or false)

Answer) False

Q.3) Alice and Bob are trustworthy clients in an organization which is equipped with Intrusion Detection System. The organization allow file-sharing between clients. However, whenever both Alice and Bob try to share files –IDS detects it as abnormal traffic. What sort of alarm did the IDS generated?

Answer) False Alarm (or false positive). Since it was a normal traffic but IDS was not configured to sense it as normal.

Q.4) SNORT is a network mapper and can not be used as IDS (State true of false)

Answer) False

Q.5) What are the three primary modes of SNORT ?

Answer) Sniffer mode, Packet logging mode, and NIDS

Q.6) A PCAP file is exclusively generated by IDS. (State true or false)

Answer) False

Assignment

Conduct a research and give example in real-world of every snort rule actions.

Answer) Whatever students will submit, compare it to section 3.4.12 explanations.

PROJECT

Conduct a research and discuss, what tools are used specifically for NIDS, NNIDS, and HIDS each respectively (i.e. software just for NIDS, one for NNIDS and one for HIDS only). Explain their functions to prove their purpose.

Answer) whatever software students will present, check the description online for each software (or hardware)'s website. It should say if its for NIDS, NNIDS, HIDS or not.

Statistical Anomaly Detection

Characterizing "Normal" Traffic

If you are a network security specialist or just a network administrator of an intrusion detection & prevention system, your primary concern is training your IPS to differentiate between normal traffic and abnormal behavior inside the traffic. In this topic we will focus on how we can differentiate a normal traffic from abnormal. For a start, it is duty of network administrator to keep record of daily traffic reports and analyze them thoroughly. He should learn how a normal transmission take place and what are their patterns. Each web-session, multimedia services over ip, and data transmission should be kept under observation for analyzing how a genuine traffic acts like. Once recorded the pattern of these activities, we produce a database and signatures of application and services that usually follows a static pattern and we will train our IDS to follow them strictly. One of the most important components of analyzing normal traffic is tracking down checksum of each connection-oriented transmission. A checksum will always let you know if the transmission has been altered or not, it is very hard for an intruder to actually predict a checksum and spoof it. All the security measurement discusses in this topic are accomplished using tools like pack analyzers as discussed in previous chapters.

An intrusion prevention system is more efficient than a normal intrusion detection system. We have already discussed about IDS in previous chapters, but in this topic, we will learn about IPS, as they are more efficient in detecting normal traffic.

Intrusion Prevention System (IPS)

An IPS generally lies in the middle of a network and monitors network traffic as the packets flow through it. It acts similarly to an Intrusion Detection System (IDS) by trying to match data in the packets against a signature database or detect anomalies against what is pre-defined as "normal" traffic. In addition to its IDS functionality, an IPS can do more than log and alert. It can be programmed to react to what it detects. The ability to react to the detections is what makes IPSs more desirable than IDSs. There are still some drawbacks to an IPS. IPSs are designed to block certain types of traffic that it can identify as potentially bad traffic. IPSs do not have the ability to understand web application protocol logic. Hence, IPSs cannot fully distinguish if a request is normal or malformed at the application layer (OSI Layer 7). This short coming could potentially allow attacks through without detection or prevention, especially newer attacks without signatures.

Being there is a large number of web applications in existence, both commercial and home grown, there will tend to be many different types of vulnerabilities available for attackers to exploit. IPSs cannot effectively cover all the potential vulnerabilities and in actuality may end up producing positives that are more false. False positives are very bad because they make already busy security analysts even busier. An overload of false positives can delay response to actual attacks or cause attacks to be accepted as normal because of an analyst trying to reduce the noise. *(see figure 102)*

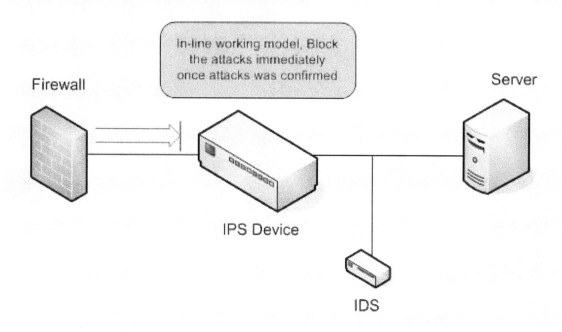

Figure 102 example of ips device

Pattern Recognition

Modern IDS are designed to detect intrusions that exploit known vulnerabilities by coding exact sequences of events related to those intrusions. Attack signatures that are tailored to each particular attack instance are required in order to avoid the risk of unfeasible false alarm rates. Unfortunately the same vulnerability can often be exploited by minor changes in the attack. As soon as an attack signature is developed and made publicly available, attackers slightly modify the attack sequence so that it does not match perfectly the attack signature stored in the IDSs. As a consequence these kinds of signatures cannot detect novel attacks or attack variations, thus requiring updating the IDS.

At present, the following issues remain open for effective implementation of IDSs based on pattern recognition techniques:

- Very little research has been carried out to produce a representative set of examples of normal traffic and attacks for training and testing. As a consequence pattern recognition techniques may suffer from insufficient training data.

- The intrusion detection problem formulated in terms of pattern recognition falls in the class of problems where data classes are very unbalanced, as attacks are very rare compared to normal traffic. The most suitable solution to this problem should be investigated further.

- As different classification errors exhibit different severities, misclassification costs may be introduced at training time to satisfy the requirement of the final user. Unfortunately, at present there is no generally agreed upon figure of merit that can be used to characterize the performance of IDS.

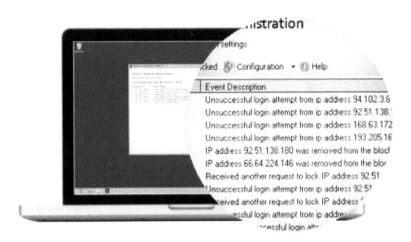

Figure 103 example of unsuccessful log in attempts

In above screenshot, you can see that several unsuccessful login attempts pattern. In this scenario, it is important to note the source and destination ip addresses. If attempting ip address is unrecognized or unauthorized then it should be reported immediate, and if it is recognized then this should be discussed with destination ip address' client.

Protocol distributions

In traffic analysis, monitoring the network to find out who and what used the bandwidth and at what time is the primary task. An analysis involves having a detailed understanding on the network protocol distribution. One may ask why is there the need to identify the protocols in the network when you see the applications being used and their related conversations.

The protocol distribution helps network administrators find the bandwidth used by each protocol in the network. This helps find if any unwanted (read as: not mean to be used) protocols are being used in the network and based on this; the network administrator can reallocate this bandwidth to more critical applications using other protocols.

Protocol distribution also helps you determine if any inactive application protocol is being used in the network taking away valuable bandwidth (such as peer to peer software). To give a real example, an administrator was expecting to see only negligible bandwidth usage by L2TP traffic in his network. He looked at the protocol distribution graph and what he found was L2TP occupying about 10% of the total traffic. Now, that is called sacrilege in network terminology!

Many of the major vendors in the market have already come up with network traffic analyzers to monitor flow format of network traffic, one does not have to wonder how to obtain such information from the routing or switching devices. Such software really does not do a big deal if you can just see the protocol distribution in the network. What you need is the ability to see the source and destination associated with each conversation corresponding to a protocol and this is exactly what a network packet traffic analyzer can also do. Below is a screen shot take from one of the commonly used network traffic analyzer known as NetFlow Analyzer.

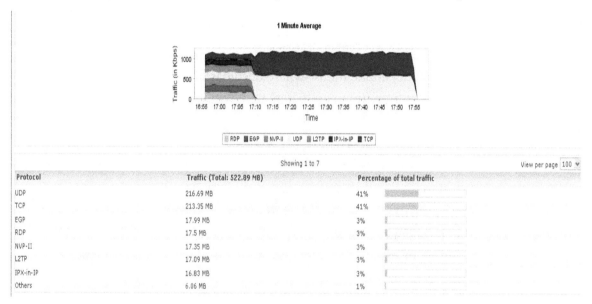

Figure 104 Proctol distribution

Address distributions

Address distribution is an act of reserving ip addresses to each client on your network according to their identity respectively. Let's say, joe is assigned 192.168.0.18 and martin is assigned 192.168.2.39. So if there is an attack or abnormal traffic analyzed on either of the ip address, the administrator would already know that to whom the ip address belong and he will discuss the issue with him exclusively. On a local network, address distribution is very easy as it is limited to following ip pools only:

10.0.0.0   -   10.255.255.255 (10/8 prefix)

172.16.0.0   -   172.31.255.255 (172.16/12 prefix)

192.168.0.0   -   192.168.255.255 (192.168/16 prefix)

But when it comes to ISP, there's a lot different kind of deal and extra measurements are taking in the procedure of address distribution. Such as an ip address, mac address of CPE, and specific gateways are assigned to each group of clients. Coming back address distributions on a local network, the mechanism of address distribution is that a protocol is under and management of proper software. The software allows the administrator to distribute ip addresses amongst the clients, while the protocol practically implements the commands given. Once of the most common protocol used for address distribution is called DHCP.

DHCP

In address distribution schema, the Dynamic Host Configuration Protocol (DHCP) provides configuration parameters to network hosts. DHCP consists of two components: a protocol for delivering host-specific configuration parameters from a DHCP server to a host and a mechanism for allocation of network addresses to hosts.

DHCP is part of client-server model applications, where designated DHCP server hosts allocate network addresses and deliver configuration parameters to dynamically configured hosts. Throughout the remainder of this document, the term "server" refers to a host providing initialization parameters through DHCP, and the term "client" refers to a host requesting initialization parameters from a DHCP server.

A host only acts as a DHCP server unless explicitly configured to do so by a system administrator. The diversity of hardware and protocol implementations in the Internet would preclude reliable operation if random hosts were allowed to respond to DHCP requests. For example, IP requires the setting of many parameters within the protocol implementation software. Because IP can be used on many dissimilar kinds of network hardware, values for those parameters cannot be guessed or assumed to have correct defaults. Also, distributed address allocation schemes depend on a polling/defense.

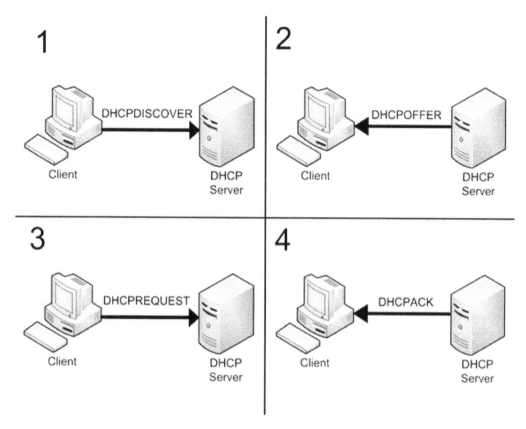

Figure 105 dhcp steps

Port distributions

In our scenario, port distribution refers distribution of physical port on a network switch our router to the network clients. As we have learned that address distribution is implemented to identify the correspondent of each ip address on a network, port distribution is similarly part of such implementation.

In port distribution, each port of the network switch or router is assigned with a mac address and sometimes ip address too. This ensures that only the reserved mac and ip will be able to pass data through the reserved port. It also prevents intruders from running a packet sniffer. In anomaly traffic detection, the role of port distribution helps in great deal as it reduces the chances of ip spoofing or identity theft.

Figure 106 24 port Poe switch

Above you can see a picture taken of a layer-2 network switch from the side where you can see its ports. These ports are basically designed Ethernet connections. Number of ports varies in model and brand of switch that you use in your organization.

Layer-2 Switches

Layer 2 switch forwards traffic based on MAC layer (Ethernet or Token Ring) addresses. It also involves bridging technology, which is segmentation of local-area networks (LANs) at the Layer 2 level. A multi-port bridge typically learns about the Media Access Control (MAC) addresses on each of its ports and transparently passes MAC frames destined to those ports. These bridges also ensure that frames destined for MAC addresses that lie on the same port as the originating station are not forwarded to the other ports. For the sake of this discussion, we consider only Ethernet LANs. Following are functions and mechanism of these switches:

Address learning: Layer 2 switches remember the source hardware address of each frame received on an interface, and they enter this information into a MAC database called a forward/filter table.

Forward/filter decisions: When a specific frame is received on an interface, the switch looks at the destination hardware address and finds the exit interface in the MAC database. The frame is only forwarded out the specified destination port.

Loop avoidance: If there's a massive traffic connections between switches are created for redundancy purposes, network loops can occur. Spanning Tree Protocol (STP) is used to stop network loops while still permitting redundancy.

Illustration below demonstrates where a network switch lies in a network:

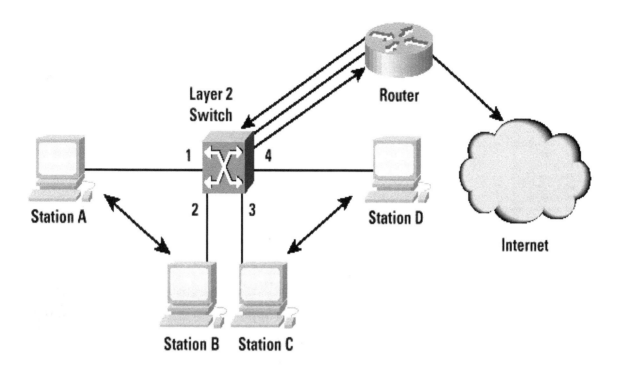

Figure 107 example of layer-2 switches

SOFTWARE LEVEL PORT DISTRIBUTION

Another approach towards port distribution is learning about what services are generally assigned to which particular port. We will discuss this in section below

COMMON PORT NUMBERS

From port 0 to 1023 are reserved for well-known services such as:

Port 80 (web server), port 25 (stmp), port 443 (ssl), port 3128 (squid-proxy), port 53 (dns), etc. While remaining ports from 1024 to 49151 are usually reserved for dynamic assigning of client-side model. That is to say, when a client request for port 80 of remote machine, its own port number will not be port 80 as well rather a random port from 1024 to 49151 will be chosen.

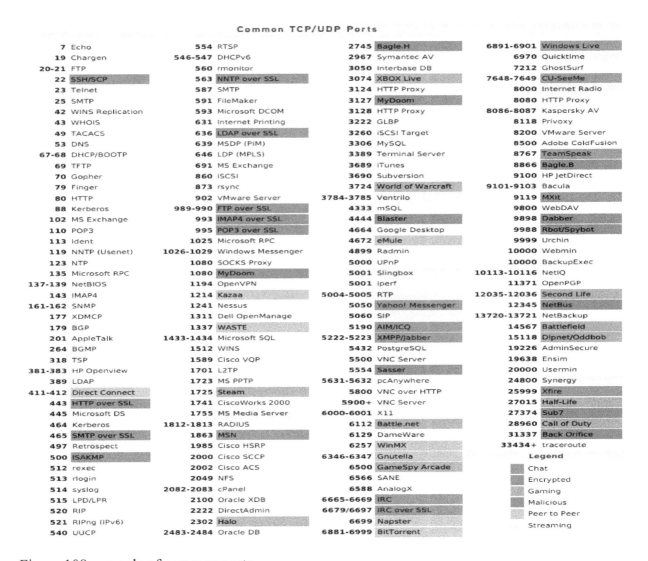

Figure 108 example of common ports

PROTOCOL STATE

Protocol state refers to various states of a protocol that it takes to reach its destination from origin of transmission. Learning about the protocol states helps you in differentiating a normal traffic from abnormal ones, as any alteration or abnormal behavior in these states could also lead to possible network threat or intrusion attempt. In this section we will focus about TCP states, as all other protocols relatively have similar work around.

TCP STATES

In a TCP connection the client application opens a connection to the server by sending a TCP segment which only the header is present (no data). This header contains a flag SYN which stands for "Synchronize" and the TCP port number to the server (application). The client is in SYN_SENT state (SYN sent).

The server (application) is now listening (listen) and on receipt of the SYN from the client, it changes of state and responds with a SYN and ACK flag. The server is then able SYN_RCVD (SYN received).

The client then receives the server's TCP segment with SYN ACK indicators and move in status ESTABLISHED. He also sent a response ACK to the server that also passes in status ESTABLISHED. This exchange in three-way handshake complete the establishment of the TCP connection can now be used to exchange data between the client and server.

The client side of the connection is responsible for the connection performs an active connection (active open) while the server performs a passive connection (passive open). In the event that a connection request arrives on the server and that no application is listening on the requested port, a segment with flag RST (reset) is sent to the client by the server, the connection attempt is

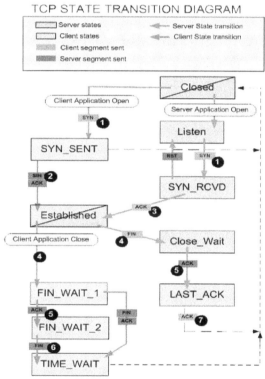

immediately terminated. *(see figure 109)*

Figure 109 example of tpc states

Exercise

Quizzes:

Q.1) What is a "normal" traffic?

Answer) Any traffic that does not violate network policies assigned by the network administrators is considered as normal traffic.

Q.2) Protocol Distribution can help you find out failed login attempts to one of your network node. (State true or false)

Answer) False

Q.3) What is the difference between address distribution based on DHCP and port distribution based on layer-2 switching?

Answer) A DHCP binds IP and MAC to give identification to each client on a network, regardless of whether there is a layer-2 switch or not in the network. Whereas port distribution are strictly based on binding of MAC and IP to physical port of a layer-2 switch.

Q.4) Protocol distribution and port distribution are same. (State true or false)

Answer) False

Q.5) What are names of TCP Flags which are utilized during all the states of a connection respectively?

Answer) SYN, ACK, PSH, URG, RST, FIN

Q.6) SYN_RCVD flag states abnormal traffic regardless of any exceptions. (State true or false)

Answer) False

Assignment

With reference to section 4.4, draw more relevant diagram to illustrate pattern recognition.

PROJECT

Use linux to deploy a DHCP Server. Assign IP Addresses to hostname bob, alice, joe, martin, Michele, and mark. Submit the dhcpd.conf file of this project.

Wireless Network Security

Access Control Fundamentals

Access Control is the process by which resources or services are granted or denied on a computer system or network. There are four standard access control models as well as specific practices used to enforce access control.

There are four main features through which access control policies are implemented: *(see table 21 for more elaboration)*

Identification: A user accessing a computer system would present credentials or identification, such as a username. He may also be bind with an IP and MAC (which will be reserved only for him).

Authentication: A process which Checks for the user's credentials to be sure that they are authentic and not fabricated or spoofed.

TABLE 21 ACCESS CONTROL FUNDAMENTALS

Role	Description	Duties	Example
Owner	Person responsible for the information	Determines the level of security needed for the data and delegates security duties as required	Determines that file SALARY.XLSX can be read only by department managers
Custodian	Individual to whom day-to-day actions have been assigned by the owner	Periodically reviews security settings and maintains records of access by end users	Sets and reviews security settings on SALARY.XLSX
End User	User who accesses information in the course of routine job responsibilities	Follows organization's security guidelines and does not attempt to circumvent security	Opens SALARY.XLSX

Authorization: Granting permission to take the action. For example, a computer user is granted access to only certain services or applications in order to perform their duties.

Action	Description	Scenario Example	Computer Process
Identification	Review of credentials	Delivery person shows employee badge	User enters username
Authentication	Validate credentials as genuine	Megan reads badge to determine it is real	User provides password
Authorization	Permission granted for admittance	Megan opens door to allow delivery person in	User authorized to log in
Access	Right given to access specific resources	Delivery person can only retrieve box by door	User allowed to access only specific data

Above are tbe basic steps taken while implementing access control policies in a wireless network as part of its security measurements.

Below table will further elaborate these roles in with more specifications:

Access Control Models

The goal of access control is to provide a predefined framework for hardware and software developers for whom it is mandatory to implement access control in their devices or applications. Once an access control model is applied Custodians can configure security based on the requirements set by the owner So that end users can perform their job functions without hassle. We further divide these models in to four categories, MAC, DAC, UAC, RBAC:

Mandatory Access Control (MAC)

In this model, the end user cannot implement, modify, or transfer any controls. The owner and custodian are responsible for managing access controls. This is the most restrictive model because all controls are fixed In the original MAC model, all objects and subjects were assigned a numeric access level. The access level of the subject had to be higher than that of the object in order for access to be granted.

Discretionary Access Control (DAC)

This model is least restrictive. A subject has total control over any objects that he or she owns. Along with the programs that are associated with those objects In the DAC model, a subject can also change the permissions for other subjects over objects.

User Account Control (UAC)

In this model, operating systems prompt the user for permission whenever software is installed. There are three primary security restrictions implemented by UAC:

- Runs with limited privileges by default.

- Applications run in standard user accounts.

- Standard users perform common tasks (i.e. no administrative rights are given).

Another way of controlling DAC inheritance is to automatically reduce the user's permissions.

Role Based Access Control (RBAC)

Also known as Non-Discretionary Access Control, this model is considered a more "real world" approach than the other models. It assigns permissions to particular roles in the organization, and then assigns users to that role. In this model, objects are set to be a certain type, to which subjects with that particular role have access.

Authentication

Authentication is basically verification procedure which ensures the identity of each client on a network. Authentication can be further defined in two contexts:

- The first is viewing authentication as it relates to access control.

- The second is to look at it as one of the three key elements of security—authentication, authorization, and accounting.

Authentication, Authorization, and Accounting (AAA)

AAA (or TripleA) refers to a security architecture for distributed systems, which enables control over which users are allowed access to which services, and how much of the resources they have used. This is fairly popular protocol in the field of wireless network security.

Types of Authentication/Credentials

Following are main types of authentication, or authentication credentials:

- **One-time passwords**: They are dynamic passwords that change frequently. Systems using OTPs generate a unique password on demand that is not reusable. The most common type is a time-synchronized OTP, they are used in conjunction with a token. The token and a corresponding authentication server share the same algorithm and each algorithm is different for each user's token. *(see figure 5.2.2a)*

- **Standard biometrics**: This technique uses a person's unique characteristics for authentication. For example, scanning of fingerprints, faces, hands, irises, retinas and storing the information in shape of credential.

- **Behavioral biometrics**: It authenticates by normal actions that the user performs, such as keystroke dynamics. It attempt to recognize a user's unique typing rhythm. Keystroke dynamics uses two unique typing variables, Dwell time, and Flight time. *(see figure 111)*

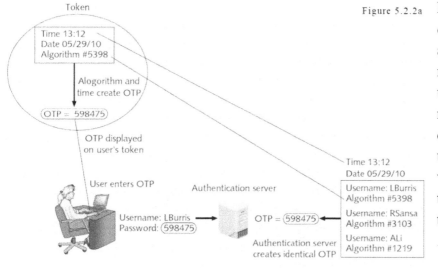

Figure 5.2.2a

FIGURE 110 BEHAVORIAL BIOMETRICS

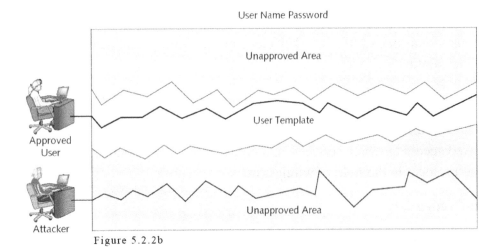

Figure 5.2.2b

Figure 111 behavorial biometrics 2

Authentication Servers

Authentication can be provided on a network by a dedicated AAA or authentication server. The most common type of authentication and AAA servers are RADIUS, Kerberos, TACACS+, and generic servers built on the Lightweight Directory Access Protocol (LDAP).

RADIUS

Radius is a server for remote user authentication and accounting. It is used on any network that needs a centralized authentication and/or accounting service for its workstations.

Kerberos

Kerberos is a secure method for authenticating a request for a service in a computer network. Kerberos was developed in the Athena Project at the Massachusetts Institute of Technology (MIT). It lets a user request an encrypted "ticket" from an authentication process that can then be used to request a particular service from a server. The user's password does not have to pass through the network. A version of Kerberos (client and server) can be downloaded from MIT or you can buy a commercial version.

Terminal Access Control Access Control System (TACACS+)

TACACS is relatively an older authentication protocol common to UNIX networks that allows a remote access server to forward a user's logon password to an authentication server to determine whether access can be allowed to a given system. TACACS is an encryption protocol and therefore less secure than the later TACACS+ and Remote Authentication Dial-In User Service protocols.

Lightweight Directory Access Protocol (LDAP)

LDAP is an application protocol for accessing and maintaining distributed directory information services over an Internet Protocol (IP) network. Directory services may provide any organized set of records, often with a hierarchical structure, such as a corporate email directory. Similarly, a telephone directory is a list of subscribers with an address and a phone number.

Performing Vulnerability Assessments

One of the most important assets any organization possesses is its data. But unfortunately, the importance of data is generally underestimated. The first steps in data protection actually begin with understanding risks and risk management.

The In information security, there is always a risk that a threat agent will exploit a vulnerability. A risk can be defined as an event or condition that could occur. And if it does occur, then it has a negative impact. Risk generally denotes a potential negative impact to an asset. And here is when the need of vulnerability assessment becomes mandatory.

The first step or task in vulnerability assessments is to determine the assets that need to be protected. Asset identification is a process which ensures inventorying and managing these items. Along with the assets, the attributes of the assets need to be compiled. It is important to determine each item's relative value. Factors that should be considered in determining the relative value are:

- How critical is this asset to the goals of the organization?

- How difficult would it be to replace it?

- How much does it cost to protect it?

- How much revenue does it generate?

Table 22 Vulnerability assessments

Attribute Name	Description
Equipment name	The name of the device commonly used, such as *Web Server 6-10*
Equipment type	Type of equipment, such as desktop or intrusion detection device
Manufacturer	The name of the manufacturer
Model and part number	The identification numbers used by the manufacturer
Manufacturer serial number	The unique serial number assigned by the manufacturer
Inventory tag number	The number assigned by the organization to the item; this is useful as a cross reference to the order inventory, which contains additional information such as the date purchased, the vendor's name, and the cost
Software or firmware version	The version of the software or firmware, including all updates and service packs installed
Location	The building and room number where the equipment is installed
Addresses	The Media Access Control (MAC) address and the IP address of the hardware or the hardware on which the software resides
Unit	The name of the organizational unit that is responsible for the asset
Function	A description of what the asset does

IDENTIFYING VULNERABILITIES

It is important to determine the current security weaknesses that could expose assets to threats. There are two categories of software and hardware tools which can be used for vulnerability assessment:

- Vulnerability scanning

- Penetration testing

VULNERABILITY SCANNING

Vulnerability scanning is typically used by an organization to identify weaknesses in the system. It needs to be addressed in order to increase the level of security. Tools required to perform vulnerability scanning include port scanners, network mappers, protocol analyzers, vulnerability scanners, and password crackers.

PORT SCANNERS

Port scanners are used to check for open ports on a system in your network. An open port which is suspected to be related to a backdoor or worm will always help the network administrators to evaluate the assessment more efficiently.

NETWORK MAPPERS

Network mappers are software tools that can identify all the systems connected to a network (by sending series of broadcast queries in specified range of ip pool). Most network mappers utilize the ICMP, and other common method is sending NBT request on broadcast level. Below is a screen shot of nmap (a network mapper) to illustrate how they assist.

```
$ nmap -sP 10.0.0.1-254
Starting nmap 3.81 ( http://www.insecure.org/nmap/ )
       at 2006-11-01 14:46
NZDT
Host 10.0.0.25 appears to be up.
MAC Address: 00:0C:F1:AE:E6:08 (Intel)
Host 10.0.0.51 appears to be up.
MAC Address: 08:00:09:9A:1A:AA (Hewlett Packard)
Host 10.0.0.70 appears to be up.
MAC Address: 00:0F:EA:64:4E:1E (Giga-Byte Tech Co.)
. . .
```

Figure 112 example of network mapper

VULNERABILITY SCANNERS

This is just a generic term that refers to a range of products that look for vulnerabilities in networks or systems. Intention of vulnerability scanners is to identify vulnerabilities and alert network administrators to these problems. Most vulnerability scanners maintain a database that categorizes and describes the vulnerabilities that it can detect. Other types of vulnerability scanners combine the features of a port scanner and network mapper.

PASSWORD CRACKERS

Even though password crackers are commonly used by hackers, but of course they are also used by network security specialists to check the strength and uniqueness of their own passwords. The harder it takes a password cracker to crack a password, the better it is. However, it is always preferred to set a password that can not be cracked by password crackers at all.

CONDUCTING SECURITY AUDITS

Security Audit is a manual or systematic measurable technical assessment of a system or entire network. Manual assessments include performing security vulnerability scans, reviewing application and operating system access controls, analyzing physical access to the systems, and much more.

PRIVILEGE AUDITING

A privilege can be considered a subject's access level over an object. Principle of least privilege is that, users should be given only the minimal amount of privileges necessary to perform his or her job function Privilege auditing. In privilege auditing it is required to have knowledge of privilege management, how privileges are assigned, and how to audit these security settings.

PRIVILEGE MANAGEMENT

Privilege management it the process of assigning and revoking privileges to objects. The roles of owners and custodians are generally well-established. Where those roles fit into the organization often depends upon how the organization is structured. The responsibility for privilege management can be either centralized or decentralized. In a centralized structure, one unit is responsible for all aspects of assigning or revoking privileges and all custodians are part of that unit.

AUDITING SYSTEM SECURITY SETTINGS

Auditing system security settings for user privileges involves:

- A regular review of user access and rights.
- Using group policies.
- Implementing storage and retention policies.
- User access and rights review

It is important to periodically review user access privileges and rights.

Auditing system security settings are for reviewing user access rights for logging into the network can be performed on the network server. And reviewing user permissions over objects can be viewed on the network server. *(see table below)*

Table 23 permissions on network server

Name	Description
Read	Allows files or folders to be opened as read-only and to be copied
Write	Allows the creation of files and folders, and allows data to be added to or removed from files
List Folder Contents	Same as Read but also allows navigation of subfolders
Read and Execute	Same as Read but also allows users to run executable files
Modify	All the above along with permission to delete the file or folder
Full Control	All the above along with the ability to change permissions

MONITORING METHODOLOGIES AND TOOLS

There are several types of tools that can be used on systems and networks to detect security-related anomalies. Anomaly-based monitoring is designed for detecting statistical anomalies. A reference set of data against which operational data is compared is also one of the techniques in this concept known as baseline. Whenever there is a significant deviation from this baseline, an alarm is raised. Its advantage is that it detects the anomalies fairly quickly.

SIGNATURE-BASED MONITORING

Signature-based Monitoring compares activities against a predefined signature. It requires access to an updated database of signatures, along with a means to actively compare and match current behavior against a collection of signatures.

BEHAVIOR-BASED MONITORING

Behavior-based monitoring is designed to be more adaptive and proactive instead of reactive. It uses the "normal" processes and actions as the standard. It continuously analyzes the behavior of processes and programs on a system.

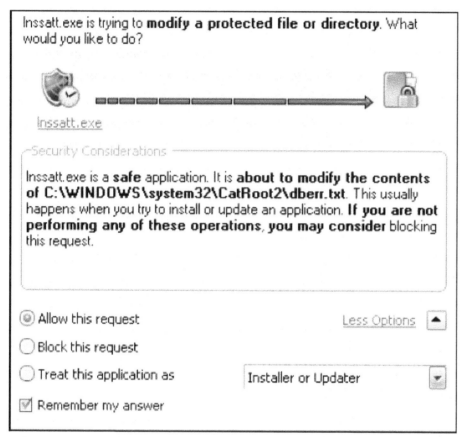

Figure 5.4.5

Figure 113 behavior based monitering

Exercise

Quizzes:

Q.1) What one of the three models of access control?

Answer) Mandatory Access Control, Discretionary Access Control , and User Account Control.

Q.2) Authentication and Authorization are same in nature. (State true or false)

Answer) False

Q.3) Password cracking tools are used by hackers. Why would network security specialists use password crackers?

Answer) For slightly contrasting reason compared to why hackers use it. That is to say, hackers use it to crack a password of their victim. And security specialists use it to check the strength of their clients to ensure they are not crackable or at least nearly impossible to crack.

Q.4) Penetration testing is a category within Vulnerability scanning. (State true or false)

Answer) False

Q.5) What is behavior-based monitoring?

Answer) Behavior-based monitoring is designed to be more adaptive and proactive instead of reactive. It uses the "normal" processes and actions as the standard. It continuously analyzes the behavior of processes and programs on a system.**Q.6) Intrusion Detection is another terminology for network mapping.** (State true or false)

Answer) False

Assignment

Using nmap, conduct a full scan of your system and submit the result.

Answer) Each student will present a unique result of their computer system respectively, but a common idea of how it will look like can be grabbed from here: http://nmap.org/book/images/zenmap-fig-tab-nmap-output.png

PROJECT

Conduct a research and discuss which wireless network protocol is most difficult to crack for hackers. Also explain why you concluded a protocol most secure.

Answer) In short, WPA2 is considered one of the strongest protocol because of its complex mechanism of securing SSID and data encryption.

www.ingramcontent.com/pod-product-compliance
Lightning Source LLC
Chambersburg PA
CBHW080147060326
40689CB00018B/3885